D0310611

SIR ALEX FERGUSON

SIR ALEX FERGUSON

THE OFFICIAL MANCHESTER UNITED STORY OF 25 YEARS AT THE TOP

DAVID MEEK AND TOM TYRRELL

SIMON &
SCHUSTER

London · New York · Sydney · Toronto · New Delhi

A CBS COMPANY

First published in Great Britain by Orion Publishing Group Ltd, 2006
This revised and updated edition published by Simon & Schuster UK Ltd, 2011
A CBS Company

1 3 5 7 9 10 8 6 4 2

Simon & Schuster UK Ltd
1st Floor
222 Gray's Inn Road
London
WC1X 8HB

Originally published under the title *Sir Alex*

www.simonandschuster.co.uk

Simon & Schuster Australia
Sydney

Simon & Schuster India
New Delhi

Every reasonable effort has been made to contact copyright holders of material reproduced in
this book. If any have inadvertently been overlooked, the publishers would be glad to hear from
them and make good in future editions any errors or omissions brought to their attention.

A CIP catalogue record for this book is available from the British Library

Hardback ISBN 978-0-85720-915-3

Printed and bound in Italy by L.E.G.O. SpA

CONTENTS

FOREWORD BY
SIR BOBBY CHARLTON

THE APPOINTMENT of Sir Alex Ferguson as manager 25 years ago was the best thing that ever happened to Manchester United. He has led our club to the forefront of the game in England and made us the dominant force, with such a stack of trophies that he has overtaken the great man of my playing days, Sir Matt Busby, as the most successful manager of all time.

He first came up on my radar when I watched his then team Aberdeen take on the mighty Real Madrid in the final of the European Cup-Winners' Cup. He was everywhere, pitch-side when there was an injury and his team always looked threatening. Reading what he said at the time, he struck me as a man of great knowledge who knew what he was talking about. He had a confidence that reminded me of Sir Matt, and like Sir Matt he knew what he wanted and how he was going to get it.

His achievement of breaking the dominance of the two big Glasgow clubs, Rangers and Celtic, spoke for itself. I thought at the time that if ever he thought about leaving Aberdeen and we needed a manager then he was perfect for us.

When it became apparent he was ready to leave Aberdeen, he was our first choice, and as I say, he was the best thing that ever happened for United. What struck me about him was his enthusiasm for football and his role as a manager, and it burns as strongly now 25 years later as it did from his first day at Old Trafford. He seems to love every minute of his job and that has never wavered either.

The bonus for our club is that he arrived thinking long-term, which is why he not only took the first team forward but found time to reinvigorate the youth system, even though he knew that it would be a few years before it produced results. That long-term approach has given us a stability and consistency that has paid dividends. It adds up to an incredible time span of a quarter of a century and, when you think that the average stay for a manager is three and a half years, you see what I mean about stability and the reason we can plan for the future.

He just goes on and on without any slackening in terms of his energy, his drive and his desire to make Manchester United the best. I look on in admiration at the way he still gets exactly what he wants from the modern-day wealthy players, so different from my day as a player. He is nothing short of fantastic and it's hard to appreciate at times that here is a man heading into his seventies.

He is an inspiration for his contemporaries and if I ever feel I should be taking it easier, I look at Sir Alex and realise that age is in the head as much as in the body. As long as he has his health, he says he won't be retiring and I think all Manchester United supporters will wish him the longest life possible.

We have just enjoyed an incredibly successful season, with Sir Alex bringing a record 19th title to Old Trafford. Yes, we were all disappointed when we were beaten by Barcelona in the final of the Champions League, but you can't win everything and three European finals in the last four years is a fair indication of where we are, and let's face it, Barcelona are arguably one of the finest teams we have ever seen, so there was certainly no shame losing to them.

The manager will simply regard it as a challenge to do better next time and I for one believe he will … that's how he has become the incredibly successful manager he is and why we are so fortunate to have him at Old Trafford.

List of Honours Won by Sir Alex Ferguson at Manchester United

Premier League champions (12): 1992-93, 1993-94, 1995-96, 1996-97, 1998-99, 1999-2000, 2000-01, 2002-03, 2006-07, 2007-08, 2008-09, 2010-11

FA Cup winners (5): 1989-90, 1993-94, 1995-96, 1998-99, 2003-04

League Cup winners (4): 1991-92, 2005-06, 2008-09, 2009-10

Charity (Community) Shield winners (10): 1990-91 (joint), 1993-94, 1994-95, 1996-97, 1997-98, 2003-04, 2007-08, 2008-09, 2010-11, 2011-12

Champions League winners (2): 1998-99, 2007-08

European Cup-Winners' Cup winners (1): 1990-91

Inter-Continental Cup winners (1): 1999-2000

UEFA Super Cup winners (1): 1991-92

FIFA Club World Cup winners (1): 2008-09

Sir Bobby Charlton congratulates the United manager after the Reds had won the Club World Cup in Japan.

1

A MAN OF PASSION

SIR ALEX FERGUSON is the most successful manager in British football. As he celebrates 25 years at the helm of Manchester United, the man is already a legend with a record that puts him alongside, if not ahead of, the game's other great Scottish leaders Sir Matt Busby, Bill Shankly and Jock Stein.

For a decade Ferguson's teams dominated the English game, reaching a peak with the unique treble of FA Cup, Premiership and European Champions League in 1999. From time to time when he has failed to deliver a trophy, the critics have been quick to suggest that the Old Trafford empire is crumbling, but he is a fighter and has always come back to prove he is as durable as he is astute.

In recent years, first Chelsea then Manchester City, both backed by huge resources, emerged as contenders to become the top club in the country, while the ambition of Arsenal, Liverpool and all the other major clubs does not dwindle – but if ever anyone was equipped to meet the present-day challenge, it's the man who ended United's 26 years of frustration by winning the Premiership in 1993.

Sir Alex Ferguson is a character of so many parts that at times he seems to have a split personality, one minute raging and swearing, the next singing at the top of his voice as if he didn't have a care in the world. He can be incredibly kind and loyal to those he feels have served him well, but he can also be hard with those he considers have let him down – a man's man in a tough world. A few miles away from Old Trafford and the Carrington training ground, though, he slips easily into a family role, still close to his three sons, Mark, Darren and Jason. He dotes on his grandchildren and accepts home rule from his wife, Cathy, without a murmur, even though she has been known to refer to football as 'that stupid game'.

Along with these many contrasts, one consistent thread runs through his life – Alex Ferguson is a winner who brings to his job in football a passion, a hunger and a determination that does not take defeat for an answer.

Typically, he decided a few years ago that he would retire from front-line management at the age of 60, while he still had his health and fitness, to enjoy other pursuits and devote more time to his family. He had just won two championships by runaway margins, and although he had twice been disappointed to fail in Europe at the quarter-final stage, it seemed the right time to seek a less onerous job. He had just about tied up all the details of his pension and agreed to become a roving goodwill ambassador for United, pulling together the club's global interests.

However, when it became clear that his final season was not going to plan and United were losing too many games, he changed his mind and asked for a new contract to stay on as manager. The directors were naturally delighted to agree and Sir Alex summed up his feelings with the words, 'I am not going to leave this club as a loser.'

That remark reflected his professional attitude, his relentless search for perfection in himself and his players. A setback only intensifies his commitment and he looks for the same kind of response from his players. He says:

'The slightest fall in the standards of Manchester United seems to invite torrents of criticism with some even ready to claim that our empire is crumbling, the bubble has burst and all that kind of rubbish.

'I suppose it's all about people's expectations. I have no problem with that but it does bring me a situation that I have to deal with. I have to get the players to understand where the people who are so quick to write us off are coming from and that they shouldn't panic in face of a bad press.

'Success over the years means that when we have a bit of a blip the roof falls in. Critics ignore the positive aspects and seize on perceived weaknesses in order to have a go at us. The more success you have, the more it is brought up in evidence, and it just gets a bigger factor all the time.

'But the players must live with it, and if they can't, then they should know they are at the wrong club. We have to be single-minded, starting with me and going right through the dressing room. When we are having everything thrown at us, we must stand together. We won't change the media, so we must build our own defences. We must understand the expectations and rise above it all. We must then deliver the kind of performances that brook no argument.'

Of course, Sir Alex is very clever at psychology, and prepares the minds of his players as well as their bodies. Over the years, if things have started to go wrong, he has often used the technique of telling his players that the world is against them and they must fight back. He has often generated a siege mentality, which has produced many a fighting reaction that has enabled them to weather a storm. Alex Ferguson's management is based on cultivating the brain as well as the brawn, although he certainly does not neglect the physical approach.

'Fergie Fury' is an important weapon in his management technique. He claims to have mellowed in recent years but his temper can still be ferocious, and he does not hesitate to lash his players when he thinks the time is right, nor does he hold back from blasting the media. His 'hairdryer' technique – so called because the hot blast of his words is said to curl your hair – as applied to journalists who have upset him, is well known in newspaper circles, and there always seems to be some paper or radio station banned from his press conferences for stepping – in his opinion – too far out of line. He maintains there is nothing wrong with losing your temper, provided it is for the right reasons, and the right reason for him is if it is in the course of striving to win.

'In the last two or three years I have mellowed,' he says. 'When you have success you have far more patience, but you have to create a little spark sometimes.

'If it's in your nature to lose your temper, let it out. Don't keep it bottled up. You can end up growling and kicking doors when you're not getting over what you actually feel. If you're disappointed with the players, then you have to tell them. I have thrown more teacups across the dressing room than I can tell you. As far as I'm concerned, anger is not a problem. I believe that losing your temper is OK – as long as you do it for the right reasons.'

Ferguson has little patience with players who are booked for dissent, because nobody is going to get a referee to change his mind, but fierce tackles and even fights with opponents within reason are countenanced, if they have been committed out of a determination to win.

The manager had no problem defending Roy Keane, despite his captain's aggression. Keane admitted in his autobiography that he had deliberately sought revenge on Norwegian Alfie Haaland because the former Leeds

After playing 480 times under Sir Alex, there was one more visit to Old Trafford as a player for Roy Keane, in May 2006 for his testimonial. The huge respect between the two men was always evident.

player had laughed at him when he had been injured in a previous incident. The Republic of Ireland captain faced disciplinary action from the Football Association and even legal action from Haaland, but Ferguson stood staunchly by his man and his book.

'The book is a fantastic read,' he said. 'Roy has just been totally honest about his life and football. He has opened up and told the truth as he sees it. I find nothing wrong with that.'

Sir Alex will stand shoulder to shoulder with his players when they have problems. He instinctively stood by David Beckham when they were burning his effigy in London following his sending off during the World Cup finals in France. It is part of his management style, and one reason why he was so successful in bringing a maverick such as Eric Cantona into line when other managers had failed to control him. Ferguson admired Cantona's talent and his high commitment to training. He recognised that the Frenchman could bring out the best in his developing young players, including David Beckham, Ryan Giggs and Paul Scholes, so he stuck by the player in his hour of need.

Cantona was sent off during a game against Crystal Palace in London and on his way to the tunnel, kung-fu kicked a taunting spectator. Following that infamous event, Cantona was first given a jail sentence – later, on appeal, reduced to community service – and there were demands for him to be banned from football for all time. Ferguson saw this as hysteria and never wavered in his support for the player. His reward was Cantona staying on at Old Trafford and continuing his vital catalyst role in midfield, which prompted the most consistently successful period in the club's history. What terrific managerial judgement!

Loyalty to his players is paramount in Ferguson's philosophy, but not blind loyalty. It doesn't mean that he is a soft touch.

Ferguson has always been a strict disciplinarian, especially with young players, nagging them on details such as making sure their hair is cut properly and that they wear jackets and ties when appropriate. He is shrewd enough, though, to recognise when it would be a waste of time to insist on an older player being made to toe the line unnecessarily. Cantona, for instance, as a free spirit, was allowed to break the club's dress code, and Ferguson also allowed Beckham a much freer lifestyle than he would have countenanced earlier in his career, because he recognised that times change. He turned a blind eye to the fashion icon's freakish hairstyles and accepted his earrings and sarong because he knew that was the

Ferguson's support for Eric Cantona, after his notorious kung-fu kick, ensured that the talismanic Frenchman returned to Old Trafford to help inspire a new generation of players.

It is in Ferguson's nature to stand by his players through the good and the bad, as David Beckham found out following his 1998 World Cup sending off.

way the world was going. Beckham had become a fantastically popular cult figure, and Sir Alex was prepared to bend in order to keep a rare talent happy at Old Trafford.

There are limits, though, such as the time Beckham gave a poor excuse for not coming in for training before an important game at Leeds. When Beckham did arrive, a day late, he was promptly sent back home and dropped for the match. It was a brave decision. When United won without Beckham, that disciplinary action was reinforced, although it wouldn't have troubled the manager had they lost, because he stands by his principles.

He can be tough when he feels it is necessary, particularly if he feels he has been let down. For instance, he did not hesitate to release Norman Whiteside and Paul McGrath, both great players for United, when he decided that their drinking habits were wrong for the club.

'I am running a football club, not a drinking club,' he growled at the time, and although a lot of supporters were upset, both players were transferred.

He similarly lost patience with Paul Ince, arguably the player of the year in his last season with United, when he felt the player was becoming too powerful in the dressing room and ignoring his tactical instructions. The Independent Supporters' Association organised a campaign to try to get Ince back from a transfer to Italy, but Ferguson was adamant. He had made up his mind and Ince, or 'The Guv'nor' as he had started to style himself, had to go, regardless of the consequences.

Ferguson has also had the happy knack of being proved right in most of his controversial decisions, obviously one of the key factors that have made him such a successful manager. As he explains, 'Unless you have control, you can't have a vision, targets, dreams.'

Pursuit of control is a major factor in his management, and is the reason he expresses himself so vehemently. Football is such a driving force in his life, or as Mark McGhee, one of Ferguson's players when he was manager of Aberdeen, says, 'He sees football as a cause to which he expects you to give a hundred per cent. Everything else is secondary, and I mean everything. He only wants people around him who are prepared to accept the challenge, as he calls it. To take on the cause, his cause – to achieve success and prove the others wrong.'

So Ferguson has always been big on discipline, and perhaps that stems from his own upbringing. As he once explained, 'I see the need for discipline. I had a disciplinarian father who worked in the Glasgow shipyards and taught me the values of life and the values within yourself. My father had a big temper, and though my mother was quieter, she was a very strong and a very powerful character.

'I had a tough upbringing but it wasn't poor. We maybe didn't have a television, a car or a phone but I considered I had everything and I did … I had a football!'

There is no doubt that, apart from his family, football has been at the centre of his life. Although he was apprenticed as a toolmaker at a type-writer factory in Glasgow when he left school, he was always 'football mad' and played part-time with Dunfermline before being taken on by Glasgow Rangers.

Incidentally, even as a toolmaker his powers of leadership were in evidence. He became a shop steward and led an apprentices' strike for better pay. Needless to say it was successful and the apprentices got their rise.

Later in life he opened a bar in Glasgow, which gave him further insight into the feelings of ordinary fans. That sensitivity has never left him and nobody can say he has led the typically sheltered life of most successful professional footballers. Perhaps because of his involvement in a wider world, he has also been able to take an interest in matters outside football. He likes music and at one point started to learn to play the piano. More recently, he decided to learn French and a tutor called weekly at the training ground, although sometimes in vain because Ferguson is a busy man. He likes reading, especially the life stories of self-made men who have become successful in their business careers, and he has also bought several horses due to his interest in horse racing.

He admits that he left the upbringing of his three sons largely to Cathy. Darren played for United and other clubs, before becoming a manager, currently at Peterborough, his twin Jason left television to become a football agent, and their older brother Mark is successful in the world of finance.

Perhaps now Sir Alex is approaching 70 he will relax more – unlikely, though. Right up to the time when he considers it right to walk away, he will be giving his all and preaching his footballing philosophy, which he once described like this:

'I want the players to enjoy each season and relish the challenge. I have felt at times that some of the players were not enjoying life when things were going wrong and that's a self-defeating emotion. A team that does not enjoy playing is not going to succeed.

'Playing football, even at the very highest level, should always be a joy, and that's the spirit I want to see bubbling at Old Trafford alongside all those other qualities, such as skill, determination, passion and hunger, that make up a winning team. They must make sure they enjoy the challenge.'

One thing for certain is that Sir Alex Ferguson will enjoy the challenge. As he says, 'I am fit and I still have a high energy level, which is one of the reasons why I decided to stay on as manager. I still have my edge, too, a hunger and an ambition for more success. I may have mellowed – but not that much!'

For the 12th time, Sir Alex Ferguson lifts the Premier League trophy.

2

A MONUMENTAL DECISION

SIR ALEX FERGUSON considers himself a Manchester United man these days and can't contemplate becoming the manager of another club.

'Old Trafford is the pinnacle of my career. I grew up a supporter of Glasgow Rangers and achieved an ambition by playing for them. I enjoyed my time as manager with Aberdeen and we had a lot of success for a relatively small club in Scotland, but when the call came to manage Manchester United, I just had to accept the challenge,' he says.

'There is a great tradition at the club established by Sir Matt Busby, and despite the enormous way the club has grown, we still like to produce our own players. I have always believed in a youth policy and while never afraid to buy in the transfer market, there is special satisfaction in bringing a player up through your academy and junior teams.

'I have had my problems at Old Trafford. Three years after I came here we came to a standstill despite spending a considerable sum of money on new players, but we got through, our youth policy began to pay off and we haven't really looked back since.

'The biggest moment, of course, was winning the treble. It is unforgettable and I doubt whether it will ever be repeated. Football never stands still, and other clubs have their ambitions, too, but we keep working.'

It was that kind of philosophy harboured by a man of steel that United needed as they struggled to recapture the glory days following the retirement of Sir Matt Busby. The grand old man of football had cast a long shadow over Old Trafford when he decided to bring down the curtain on his 25-year reign as manager of United. He was tired after a traumatic and glorious career. Close to death in 1958 after the Munich air crash, he recovered to enjoy victory as the manager of the first English club to win the European Cup just 10 years later. The effort cost him and left him without the will and ruthless edge to do what needed to be done in terms of breaking up a successful team to start all over again. The result was a squad of illustrious players who were too long in the tooth, and his successor was always going to be faced with a massive rebuilding job.

It would take time, something that was not available to Wilf McGuinness, who was moved aside after 18 months. Frank O'Farrell is still bitter that he was also given just 18 months before he was sacked. His successor, Tommy Docherty, looked like he could restore the glory days but ran away with the wife of the club physiotherapist, and was dismissed.

Dave Sexton and Ron Atkinson took the club to cup finals but United, brought up on Busby-style success, wanted more. Atkinson never finished out of the top four when he was manager, but by then the need to win the championship after 20 years was pushing the United board into yet another management change. They wanted a winner, and their collective eye was caught by a young man in Scotland who was moving mountains.

It was Martin Edwards, who inherited the club from his father Louis, urged on by Sir Bobby Charlton, who made the monumental and, indeed, inspired decision in November 1986 to appoint Alex Ferguson as manager of Manchester United. It proved to be one of the most significant decisions ever made at Old Trafford, and as Martin Edwards, owner and chairman, later chief executive and now honorary life president, explained, 'I had met Alex Ferguson when we signed Gordon Strachan from Aberdeen and I was impressed. I also knew of his reputation as the manager of a small club who had taken on the two big clubs in Glasgow and come out on top. It seemed to me that the qualities it had taken to do that were just what we needed at Old Trafford to take us that final step towards the championship after so long knocking on the door.

'He had also shown that he could cut it in Europe by winning the European Cup-Winners' Cup with Aberdeen, beating Real Madrid of all people in the final.

'He struck me as the young turk of British football who was destined for success, and history has shown that we made the right appointment. In 12 years he took us from also-rans to total domestic dominance, overtaking Liverpool and keeping us up there. It wasn't just Liverpool, either. He also dealt with Blackburn, Newcastle and Arsenal when they made their title challenges.

'In terms of league football he has been fantastic, superb. In Europe, I think even Alex himself might look back and consider that we might have done better. Winning the Champions League in '99 and 2008 was tremendous of course, but it's been disappointing to find us stalling at the quarter-final and semi-final stages so often in other seasons.

'I always had great faith in Alex, even in the relatively early days when things were not going well and there was a lot of paper talk that the board would be considering his future. It was never an issue with me or the board because we knew what was happening further down in the club. With the reorganisation of the scouting set-up and coaching, we were on the point of producing the exciting young players who would emerge as the backbone of United and England.

'Alex turned things round and has given us some marvellous memories from his 25 years as manager of Manchester United. We had a magical spell when Eric Cantona and Mark Hughes led the attack with Ryan Giggs and Andrei Kanchelskis on the wings. That, for me, was our most entertaining time, matched only by the treble season when Andy Cole and Dwight Yorke, backed up by Teddy Sheringham and Ole Gunnar Solskjaer, shot us the unique treble.

'The emergence of Chelsea as a commanding force in the game made it more difficult for us, but we rose to that challenge, and continue to do so whoever comes along, so I'm looking to the future with every confidence, and rightly so because Sir Alex Ferguson is still at the helm.

'He now stands alongside Sir Matt Busby as the club's pre-eminent manager and he deserves the congratulations of us all for what he has achieved in his 25 years in charge at Old Trafford. Winning twelve league titles, five FA Cups, four League Cups, two Champions Leagues and the European Cup-Winners' Cup is a record second to none and a remarkable story.'

Ferguson approached his task in November 1986 with the confidence born of his success in Scotland. He had his moments as a player with Glasgow Rangers but fell victim to religious bigotry as a Protestant married to a Roman Catholic. He must have quite enjoyed turning down their offer when they were forced to recognise his achievements with Aberdeen and come cap in hand to ask him to be their manager. He was the obvious man for the job after breaking the Glasgow stranglehold and winning three championships, four Scottish Cups, one League Cup and the European Cup-Winners' Cup. The Ibrox loss was Manchester United's gain, and

Alex Ferguson, the man who broke the Old Firm duopoly in Scotland, arrives at Old Trafford with the challenge of making United once again the best club in the land.

Action from United's famous 5–0 victory over Manchester City in November 1994. (Top) Andrei Kanchelskis scores one of his three goals that day, while (below) goalscorer Eric Cantona wins the ball in midfield. For Martin Edwards, this was his favourite era as United rattled in 115 goals in the campaign.

Martin Edwards got a quite different reception when he went calling at Pittodrie. Sir Alex describes it:

'It was a beautiful sunny morning as I drove back to the ground from a training session and I saw the chairman's car there. I went into my office and he was sitting at my desk with his hand on the telephone. He threw me a piece of paper with the name and phone number of Martin Edwards. He said, "Do you want me to phone him?" and I said I did. I went back up after going down to the dressing rooms and he said that Mr Edwards was flying up straightaway and would go to my house. He said, "If you want the job, there's nothing we can do to stop you."'

The family didn't at first want to leave Aberdeen because they felt it was a lovely city and the three boys were all settled at school, but Cathy said he had to take the challenge. So began a roller-coaster ride for everyone connected with Manchester United, including the media. As co-author David Meek, a *Manchester Evening News* reporter for 37 years, recalls from personal experience, 'Lots of journalists have been given the hairdryer treatment, and it can be a frightening experience as Sir Alex wipes the floor with you, but as my turn on the end of his apparent blistering rage indicated, the hairdryer is used for a purpose.

'In my case, the *Evening News* had upset him by publishing a story he felt would have been better left unreported, and he retaliated by refusing to accept my telephone calls. I went down to try to clear up the problem only to run into a storm of abuse rubbishing the paper and my editor. I was a bit miffed and, as it was just a few days before Christmas, I turned on my heel with a muttered sarcastic, "Merry Christmas." At that his arm shot round my shoulders and, with a big smile on his face, he said, "Nothing personal, you know!"

'I'm sure it wasn't, either. It was just Sir Alex's way of making sure that when I went back to the office I would be impressing on the editor how angry he had been and that we perhaps should listen more carefully the next time he made a request. Most of his outbursts are intended to make maximum impression, be it on players by hurling teacups across a dressing room or kicking the boot that regrettably hit David Beckham. That wasn't anything personal, either, just an unfortunate accident, but at the same time it was designed to make a point. He cares about winning, and always has done.'

As his brother Martin, one year younger, once told Gerry McNee of the *Scottish Sunday Mail*, 'When we were kids, Alex always had a hot temper.

He could cause a fight in an empty house. He was always competitive and would do anything to win. He liked a game of cards and very often he's taken my pocket money off me. At primary school, he didn't like you to take the ball off him. If you did, he'd kick you. He was always a bad loser.'

That is just one side of the deeply layered Alex Ferguson. In total contrast, he goes well out of his way to attend the funerals of old friends, and despite a hectic working life, he will always find time to pop in to a leaving do or a special party being thrown by somebody he considers a friend. In the case of players who have given him good service, he makes a point of helping them find new clubs and perhaps a good money deal rather than leaving them wasting away in his reserve team on the off chance that he might need them. He is genuinely pleased if one of the players he has released enjoys success somewhere else.

'My hairdryer treatment seemed a long way off when I was convalescing at home following a spell in hospital,' says David Meek. 'The phone rang and a voice at the other end informed me that, "The Scottish beast is on his way." Twenty minutes later he was there to give me his good wishes for my recovery, the soft side to an iron man.'

Certainly, Manchester United needed a strong, resolute character to follow Ron Atkinson, if only to escape the Busby shadow. That never seemed to be a problem for Ferguson. As he once explained a few years into his management, 'I can honestly say I have never felt inhibited by Sir Matt Busby's success at Old Trafford. I had heard what I regarded as rubbish and thought why should this be? I was proud to be going to a club with a great tradition, and it was a tradition built by Sir Matt. Quite frankly, there are very few clubs with this kind of tradition, so I felt lucky rather than intimidated.

'I don't see history as an obstacle at all. Indeed, I wish Sir Matt had been younger so that I could have drawn more knowledge from him. He was always helpful to me and he was helpful to everyone. I believe that any manager who has tried to say he was inhibited by the shadow of Sir Matt was making an excuse, except perhaps Wilf McGuinness, who was so young and inexperienced when he was asked to take over. There was a kind of father–son thing about that appointment. No other manager could possibly say his job was made more difficult by interference from Sir Matt. So I certainly did not have any hang-ups about a Busby shadow when I decided to break away from my comfortable life in Aberdeen to step into the unknown with Manchester United.'

(Top) Matt Busby celebrates winning the European Cup in 1968. (Below) Many others had been daunted by his shadow, but Alex Ferguson knew he could move the club on to a great, new era.

Most Goals Scored for Sir Alex Ferguson

Ryan Giggs	159
Paul Scholes	150
Ruud van Nistelrooy	150
Wayne Rooney	147
Brian McClair	127
Ole Gunnar Solskjaer	126
Andy Cole	121
Cristiano Ronaldo	118
Mark Hughes	115
David Beckham	85

Ryan Giggs is the leading Premier League goalscorer, with 105; Paul Scholes and Wayne Rooney, both with 102, are the only other players to score more than 100 goals in the Premier League.

Brian McClair and Ruud van Nistelrooy have scored most FA Cup goals (14). Brian McClair tops the League Cup goalscorers' chart with 19.

Ruud van Nistelrooy's incredible Champions League record was 38 goals in 47 games.

3

LIKE A BEAST

NOBODY KNOWS Sir Alex Ferguson better than the man who was at his side for nine years, first at Aberdeen and then at Old Trafford. Archie Knox had been Alex's assistant and coach at Aberdeen for four and a half years when Ferguson got the call from Old Trafford and the new boss immediately asked his right-hand man to continue the partnership in Manchester. Archie, now working as assistant manager at Aberdeen, didn't need asking twice, as he explained:

'I first linked up with Alex when I was player-manager at Forfar and he invited me to be his coach at Aberdeen in place of the departing Pat Stanton. It didn't take me very long to agree and I had nearly five great seasons with him at Pittodrie.

'Then I was out training one afternoon when his car came reversing into the car park and he got out to tell me that, out of the blue, he was going to Manchester United. He said I would probably get the manager's job at Aberdeen if I stayed but I could go with him to Manchester if I wanted. It took me all of two minutes to decide that it was just too much of an opportunity to miss, and that's how it turned out. It was a fantastic experience and to say it was always interesting is a massive understatement.

'The club has grown enormously since I was there, but even then you never knew what was going to happen next, both on and off the pitch.

'Alex was great to work with. We got on fine. There were the usual tantrums of course, but if you have an opinion, that was bound to happen, and I don't think he would have had me as his assistant if I hadn't had opinions.

'His strengths as a manager are well documented with all the success he has enjoyed through the years at both Aberdeen and Manchester United, but the uppermost quality has always been his drive and desire. Winning is a drug for him, being on top, be it football or tiddlywinks.

'I left United in 1991 to go back to Scotland to become assistant to Walter Smith at Glasgow Rangers. Maybe Alex was a bit disappointed at the time, but it was a tremendous offer and I think everyone has to take the best they can, just as Alex did when he left Aberdeen. For me, it was a career move and no slight on the relationship I had with Alex. It was a bit awkward at the time but no problem now. We are in touch. In fact I played golf with him in Scotland not long after my departure.'

Alex always described Archie as someone who 'worked like a beast' – a quality that was particularly necessary under the Ferguson regime in England because, in addition to sorting out the first team, Archie was back in the evenings helping the manager get to grips with a failing youth system. He would turn up at the Cliff training ground to work alongside Eric Harrison, the youth-team coach. Harrison had been appointed by Ron Atkinson and had been at United for five years before being caught up in the upheaval that accompanied the arrival of Ferguson and Knox. He wrote about their impact in his book, *The View from the Dugout*, and says life changed dramatically for everybody at the club.

Alex Ferguson took over when United were in the bottom half of the First Division and within days had stamped his authority on every corner of his new domain. For those of us involved with the youngsters, his arrival was manna from heaven. It did not surprise me when the Boss made it perfectly clear to every member of staff that the way forward for the club was in producing our own players. Yes, you could always strengthen your squad through the transfer market but the squad had to be based on a rolling production line of home-grown talent. Although we had done pretty well, he said, we were miles short of perfection. United, he insisted, were the great under-achievers.

I thought he was having a go at me. Probably being a little sensitive I told him: 'Get me some better material to work with and I will produce more first-team players for you.' He took the message on board.

The Boss and Archie Knox had the same temperament – fiery with a capital F. A whirlwind hit Manchester United from day one. There was an abundance of passion, enthusiasm and motivation around, but it was not all just gung-ho. A lot of thinking and serious planning were going on, too. The Boss has excellent skills in spotting natural football talent – just look at

Alex Ferguson and Archie Knox worked together for five years at Aberdeen before coming to Manchester. Knox eventually moved to Rangers in 1991.

Youth-team coach Eric Harrison, with three of his former charges in 1996 – David Beckham, Gary and Phil Neville. With around 1400 appearances for United between them, not to mention almost 260 England caps, he has every right to smile.

the number of home-produced players in Manchester United's squad over the years. He is also very supportive of his staff and prepared to listen to their opinions before making his own judgement.

Alex's ferocity did not worry me. After all, I had dealt with Brian Clough when I was a young player at Hartlepool, and had always been mentally strong where football was concerned. One Saturday morning, however, a situation got a little out of hand.

My youth team were playing Burnley at our training ground at the Cliff. If the first team were playing at home, the Boss and Archie always watched the kids – I have been in football well over 40 years and I have never met two harder working men. The Boss was watching the game as usual from his office upstairs and I was watching from the coaches' room next door. This was my usual practice because I got a perfect view from there.

We were winning the game, only 1–0 but quite comfortably, when Archie came flying through the door and got stuck into me. He kept shouting: 'Can your forwards only play one-twos around the box? Haven't they got any other ideas?'

Archie didn't realise that I could be as volatile as him and I forgot all about the game and launched back at him. He retorted by saying that he thought we were a pretty poor team (though 'poor' was not the exact word he used). He said the youth team at Aberdeen would beat us 6–0. That was like a red rag to a bull and I told him to get Aberdeen down here so we could see. The Boss had to come out of his office to calm us both down. It just showed the incredible passion at the club, a determination to win at whatever level. Players and coaches quickly got the message, 100 per cent effort was demanded at all times, in matches and in training.

I got to know Archie Knox more quickly than I did the Boss. This is the usual way in football because coaches spend a lot more time together. I grew to like Archie because he was my kind of man. He was passionate about football, worked hard and loved a night out for relaxation. It took me longer to get to know the gaffer but I quickly realised what he wanted on the football side: 24 hours a day commitment to Manchester United.

This was fine by me because I was desperate to be successful as youth-team manager. After a playing career at outposts of the League on the books of clubs that were struggling to exist, never mind succeed, here was my chance to enjoy success with one of the biggest clubs in the world.

As I settled in at Old Trafford I thought many, many times about the Busby

Babes. My mission was to try to develop a generation of young players to be just as good. I had heard all about the work that Jimmy Murphy, who nurtured the Busby generation, had done and the success he had achieved. It was the hardest possible act to follow.

Older supporters would constantly regale Eric with stories about the Babes, so it was a particular pleasure when, later on, both Matt and Jimmy took time to compliment him on the job he was doing. Indeed, David Beckham is quoted in Bryan Robson's book as saying that Eric is the greatest youth coach in the country – a little further down the line, Beckham and the new babes took both United and England by storm.

However, there was still a lot of work to do as Ferguson got down to revamping the scouting system, which he felt was out of balance. A stack of scouts in Scotland far outnumbered the club's representatives in Greater Manchester, despite the fact that the Manchester area has a population nearly as big as Scotland's.

It was painful but nonetheless true to discover that Manchester City had forged ahead in the competition for young talent, a fact they rammed home when they beat United in the 1986 final of the FA Youth Cup. Only two players from that year's youth squad made the first team – goalkeeper Gary Walsh and full-back Lee Martin. Six years later, how things had changed! The 1992 Youth Cup winners provided the backbone of both the United and England team with players including David Beckham, Gary Neville, Paul Scholes and Nicky Butt, and Ryan Giggs, who went on to play for Wales.

At least in the early days United had managed to sign Ryan Giggs, or Ryan Wilson as he was before changing his name, but that was only courtesy of Harold Wood, the training ground steward. He drew attention to the Salford youngster, who was already going for coaching at City.

Again, it was only through someone outside the scouting system – Len Noad, a football journalist who had retired to live on the south coast – that Ferguson was alerted to the promising talent of Lee Sharpe as he worked his way through Torquay's junior and reserve teams.

Giggs and Sharpe were to serve United well but the new manager knew he must improve the basic set-up. City had also left United standing with the introduction of a successful supporters' club for youngsters. The Junior Blues linked City even more closely with the concept of youth development.

Ferguson culled the scouting system, sacking some staff and making

new appointments, especially locally. He held meetings and told the scouts
he wasn't satisfied with the standard of youngster they were bringing to the
club.

'I think they were hurt and shocked but it had to be done. I said they
must not just bring me the best boy in the street but the best in the country. I told them I didn't want any bad players,' said the manager.

Eric Harrison says, 'The Boss really got his teeth into the youth policy
and the system was expanded. He called the scouts together and spelt out
to them that without good scouts, Manchester United could not become as
successful as he wanted. He made them feel important, no, vital, to his
ambitions. They went away more committed than ever to unearthing a
great generation of United players.'

Eric Harrison and Archie Knox became key figures in Ferguson's plans
to wake what had become something of a sleeping giant and build for the
future of the club. His vision and determination were already marking him
out as the right man in the right place at the right time.

Harrison, still living in Halifax in his native Yorkshire, says, 'After the
Boss had examined, with his usual professionalism and precision, my personality and coaching ability, I finally got to know him. I respected him for
what football meant to him and for what Manchester United meant to him.
Years on, I feel that we are now good friends and I tease him that he is much
softer with players now than he was in his initial seasons.'

It's true that the Alex Ferguson of the present day has mellowed a tad
compared to the days of headlines along the lines of 'Fiery Fergie' and
'Fergie Fury'.

Archie Knox was an equally determined driving force until he suddenly
stunned his mentor by leaving to become Walter Smith's coach at Glasgow
Rangers. Ferguson considered it a backward step in terms of quality of football and he also felt rather betrayed. The timing of the move certainly
shocked him, coming as it did just a couple of days before a tough semi-
final against Legia Warsaw in the European Cup-Winners' Cup.

United made him a big offer to stay but it didn't match what was on the
table at Ibrox, so off he went back to Scotland. It is a matter for conjecture
if he ever regrets what he missed after playing such an important part in
building the foundations of a great era. He undoubtedly realised that
Ferguson would survive without him. After Rangers, Archie followed Walter
Smith to become his assistant at Everton. He then had a spell with
Coventry, but is now back in Scotland, working with Craig Brown at
Aberdeen. In the interim, he had a range of posts, working as assistant man-

ager at Bolton Wanderers and Blackburn Rovers (under Paul Ince) as well as coaching Scotland Under-21s during Walter Smith's time in charge of the senior side.

Looking back and talking about Ferguson's early days at Old Trafford, Archie says, 'I always knew he would cope. United's past can be a millstone around your neck and it proved too much for some bosses who came before Alex, but he handled it well. The pressures start from the moment you arrive. You get the past rammed down your throat from day one – there's no escape. Nobody lets you forget what has been achieved and what is wanted again. Ferguson respected their past – you have to admire what went before, but you mustn't be scared of it, and Alex was never scared. He just didn't let it play on his mind like some of his predecessors did.'

Most Appearances for Sir Alex Ferguson

Overall		*League*	
Ryan Giggs	876	Ryan Giggs	613
Paul Scholes	676	Paul Scholes	466
Gary Neville	602	Gary Neville	400
Denis Irwin	529	Denis Irwin	368
Roy Keane	480	Brian McClair	355
Brian McClair	471	Roy Keane	326
Gary Pallister	437	Gary Pallister	314
Steve Bruce	414	Steve Bruce	309
Peter Schmeichel	398	Peter Schmeichel	292
David Beckham	394	Nicky Butt	270

Gary Neville became the first United player to make 100 appearances in the Champions League during the game against Benfica on 26 September 2006, going on to a final total of 115; Ryan Giggs (136) and Paul Scholes (128) also reached the landmark.

[4]

SOMETHING ABOUT THE MAN

THERE IS NO DOUBT that Aberdeen found it difficult to part with Alex Ferguson. He had been a brilliant manager for them and had enjoyed a great relationship with Dick Donald, the Pittodrie chairman. As Ian Donald, the chairman's son, who spent a few years with United as a junior and reserve player, says, 'Alex Ferguson set new standards for our club and set the area alight. In fact, he put Aberdeen on the map.'

Inevitably, his work at Aberdeen had attracted offers in addition to the abortive approach from Rangers. He turned down both Wolves and Spurs before taking the Old Trafford post, and he arrived with a quite clear dec-laration of intent, as he spelt out to co-author Tom Tyrrell, then Piccadilly Radio's United reporter, in one of his first interviews as the new boss:

'It's luxury for me here. For a start, at Aberdeen we didn't have our own training ground. We used school pitches and that kind of thing, so it's a real change for me. Here at Manchester United the facilities are marvellous and I hope we can put them to good use.

'We are not in a desperate position. My job is to come here and win every game I am involved in, and that's the only way I can attack it. It is the same attitude that I had at Aberdeen. There is a game to be played tomor-row and we must be positive in our approach to every game.'

Ferguson generously resisted the approach of many newly appointed managers, who so often complain about the state of the club to emphasise the enormity of the task facing them. Alex was most complimentary about Ron Atkinson, paying tribute to his knowledge of the game, and adding, 'I know the club's had injury problems and my sympathy goes to Ron Atkinson. You need luck in football, and he didn't have any. I just hope I get better luck with injuries.'

(Above) Alex Ferguson watches his new charges from the dugout: 8 November 1986. Despite solid defence from Paul McGrath (below), what he saw was not good, as United stumbled to a 2–0 defeat against Oxford.

Atkinson was sacked on 6 November 1986, two days after United's crushing 4–1 defeat at Southampton in a Littlewoods Cup third-round replay. This match, on top of a slipping league performance that had landed them second bottom in the table, spelt the end for Ron.

Three hours after sacking him and assistant Mick Brown, Martin Edwards flew to Aberdeen. He hadn't wasted any time and nor did Ferguson, who reported for duty at Old Trafford the following morning. He couldn't afford to dawdle because the very next day United were playing Oxford United away in the First Division. The team he sent into action was: Turner, Duxbury, Albiston, Moran, McGrath, Hogg, Blackmore, Moses, Stapleton, Davenport and Barnes. Sub: Olsen.

On paper, it wasn't the most formidable of fixtures but the game was lost 2–0. The following week United drew 0–0 at Norwich before coming home to give Ferguson his first win, beating Queens Park Rangers 1–0 with a goal from John Sivebaek.

The new manager bided his time and on the surface there were few changes as he quietly assessed the situation and took stock of his players. In the early days he contented himself with tightening up discipline among the junior players, insisting on short haircuts and a dress code on match days. Most players are able to raise their game for a new boss because they know judgements are being made, so Alex waited until things had settled down and he could assess their true worth.

As he anticipated, there was a slight improvement but it didn't last, and with five of the final 12 fixtures lost, United finished 11th in the League, their lowest since their relegation year of 1974. They won a league game at Liverpool and knocked Manchester City out of the FA Cup but they were unable to sustain their form.

Like Atkinson before him, Ferguson continued to suffer injuries. Goalkeeper Gary Bailey was forced to retire from football at the end of the season, and Remi Moses quit with a damaged ankle. In all, he used 23 players in his first season, so nobody could complain he had not been given a chance under the new boss.

At the end of that first season Ferguson decided that he had too many players in the 30-plus bracket and not enough in their mid-20s. During the summer he set out to bring down the average age by signing Brian McClair from Celtic. The relationship they struck has continued and, as well as playing for him, Brian has coached for him and now manages the youth academy at the Carrington training ground. Nobody knows Ferguson better, and nobody has more respect for the manager's authority and leadership qualities.

'Obviously, I was aware of Alex Ferguson when I was still playing for Celtic,' explained Brian, 'because Aberdeen and one or two other clubs, such as Dundee United and Hearts, were making Scottish football much more competitive. Aberdeen, under Ferguson's management, had a lot of particularly good players, and there were a number of close-run championships.

'I remember meeting him for the first time. I was in Monaco as the winner of the Golden Boot award for being the top league goal scorer. Alex Ferguson was there to receive some award on behalf of Aberdeen, and after the dinner and presentations I bumped into him. It was only 10 o'clock and he asked me what I was doing. I told him that I thought I might as well make the most of being in Monte Carlo and intended spending a couple of hours in the casino.

'He replied, "Oh no you're not, you're going to bed!" It was the end of the season and he wasn't even my manager, but the strange thing is that I did exactly what he said. There was just something about the man that I didn't want to argue with. He has a natural authority. Somehow you just accept that what he says is right.

'I was young, of course, but even so that first experience of meeting him has never left me. Perhaps it was something to do with the fact that I had grown up a Manchester United supporter from about the age of 10. I started following them after they were relegated because I enjoyed their promotion season so much. Stuart Pearson, Steve Coppell and the rest were really exciting to watch and they played great football, home and away. At Old Trafford they played in front of crowds of fifty thousand every week. There was always a story about them to read, too, and even after I started playing for Celtic, I was always attracted to them.

'I was very happy at Celtic Park and in my last season there I scored 35 goals so things were going well for me. I was at the end of my contract, though, so when Manchester United came in for me I was thrilled. When Alex Ferguson said he wanted me it was a great feeling, a real boost to my confidence.

'Of course, Alex is a good salesman and he has a very persuasive approach. He tells you that he wants you in his team, that he will look after your interests and that joining him would be the best thing for you to do. He means it, too, it's not just talk, and I was just so glad to be joining Manchester United.

'They weren't winning trophies at the time, but they still had these huge crowds and I just felt that something was going to happen.'

For both United and McClair, it certainly did happen. Brian scored 24 league goals in an ever-present first season, plus bagging another seven in the two domestic cup competitions. He maintained that level of scoring over the next five years, along the way picking up an FA Cup winner's medal and sharing in the European Cup-Winners' Cup success of 1991 the following year.

His move highlighted Ferguson's ability to strike a hard bargain in the transfer market, at least until the flood of television money destroyed everybody's financial values with rocketing fees for players and inflated salaries. Celtic wanted £2 million for McClair. However, the player was at the end of his contract, so Ferguson took them to a league tribunal, which ruled that a fee of £850,000 was more appropriate. That decision did not please Celtic, but for United it represented a cool move, if not daylight robbery!

McClair – or 'Choccy' as he became known to team-mates because of the rhyme with chocolate éclair – was always so well behaved, disciplined and successful that he came to be regarded by players and fans alike as the manager's favourite. He responded to the teacher's pet jibes with his usual laid-back approach.

'I could always handle the banter. I like to give it out, so I always had to be prepared to take it, too, and I suppose it was true that for a long time the manager never dropped me. He had great faith in me, though I certainly like to think I repaid the trust he showed in me. I always knew, though, that when it came to my turn to be chopped, I wouldn't be shown any favours. However, I must admit I did get a shock on one occasion when I least expected it.

'We were going to an away match and he phoned to ask me to take his bag to the ground because he was going somewhere else before meeting up with us. So I duly looked after his bag and thought, well, that's my selection pretty secure, only to discover the following day that he had dropped me to a place on the bench. That was for the 1994 FA Cup final against Chelsea. At least I came on as a sub and scored in the 4–0 win.'

The arrival of Ole Gunnar Solskjaer, Andy Cole and Teddy Sheringham spelt the end of Brian's playing career at Old Trafford and he went back home to Motherwell before joining Brian Kidd as an assistant at Blackburn for a year. Then, after a spell out of the game, or a sabbatical as he puts it, he returned to United as a coach following the departure of Steve McClaren for Middlesbrough to become their manager.

'Working for him as a coach was not a lot different in principle from being one of his players. He likes people to be positive and he is good at making decisions himself. He is guided always by what is best for Manchester United,

Brian McClair celebrates his first goal for United, on 22 August 1987 against Watford. He was one of Alex Ferguson's first signings, and arguably one of his very best.

Nearly 20 years later, in September 2006, Brian McClair watches on as United's Reserves take on Manchester City.

and then you get on with it. He won't blank you, he will always take time to explain his decisions and he will listen to you, even if his conclusion goes against you. If a player is upset at being dropped or something like that, he will suggest that the player comes in on the Sunday morning for a chat, but he's clever because he knows that by the next day, faced with getting up on a Sunday morning and driving into the training ground, the player might not see the problem as quite so pressing.

'He told me once that he didn't pick teams on personalities but on what is the best side to win a game. The manager has an idea and sixteen players have theirs, too, but once he makes up his mind he goes with it. It can seem brutal or hurtful at times but that's life under Alex Ferguson. You either deal with it and get on with your career, or decide to go and do something else, somewhere else. It's inevitable in football that you will reach a point where things are not going to suit every individual. If you don't want to stay and be part of the set-up, then the manager has never stood in anyone's way. He's quite happy to let them go.

'He always wants to win. Throughout his life, winning has been so important to him. He has that drive, and because he has it he can drive other people along. His desire for success makes him always want to be the best, the best player when he was a player himself, the best landlord when he ran two pubs in Aberdeen, and nowadays of course the best manager. He wants to win at everything, even away from football. He gets just as passionate playing cards or taking part in one of the quizzes he organises on away trips between players and staff. It's all part of his high standards.

'He's a very clever man, of course. He can shout and bawl when it's necessary, but he can also be kind and encouraging if he thinks that's the best policy. Always, even when he's furious, he's under control. When he kicked the boot that hit David Beckham on the head, people tried to suggest that he had done it deliberately. Well, yes, he was angry, and he let fly to show his anger by kicking the boot. It's nonsense, though, to say he aimed to hit David. I've seen him play and he was never that good!

'There is a caring side to his nature. He's always there to help players away from football, and he does a lot for charity, as well as not losing sight of his roots. He's always going back to Scotland to do something for his old boys' club at Harmony Row in Glasgow. He has his charity golf day and is keen to support the club charity, UNICEF, and encourages the players to become involved.'

Brian McClair is now playing yet another role for Sir Alex Ferguson, following his appointment to succeed Les Kershaw as manager of the club's academy for young players. He is well suited to the job. Having coached the academy teams and shown a wide grasp of their needs, he had already been asked by the manager to advise several of them in their contract negotiations with the club.

McClair has enjoyed his responsibilities as director of United's academy. He knows what is expected from him by Ferguson, because those demands do not differ very much in principle from what was expected of him as a player and coach. He knows, too, that he can count on the full backing and encouragement of the manager.

'If you give Alex Ferguson everything in terms of respect, effort and performance,' says McClair, 'he will pay you back in abundance. Character has always been as important to him as a player's ability and it's something we recognise at academy level. I'm pleased to be involved because he believes in a strong youth policy. He is always interested in what is happening at academy level, has a good grasp of the work involved and gets as much pleasure from seeing one of the boys come through as we do. At the same time, he lets you get on with it and trusts you. He has turned United, a big club that hadn't been as successful as it should have been, into winners.'

*Viv Anderson tangles
with John Barnes:
'I wouldn't have
swapped playing
for Alex Ferguson
for the world.'*

(5)

FLYING TEACUPS

ALEX FERGUSON TOOK STOCK of his defence as well as his strike force
at the end of his fact-finding first season, with the result that in addition to
signing Brian McClair, he also brought in Viv Anderson.

As a schoolboy, Viv had spent all his school holidays for a year at United,
but he was unsuccessful. Instead, he joined his home-town club
Nottingham Forest, where he went on to win both European Cup and
League Championship honours. He then moved to Arsenal and became the
first black player to play for England, winning 30 caps.

The new United boss was attracted by Anderson's experience and the fact
that he had hardly missed a game while at Arsenal. Ferguson got him for
£250,000 and Anderson jumped at the chance finally to join Manchester
United.

'I got a call from Bryan Robson, whom I knew of course from playing
with him for England. He was acting on behalf of United and he asked me
if I was interested in joining them. I was at the end of my contract with
Arsenal. We had just beaten Liverpool to win the Milk Cup and although
I was offered a new contract to stay at Highbury, it took me two seconds to
pack my bags,' he explained.

'I didn't know Alex Ferguson, except by reputation as a fiery Scotsman,
but when I met him he was very positive and enthusiastic. United were in
the doldrums and he wanted his own people for his attempt to build them
back up again.

'I didn't have long to wait to experience his angry side. United were playing at Hartlepool in a pre-season friendly and I remember him taking Brian
McClair and me, as the new boys, by car. It was a fair side we had out, with

Bryan Robson, Paul McGrath, Kevin Moran, Mike Duxbury, Gordon Strachan, Norman Whiteside and Mark Hughes. I was at right-back and I'll never forget it when we came off at half-time 5–0 down.

'My, did the manager go for us – teacups across the dressing room, the lot! It certainly had an effect because the second half was drawn 1–1, although we still came away with a 6–1 defeat, which he certainly wasn't happy about.

'We did quite well in the manager's first full season, following the arrival of Brian and me, and finished runners-up to Liverpool. The following season, 1988-89, wasn't so good. We finished eleventh and, personally, it was a bit of a disaster. I had a heel injury and everything was stop-start. I don't think United got full value out of me, which was disappointing because at Arsenal I think I missed about three games in three or four years. I'm sure one of the reasons Alex Ferguson bought me was because he thought I was a durable kind of player he could count on for regular appearances.

'It was not to be, but I've got to say that he isn't one of those managers who doesn't want to know you if you're injured. He's very loyal and supportive with injured players. He waited a year for Ruud van Nistelrooy and look at the way he has stood by Ole Gunnar Solskjaer during the course of his injury problems. He was very good with me, too, and even after I left to join Sheffield Wednesday, he used to get me back for the European games after United had qualified for the Cup-Winners' Cup.

'United had been out of European competition for some time because of the ban on English clubs, and they didn't have a lot of European experience in the team. Playing in Europe is totally different in terms of atmosphere, tactics and tension, so Alex had me like a wise old head in the dressing room on European nights. I had been around the scene with Nottingham Forest whereas it was something new at the time to Ryan Giggs, David Beckham and the others.

'I was delighted to help, and at the same time it was good of Alex to think of having me back. I felt it was quite a shrewd move, but then he is a shrewd manager. I'm sure he also did it because he knew it would help me, too.

'Although I didn't play as many games as I would have liked, I wouldn't have swapped playing for Manchester United and Alex Ferguson for the world. After Sheffield Wednesday, I went as Bryan Robson's coach to Middlesbrough. I enjoyed the ups and downs there and tried to put to good use what I had learned from the managers I had played for – Brian Clough, Bobby Robson, Ron Atkinson and Alex Ferguson. I'm sure I took a few things on board from my time with him.

'I had the opportunity to go with Bryan to Bradford after Middlesbrough, but I thought that was a bit of a poisoned chalice so I linked up with with Mike Beresford, the former athlete and runner, at North West Events, based in Altrincham. We organised corporate sports functions – everything from football to Formula One motor racing. I have also been involved in a football set-up in Dubai, where we hosted training camps for professional teams and ran coaching schools for youngsters.'

Naturally, with new players coming in, some had to go to make room for them. Frank Stapleton was probably the biggest 'name' to depart, sold to Ajax after Ferguson had decided that Frank, for all his achievements at Arsenal, was going downhill. Gary Bailey and Remi Moses left because of injuries but others had to go because they were on the wrong side of 30, including Colin Gibson, Arthur Albiston and Kevin Moran. Terry Gibson, John Sivebaek and Jesper Olsen were considered less suited to English football. Goalkeeper Chris Turner, Peter Barnes and centre-half Graeme Hogg also left.

Peter Davenport was another casualty, although he actually asked for a transfer when, following the return of Mark Hughes from Barcelona in the summer of 1988, it became clear that the new strike force would be Hughes and Brian McClair.

What did it feel like to be eased out in the upheaval brought about by the new manager? Was Ferguson as persuasive and caring with those leaving as he was when charming new players to the club? If the experience of Peter Davenport is anything to judge by, Alex Ferguson continued to play fair with the players he was moving on.

'I have no complaints,' said Peter. 'The manager explained to me that he had to try Mark Hughes playing alongside Brian McClair, which left no place for me, but he was OK about it. He knew that after breaking the monopoly of Celtic and Rangers with Aberdeen in Scotland, he now had to do the same with Liverpool and Everton, and I don't think he found it very easy.

'He soon realised that English football had a strength in depth that was missing in Scotland, and that there were eight or nine teams all capable of beating each other, so he needed to strengthen his team, and I paid the price for the arrival of McClair and Hughes. I moved to Middlesbrough. Later, when I was playing for Sunderland, I got a phone call on the morning of our 1992 FA Cup final against Liverpool. It was Alex Ferguson to wish me good luck. I'd been gone from Old Trafford four years but he took the trouble. I've not forgotten that gesture. It tells you a lot about the man.

'Initially when he arrived, he seemed nervous when he talked to the players. I suppose he was hyped up about the job and perhaps nervous of the expectations, which might explain the embarrassment for both him and me at a meeting before one of our first games. He ran through who was playing in the various positions and then said up front there would be Frank and Nigel. The lads knew all about Frank Stapleton of course, but who's Nigel they asked. "You know, Nigel Davenport, there," he said. He'd mixed up my name with the actor's, much to the amusement of the boys.

'Perhaps it's my name that's tricky. Bobby Robson, who had a reputation for getting things wrong with names, didn't let me down when I was on the bench for my one and only England cap. He turned to Don Howe, the coach, and said, "Get Devonshire on." So Alan Devonshire alias Peter Davenport duly came on to replace Tony Hateley!'

Far from his fiery image, Alex Ferguson is fond of making the kind of good-luck phone call he made to Peter Davenport – and you don't have to have played for him. Martin Buchan, United's elegant centre-half in the 1970s who is now with the Professional Footballers' Association, received a call on the morning he was just about to set off from home for his first league game as the newly appointed manager of Burnley.

'Alex said he was calling to wish me all the best and to offer me two pieces of advice. He said I should always make myself available to the press so that you can have some control of what they write, and that I should never seek confrontation with my players. He said you shouldn't manufacture a row with someone just to show who is the boss.

'I replied that I appreciated the call but the advice had come a couple of weeks too late. I'd thumped one of the team. That punch, incidentally, sealed my career as a manager. In all my time playing in England I had never been involved in a fight. I had never been sent off and had just five bookings to my name. I realised that if I was lashing out, and at someone on my own side, then management wasn't for me. Oh, why didn't you ring earlier, Alex?

'I never played for Alex but I did play against him, when he was with Rangers and Dunfermline and I played for Aberdeen. He was a centre-forward and I found him a handful, very competitive. You could certainly say he left a big impression on me!

'I like to think I played a part, in a small way, in getting him to Old Trafford as successor to Ron Atkinson. Obviously, the United board knew all about his success with Aberdeen in Scotland, especially beating Real Madrid to win the European Cup-Winners' Cup, but I gave the directors

Peter 'Nigel' Davenport, United's top scorer in 1986–87, chases a through ball on QPR's artificial surface.

Martin Buchan and a young Arthur Albiston celebrate winning the 1977 FA Cup. Buchan had more painful memories of playing against Alex Ferguson.

the chance to meet him when he agreed to bring Aberdeen, my previous club, down to Manchester to play United in my testimonial match. Maybe I helped him on his way with that introduction to the Old Trafford people.

'Incidentally, it was typical of him to turn out a team for a testimonial for one of the club's former players. He has a great sense of doing the right thing in football and upholding what's good for the game, as I have also discovered in my work for the Professional Footballers' Association. My job frequently takes me to United and he is always helpful. For instance, when drugs were high on the agenda, the PFA took an expert round the clubs to talk to the players about the dangers and that kind of thing. Alex took it very seriously and made sure that every player, from the most seasoned international to the newest recruit, was there for the talks when we went to the Carrington training ground.

'He takes the education side very seriously and is meticulous. He can remember people's names, which I don't think is a gift but just plain hard work. He's a busy man but he makes time for people and has never allowed himself to get carried away with his own importance. For instance, when I used to go back to Aberdeen while he was the manager there, I always used to call in at the club for a chat with Teddy Scott, the second-team trainer who had been there for years and was a real character. I used to like showing people round my old club, too, and on one occasion we bumped into Alex Ferguson, who invited us to have a cup of tea. Instead of dispatching someone to make a pot for us, he took us down to the groundsman's place and made it for us himself. It's only a little thing, but it's these touches that mark him out as an exceptional man as well as a great manager.'

The more different people talk about Alex Ferguson and his achievements, the more the many contrasting sides to his character become apparent. Harry Gregg, United's former Northern Ireland goalkeeper and a Munich survivor, remembers that, as well as being kind, Sir Alex is never far from militant mode:

'I was a coach at United under manager Dave Sexton and the club sent me up to see Alex Ferguson to discuss a tournament we were going to play in at Aberdeen, along with Southampton.

'I was sitting in the stand with Alex, watching some of the lads training, when he suddenly began shouting at one of the players. His training was being ripped to pieces by his manager, who up until that point had been chatting very pleasantly.

'I knew that Alex was a down-to-earth kind of man with no frills, but I was staggered. On my way back to Manchester I couldn't help thanking my lucky stars I had never played for him because I don't think I would have lasted five minutes without doing something stupid if he had given me that kind of treatment. Perhaps the player was used to it and took no notice, but I would have found it tough.'

Sir Alex Ferguson's Record against Selected Opponents

Arsenal

Competition	P	W	D	L	F	A
Premier League	38	16	11	11	49	36
Division One	11	3	4	4	13	12
Cups	18	8	4	6	25	22

United have met Arsenal in only one final (FA Cup 2005); the match was drawn 0–0, but United lost on penalties.
The clubs have met five times in the Charity/Community Shield, United winning twice after a penalty shoot-out and losing the other three.

Chelsea

Competition	P	W	D	L	F	A
Premier League	38	11	14	13	47	49
Division One	9	3	3	3	14	12
Cups	15	8	4	3	21	11

United have met Chelsea in three finals: they won the 1994 FA Cup 4–0, lost the 2007 FA Cup 1–0 and then drew the 2008 Champions League final 1–1, winning on penalties.
The clubs have met in five Charity/Community Shields: United won one, three went to penalty shoot-outs (United winning twice), and Chelsea won one.

Liverpool

Competition	P	W	D	L	F	A
Premier League	38	20	7	11	56	45
Division One	12	3	5	4	11	15
Cups	8	4	1	3	9	8

United have met Liverpool in two finals, winning the 1996 FA Cup by 1–0, and losing the 2003 League Cup by 1–0.
The clubs have met twice in the Charity/Community Shield, sharing the trophy once, and United losing once.

Manchester City

Competition	P	W	D	L	F	A
Premier League	28	17	6	5	47	28
Division One	7	2	4	1	9	10
Cups	6	4	0	2	11	7

6

THE DRINKING CLUB

ALEX FERGUSON might not have acted hastily, but once into his stride, there was no holding him. As well as the long-term injured, the over 30s and those who didn't suit, the massive rethink of players included another category. This one covered an area that he considered had got out of hand and called for drastic action.

As the manager explained, 'One of my concerns when I arrived was that I had to get rid of the idea that United was a drinking club rather than a football club. I had enormous difficulty with Norman Whiteside and Paul McGrath.

'I believe most of Norman's trouble was down to disappointment and possibly depression with his continual injuries. I think he sought refuge in a lifestyle that created conflict with my concept of a Manchester United player.'

Ferguson showed great patience but Norman and Paul seemed to encourage each other in their excesses. The inevitable result was that he put both players up for transfer. Whiteside was sold to Everton in August 1989 for £750,000, while McGrath joined Graham Taylor at Aston Villa where, despite his knee problems, he pulled himself together to make more than 250 league appearances, more than he had logged up for United.

Norman was not so fortunate at Goodison Park. Despite a bright start and scoring regularly, including one against United, he was able to make only 27 league appearances before further injury forced him into retirement 15 months later. At his peak, the top Italian clubs had chased him, but he was a big, heavy man and his body just couldn't take the wear and tear, so he spent increasing amounts of time on the sidelines. He became friendly with Paul McGrath, another Irishman, albeit from the south, who had even more baffling problems with alcohol. Together they would go on sprees that soon put them on a collision course with the new manager.

Norman was still a 16-year-old apprentice when Ron Atkinson gave him his league debut as a substitute at Brighton in April 1982. A month later, in the final game of the season, he was in the starting line-up for a full debut and marked the occasion by scoring in a 2–0 win over Stoke City.

His impact was startling. Northern Ireland had had their eye on him and that summer they decided that if he was good enough for Manchester United, he was good enough for them. They took him to the 1982 World Cup in Spain and gave him his international debut against Yugoslavia in Zaragoza. At 17 years 41 days, he became the youngest ever World Cup player, younger even than Pelé had been when he arrived on the scene for Brazil. Norman appeared in all five of Northern Ireland's matches in the tournament on the way to a total of 38 international caps.

The following season, back in Manchester, he was a regular in the first team and created another record by becoming the youngest goal scorer in an FA Cup final when he headed United's second goal in the 4–0 replay victory against Brighton. He had also scored in that season's Football League Cup final when United lost 2–1 to Liverpool, setting another record by scoring in the two domestic cup finals in one season.

The FA Cup always seemed to bring out the best in him. Fans will remember his superbly struck shot that curled from a narrow angle round the goalkeeper to give United a 1–0 win over Everton in the 1985 final at Wembley. Sadly, it was to prove his last notable achievement in the game because for the next three years he fought what became a losing battle against injuries. By the age of 23 he was struggling with his knee, and although he was still capable of producing some outstanding displays, he had to keep dropping out of the action. He was out of the game by the age of 26.

Alex Ferguson has never lost his admiration for Norman as a player and says, 'If he had had one more yard of pace, he would have been one of the greatest players ever produced in British football. But for continuous knee problems affecting him, he would without doubt have become a truly world-class star.

'As it was, he still managed to make a tremendous impact on English football. He had incredible quality, an ice-cold temperament, wonderful vision and a good touch on the ball, all topped off with his infamous aggressive streak, which often had supporters as well as opponents cringing.'

Certainly, United fans appreciated and enjoyed Norman's total commitment. Anyone who watched his impact on Liverpool and Steve McMahon, for instance, when he came on as a substitute at Anfield in 1988 in one of his last appearances for United, will never forget the way he drove at the opposition to turn the game around. From 3–1 down, the game ended in a 3–3 draw.

When it became clear that he could not carry on as a player, far from feeling sorry for himself, Norman took a positive stance. 'It was hard to take when my playing career ended,' he said, 'but there was no point sitting around looking for sympathy. So I went back to school.'

He graduated in sports science at University College, Salford, and is now a qualified podiatrist, an expert on the study of the lower limb. He worked for several years for the Professional Footballers' Association, visiting clubs and screening their young professionals for lower limb abnormalities.

'A few of the big clubs have their own podiatrist,' he explained, 'but one year I visited 60 clubs to check the young players for flat feet and poor posture. I carried out gait analysis, watching them walk and run, and then tried to find a remedy for any defects.'

He opened a private clinic in John's Street, Manchester, with rooms next door to Jim McGregor, the former United physiotherapist, who first set him on the medical path by giving him the names of the bones in the body to learn.

Some might find it difficult to equate the professional medic of today with the macho figure he cut in his playing career, but there is much more to the man eased out of Old Trafford for drinking than his love of a tipple. For instance, how many know that he doesn't smoke or swear and hasn't done so since giving up on bad language when he went to secondary school at the age of 11? He has a match-day job at Old Trafford as one of the club's hospitality hosts at home fixtures. That role and his after-dinner speaking, in addition to his clinic and then writing a book, *Determined*, which was published in 2007, about his journey through life, as well as appearances on Soccer AM, make him a very busy man.

So does he harbour any bitterness about being shown the door at Old Trafford? Does he feel Ferguson gave him a raw deal?

'Not a bit. I'm fine with Alex Ferguson,' he says.

'I knew from the moment he arrived who was going to be boss and that he didn't care who the players were or how big their reputations. He knew all about the drinking culture that existed at the club at that time, too.

'I remember quite clearly when he came down the stairs at the Cliff

Paul McGrath, with Bryan Robson and Norman Whiteside, after scoring against Arsenal in August 1985: cue the celebrations! Alex Ferguson was not impressed with the drinking culture he found at United when he arrived.

training ground to meet everyone and introduce himself that he was intent on making sure we all knew who the new manager was. It was not so much what he said as simply the tone of his voice. Our first game was the next day and he wanted everyone there, including the injured. That meant me and Robbo – Bryan Robson – who was another on the sick list at the time. We drove down by car after treatment to join the rest of the team at Oxford.

'I also remember his first team talk. The point that sticks in my mind is that he said if you want to play football, keep the ball on the park, no belting it off the pitch. You always have a better chance that way, he said, which I suppose makes sense.

'Naturally, he changed things but one of the strangest rules he introduced, which I still can't understand, is that he insisted all the injured players should stay at the ground after training and go for lunch in the restaurant that United had at that time at Old Trafford. His idea was that we should mix with the public and supporters, who were also in for a meal. The problem was that when you are injured and can't train, you worry that you will put on weight, and yet here we were stuffing ourselves every day with rich lunches just so we could talk to fans. He was making "Billy Bloaters" of us!

'Perhaps he thought the drinking was already doing that, because it wasn't long before he had his hooks into Paul McGrath and me. Paul was also having a difficult time with injuries and liked a drink. We had too much time on our hands. I think I took the wind out of the boss's sails a bit, though, because whenever I had been out on the tiles I would knock on his door the next day and, before he could say anything, I would say, "I was out last night, Boss, sorry."

'The result was that we were always honest with each other, no lies or excuses on my part, though naturally some straight talking from him.

'He understood my frustration, though. It's horrible when you're a professional footballer and have long stretches out of action. I'm not even a good watcher and he knew it was a hard time for me. I just regret he didn't see the best of me.

'It was no surprise when I came back from Northern Ireland and he said that Colin Harvey wanted to take me to Everton. It was a transfer that suited United, Everton and me. The fee was £600,000, which was good for United, with another £150,000 if I made a certain number of appearances, which I never reached so that was OK for Everton. I was given a good deal. In fact, I made more money in my transfer year than I had been earning at

Norman Whiteside, supported by Mike Duxbury, sees off the challenge of Alan Smith and David Rocastle. Ferguson thought that with a little more pace 'he would have been one of the greatest players ever produced in British football'.

Arthur Albiston (right) played for United for 14 years and made nearly 500 appearances, but there were no hard feelings when the new manager decided it was time for a change.

United because I had been left behind in the wage structure and had hardly been in a position to ask for more.

'Alex said a fresh challenge would be good for me, and he was right. Despite all the problems, I always got on well with Alex and I have the greatest respect for both him and Manchester United. When I left the club, I was offered £50,000 by one newspaper to have a go at him but I turned it down. It was a lot of money at the time but I would never do that, and I won't be slagging anyone off in the future, either.

'One of the good things from that is that I can work in the hospitality lounges on a match day with my head held high. Alex Ferguson, who I think found out about the newspaper offer, stops and talks to me, and he used to invite me to bring the kids down to watch the training, which was nice.

'I don't see much of Paul these days. He's back home in the Republic of Ireland, living in Wexford, and he's also written a book. His story has helped people understand the troubled times he had growing up, which perhaps accounted for his drinking sprees and the car crash that finally triggered his exit from the game.'

Alex Ferguson certainly retains a fondness and an admiration for Norman Whiteside, but at the time, typically, he did not let sentiment stand in the way of his drive to bring success to his new club. All successful managers share that quality to a degree and Ferguson never shied away from it. Norman Whiteside took both his injury misfortunes and departure from Old Trafford without ever losing the tremendous respect he has always had for Alex Ferguson.

In fact, such is the respect Sir Alex commands that very few of the players he shows the door bear any ill will, certainly not Arthur Albiston, a staunch United man if ever there was one. The Edinburgh-born Scot had had 14 years of first-team football at Old Trafford when he moved to West Bromwich Albion in 1988, and there was still more to come, but he accepted the manager's decision with good grace.

As he explained, 'I knew Alex a little bit before he arrived at United as our manager because I had been in the Scotland squad when he was in charge following the death of Jock Stein. So I already knew he was very well organised and was not surprised when that continued with United. He was meticulous, paying great attention to detail, and he had a good memory. I was impressed with him very quickly. He knew exactly what he wanted and was hard but fair. Coming from the background he did in Glasgow, he didn't suffer fools gladly, and he also liked people to earn what they achieved. I was brought up in a similar way and appreciated that he didn't like people to have an easy route to the top. He likes players to work hard so that they realise their full potential, and he can come down like a ton of bricks if he feels his guys are underachieving.

'One of his strengths is getting performances out of players. He is not afraid to make hard decisions and of doing what needs to be done for the sake of the club.

'It was difficult for me at the end, when I wasn't playing regularly in the first team. After such a long time as a first choice for my position, it comes hard, but I respected his judgement. I felt I was capable of playing for another year or so at United but when the manager decided otherwise, it wasn't a problem. It's sad when you are no longer part of the team, even though you know it can't last for ever, but there was no bitterness on my part. You have to get on with it. It's no use feeling mopey.

'When Alex took over he had his agenda and, because of the respect we had for him, players accepted his decisions. It certainly wasn't a problem for me. He doesn't make many mistakes with his judgement of players, as his record bears out. He is right far more often than he is wrong.

'I like to think I contributed to the club. It's not my style to create problems. I wasn't going to go begging, either. In fact, even when I wasn't playing, Alex kept me involved with the squad.

'Overall he had some tough decisions to make because I think the club at that point were underachieving. We had a lot of international players but they were inconsistent in terms of the league. He turned it round. After he had got the mentality right and won the first trophy, he has compiled a record second to none.'

7

THE KNIVES WERE OUT

ALEX FERGUSON WORKED HARD trying to build a team capable of honours. His first three seasons were a transfer merry-go-round with players departing and arriving. Steve Bruce was signed from Norwich for £800,000 and Jim Leighton came south from Aberdeen for £750,000 to take over in goal.

Gordon Strachan was moved out to Leeds, a controversial decision that came back to haunt Ferguson when the Scot inspired his new team's return to the top division and then, three years later, helped them to pip United for the championship. Ferguson is not a man to let doubts eat away at him, though, and once he had decided that Strachan, whom he had first managed at Aberdeen, had run out of steam and needed a change of scene, he had to go.

After experimenting with the 'Fergie Fledglings' led by Russell Beardsmore, Ferguson really let rip in the transfer market in the summer of 1989, spending what was then the tidy sum of £7 million to capture Neil Webb from Nottingham Forest, Gary Pallister from Middlesbrough, Danny Wallace from Southampton, Paul Ince, after a medical hold-up, from West Ham, and Mike Phelan, the Norwich City captain. That spree was prompted by the club slipping to 11th in season 1988-89, which was a disappointing backward step after finishing second in his first full season.

So with a stack of new players bolstering his squad, Ferguson set off on the new season with high hopes, but as he later admitted, 'I was in too much of a hurry and overambitious.' He vowed that never again would he buy so many players at the same time. The problem was that it needed time to bed in the new boys and to find the right balance. Individually, there was no doubting their quality, but as a team they just weren't gelling and it was a grim Christmas with the Reds plunging down the league table.

The knives were undoubtedly out. The media were ready for a big story but it wasn't just the media who were whipping things up – a lot of fans were moaning.

It was a crazy season right from the start. Martin Edwards was anxious to recoup the money he had invested in the club by selling, and it looked as if he had found a buyer when a £10 million deal plus a promise to rebuild the Stretford End was reached with Michael Knighton. The prospective new owner celebrated on the opening day of the season by running out on the pitch, juggling the ball and lashing it into the back of the Stretford End goal. United's hierarchy were embarrassed but it didn't seem to affect the players, who promptly went out and beat Arsenal 4–1.

Overall, though, the Reds made an erratic start to the season. Demolishing Millwall 5–1, in a match featuring a hat-trick from Mark Hughes, ended a run of three defeats, but then they went downhill again. Ferguson describes the 5–1 defeat by Manchester City at Maine Road as one of the worst days of his career. United held their own in terms of possession but after the teams had been taken off following crowd trouble in the Kippax Stand, City came back out to score two quick goals, and that was the beginning of the end. Ferguson said he drove home and went straight to bed, putting his head under the pillow in complete shock.

He needed all his famous powers of recovery to get his team back on track and they did well with a 4–1 win over Coventry City, but between the end of November and February they played 11 league games without a win, losing six and drawing five. United slipped into the bottom half of the table and finished the season in 13th place.

One of the low points came at home to Crystal Palace, when the manager chose to drop the popular Mark Hughes and the crowd let him know what they thought of his decision, which wasn't much. They chanted Hughes' name and Ferguson duly brought him off the bench to replace Lee Sharpe, but the match still ended in a 2–1 defeat and the media scented a sacking. The popular perception was that if United failed to put a run together in the FA Cup, Ferguson would become part of the post-Busby pattern of managers staying for three or four years before making way for someone else to be given a chance.

All eyes were on the third round of the Cup and when United drew Nottingham Forest away, even Ferguson's heart sank. It was a tough tie and Sir Alex described the run-up to the match as the blackest period he had ever experienced in his football life.

The press were certainly scenting blood this time, and Jimmy Hill even commented that United looked like a beaten team in the warm-up. Bryan Robson, Neil Webb, Paul Ince, Danny Wallace and Lee Sharpe were all sitting in the stands, injured, and Forest were clear favourites to win.

Ferguson had his back to the wall and, as chairman Martin Edwards said later, 'If I had paid attention to letters from fans, it would have been easy to sack the manager.' The fact that he didn't owed much to the trust and confidence that Ferguson had built up with the board during his three seasons at the club. As Martin Edwards also said, 'Those close to the club knew all the sound things Alex Ferguson was building for the future, and we believed it was only a matter of time before things came right.'

Privately, the chairman reassured his manager that even if he lost against Forest, his job was safe.

Not everyone had the same faith. The then editor of the *Manchester Evening News* ran a phone-in asking readers to vote on whether Ferguson should be sacked or not. The result of the poll showed a majority in favour of the bullet, and the editor gave this to his United reporter, David Meek, who says, 'I had the job of analysing the figures and clearly the editor expected me to write a piece saying the fans wanted Ferguson sacked. But this didn't make sense to me because, like the chairman, I knew there was a blossoming crop of young talent around the corner and that, in any case, there was just too much talent in the squad for it not to come good eventually. Perhaps I had also fallen under the Ferguson spell because I still felt he was the man to turn things round. The result was that I pointed out that if you deducted the votes from City fans wanting to cause mischief and allowed for those United fans who were content but who couldn't be bothered to telephone, you were left with an overwhelming vote of confidence in Alex Ferguson.

'It was of course spin before the word and Alastair Campbell were invented, but who proved right in the end? Alex Ferguson is a man who can sway pressmen as well as players!'

Nevertheless, it was a tense time as the crucial match approached and the manager needed to dig deep. When the chips are down, Ferguson is at his best and his players responded with a 1–0 victory, courtesy of the relatively unknown Mark Robins, who headed in a cross from Mark Hughes after 56 minutes. Sir Alex was off the hook, at least for the time being, once again showing his calibre as a manager capable of coming back off the ropes. His verdict on Robins, a local Oldham boy who had come up through the

Mark Robins wheels away in celebration after scoring the vital goal in United's third round FA Cup tie against Nottingham Forest in January 1990. Many in the media saw this result as the turning point in Alex Ferguson's career.

youth team and was the youngest player in the side, was simply: 'Bless him.'

The rescue team that day was: Leighton, Anderson, Bruce, Pallister, Martin, Blackmore, McClair, Phelan, Beardsmore, Robins, Hughes. Subs: Duxbury, Milne.

Afterwards, Ferguson commented, 'A nice touch was that the chairman called me up to his office the day before the match. We were in the midst of a crisis and the press had been badgering him for a statement about my future. They wanted him to give me a vote of confidence before the Cup-tie and they hoped he would say that if we lost, I would be sacked. The media had been working very hard at creating pressure and they wanted Martin Edwards to respond to the speculation. I have to acknowledge that the chairman and the board were brilliant. They trusted me and supported me in all my decisions concerning the buying of new players and those leaving.'

The pressure was off. The next round was not quite so formidable – a trip to Hereford where, on a muddy pitch and with nerves still jangling, they won 1–0, a goal from Clayton Blackmore sealing the victory.

The fifth-round draw presented them with another away game, and they won an exciting match at Newcastle 3–2. In fact, the entire Cup run was made up of away ties. They beat Sheffield United 1–0 in the sixth round, and progressed to meet Oldham Athletic in a memorable semi-final. That game produced a thrilling 3–3 draw after extra time at Maine Road, and three days later United won the replay 2–1 at the same ground. Once again, the hero was young Robins, who came on as an extra-time substitute to score the winner.

Twice he had saved Ferguson's bacon. Reaching Wembley took the sting out of the criticism that, to a certain extent, was still in the air as the Reds continued to stutter in the league. Robins finished the season with a tally of 10 goals in league and cup from only 13 starts, a decent strike rate, especially considering that leading marksman Mark Hughes managed just 13 goals after playing virtually the whole season. Brian McClair limped along with a meagre eight in league and cup.

The goal-poaching prowess of Robins got him no nearer the Cup final action than a substitute appearance, and the following season he seemed to sink without trace until he joined Norwich City in August 1992. Alex Ferguson will never forget him, though, and with good reason.

He didn't forget the gritty performance of Oldham's left-back, either, because that summer he went back to the Latics to buy the player for £625,000. He never regretted that decision because Denis Irwin became a linchpin of the team as the players started to sweep all before them.

First there was the Cup final. A victory would make everyone forget their woes and buy him time to work towards the consistency that is the essence of success in the league, and a quality that the club singularly lacked at the time.

Their opponents, Crystal Palace, shocked the Reds with the vigour of their approach, which somehow seemed out of tune with the character of manager Steve Coppell. The former United and England winger had been a refined player with a studious bent. He had successfully completed a degree course at Liverpool University, following his transfer from Tranmere, but his brush with academia had done nothing to soften his team's physical approach and man-marking tactics.

The Londoners' man of the match didn't even start the game, but when Ian Wright came on he rocked the Reds by scoring an equaliser to make the score 2–2 and send the game into extra time. The dashing, bustling striker, later to become a star at Arsenal, scored again, early in the extra period, and it took a goal from Mark Hughes to make it 3–3 and send the final to a replay.

The build-up to the second game was agony for Alex Ferguson. Finally, and against his better nature, he dropped Jim Leighton in favour of the extrovert and cheerful Cockney, Les Sealey. The axe for the player he had nurtured at Aberdeen had been close for a game or two and, after accepting that the goalkeeper's confidence had gone, Ferguson called on the ruthlessness that is an essential part of a top manager's armoury and delivered his bombshell.

'I felt for him,' said Ferguson, 'but I had made the decision and had to stand by it because Alex Ferguson's feelings come second to the needs of Manchester United.'

The replay suggests he made the correct decision. The Reds made no mistake this time, winning 1–0 with a goal from Lee Martin, the full-back who nearly didn't play. Martin had been going down with cramp for a match or two and the manager was concerned that he might not last if the final went into extra time. Martin assured him he would be OK, Ferguson selected him and Lee Martin emerged the hero who grabbed the lifeline that could be said to have clinched his manager's future at Old Trafford. Lee says he had no idea how significant the game was to his manager's security.

'Supporters tell me now how important that goal was for Sir Alex, like the one Mark Robins scored at Nottingham Forest to see us through the third round that season, but as a young lad of 20, I wasn't aware of all the talk about his job.

An unlikely hero. Full-back Lee Martin scores the winner in the 1990 FA Cup final replay against Crystal Palace – it was Ferguson's first trophy at United, and opened the floodgates over the years to come.

'I know we finished about 13th in the league but it never entered my head at the time that there was any possibility of the manager getting the sack. You had enough on your plate just coping with the pressure of needing to do well yourself without thinking too much about the Boss's position,' he explained.

Nevertheless, it was a valuable goal for Ferguson and a bit special for Martin. In fact, he says he is still dining out on it.

'How could I forget that goal?' asks the defender who burst forward to hammer in the rocket that won the replay. 'After all, I only scored one other goal for the first team in my 10 years at Old Trafford, and that was a fluke against West Ham. Alvin Martin kicked the ball against my legs and it went back past him into his own net,' he recalls.

'People often mention my Wembley goal but I never get fed up with hearing about it because it was the highlight of my career. I just remember Archie Knox, our coach, shouting from the bench for me to get forward and so I made a run. Neil Webb picked me out perfectly and I just whacked it. To be honest, it could have gone anywhere, and they usually did when I got near goal, but this one flew in,' he said.

'I had been a regular all season and I played most of the following season. After that, though, I struggled to hold my place and by 1994 I was on a monthly contract. Then, out of the blue, I had a call from Lou Macari asking me if I was interested in going to play for him at Glasgow Celtic.

'Carl Muggleton from Stoke City was the only other Englishman there but the Scots made me feel very welcome and I enjoyed my two and a half years at Celtic Park. Unfortunately, I had a bad time with injuries. I broke my leg, then my arm and finally I slipped two discs. I spent a couple of years with Bristol Rovers but my back just got worse and worse. I could hardly run and had to have an operation. I finished there in May of 1998.'

Lee returned to the Manchester area and settled in Glossop, close to Hyde where he grew up. He ran a sports shop for a while. Sir Alex, an appreciative man with those who have served him well, demonstrated he had not forgotten the Wembley goal when, immediately after achieving the treble, he sent a testimonial team to play Bristol Rovers in aid of a player who didn't score often, but when he did, it counted!

8

BACK IN EUROPE

THE ARRIVAL OF THE FA Cup at Old Trafford was not only a job-saver, it was also the Reds' ticket to Europe. The ban on English clubs was being lifted and United were allowed to enter the European Cup-Winners' Cup tournament. The glamour of European football has always held a particular attraction for United's fans and to a certain extent the fact that their team were back on the European stage after a five-year absence eased the pain of their struggle in the league.

Season 1990-91 was to be the real test for Alex Ferguson – was the FA Cup victory a mere flash in the pan or was the new man really making progress with his team-building? His credibility in the transfer market was on the line, following the questions posed by his dealings the previous year.

They went out of the FA Cup early but flourished in the Rumbelows, the old League Cup, meeting Ron Atkinson's Sheffield Wednesday in the final. Ferguson felt there was a strange atmosphere in the dressing room at Wembley. He didn't know at the time but this was the moment Archie Knox was preparing to reveal his decision to leave Old Trafford to join Walter Smith at Rangers. Ferguson reckoned his second-in-command was subdued and it can't have helped because ordinarily Archie is an inspirational motivator.

United had knocked out Liverpool, Leeds and Arsenal on the way to the final and hopes were high when they found themselves up against Sheffield Wednesday. At the same time, Big Ron obviously had his team well prepared and he wouldn't have been human if he hadn't wanted to put one over on his successor and the club that had sacked him.

Wednesday won 1–0 with a goal from John Sheridan but United hadn't time to feel sorry for themselves because three days later they had to play the second leg of their Cup-Winners' Cup semi-final against Legia Warsaw.

They had been convincing on the European trail, easing comfortably past Pecsi Munkas in the opening round, winning the first leg 2–0 at Old Trafford and the second 1–0 in Hungary. It seemed like Christmas when they drew modest Wrexham for the second round, winning 3–0 at home and then 2–0 at the Racecourse Ground. The only regret was that injury had robbed Mark Hughes of the chance to play in his home town.

The Welshman saw plenty of action in the quarter-final against Montpellier, though, and became the centre of controversy when he went down and stayed down after full-back Pascal Baills had head-butted him. The Frenchman claimed innocence but it looked bad and he was sent off. Hughes explained that he had stayed on the ground because it seemed the best way of avoiding a confrontation that could have led to his own dismissal as well.

The Montpellier president said that Hughes would not be welcome in his town but the United man kept his cool for the return and watched with satisfaction as his Welsh team-mate Clayton Blackmore scored a stunning free kick and later earned a penalty that was converted by Steve Bruce for a 2–0 win. Ferguson was delighted with the performance, which he considered top drawer, and hopes were high for the semi-final against Legia Warsaw. Big guns Barcelona and Juventus were paired in the other semi.

The Reds won 3–1 away, a superb result, and Lee Sharpe scored at Old Trafford for a 1–1 draw. That added up to an impressive 4–2 aggregate win. Barcelona had knocked out Juventus and so the final, which was to be played in Rotterdam, had the added piquancy of pitting Mark Hughes against the club that had interrupted his Manchester career. Mark had had an unhappy time in his two years at the Nou Camp until Alex Ferguson rescued him, and it was now payback time, which is exactly how it worked out.

Says Hughes, 'I shall always be grateful to Alex Ferguson for bringing me back to Old Trafford. Rotterdam was a great night for me, for Manchester United and for British football. It was a difficult game for us because they were a very good side, but I think on our second-half performance we deserved to win.

'I said before the final that I felt I had something to prove to Barcelona and after the game I knew I had made my point. I had no real axe to grind with them. I had had a chance when I was at the club and I didn't take it.

'To win the European Cup-Winners' Cup for Manchester United meant a lot. To do it in front of so many supporters who had gone across to Holland made it a great moment. It was a very emotional night.

'The lads could hardly believe we had gone out and won because we were under a lot of pressure before the competition started. We were the first English club allowed back into the competition and, as it went on, we realised we were carrying the flag for British football. To get to the final was a great achievement and we knew if we could win it, it would be such a boost for British football following all the setbacks.

'As for the goals, I was delighted to claim them both. The first came from Steve Bruce. It was definitely going in but I made sure by kicking the ball over the line. The record books will show that I scored, but really it should go down as one for Steve.

'I said before the game that my ideal would be to score a special goal against Barcelona and, while I am not claiming that the second fitted the bill, it meant a lot to me. Some of the lads thought I had taken it too wide, some were expecting a cross, but I could see a lot of the goal and I was confident in what I was trying to do. I made good contact, and in it went.

'It's one game I will never forget. It was a special night and the beginning of some great times at Old Trafford.'

Mark Hughes always maintained that he wouldn't go into management at the end of his playing career, but like many who are hooked on the game, he did, taking over as manager of Wales for a period. After that, he moved to Blackburn Rovers, taking charge early in the 2004-05 season when they appeared to be relegation candidates. After keeping them up, he led them to three successive top 10 finishes, before moving to Manchester City in the summer of 2008. He left that club late in 2009, before having a year as manager of Fulham.

Ferguson has always talked in glowing terms about the player he brought back home from Spain. In fact, for an insight into the character of Alex Ferguson, mark the words he uses to describe Hughes. They tell you an awful lot about what he respects and admires in the game of football and the people who play it.

'I felt it was a mistake for the club to have sold him in the first place. I have never seen a player with so much strength. He's really an awesome sight at close quarters,' he said. 'He is a warrior on whom you could put your life. He always maintained an unbelievably high standard and never wavered as a fierce competitor. He had 10 great years at Old Trafford after arriving here from school in Wrexham and although he went away for a couple of years to sample European football, I made it a priority when I was

Mark Hughes, a man on a mission against Barcelona, scores one of his two goals against his former club to bring the European Cup-Winners' Cup to Old Trafford for the first time.

May 1991: United again proved they have a keen eye for Europe when they won the Cup-Winners' Cup in 1991, their second European trophy – and Alex Ferguson can't contain his joy.

appointed manager of Manchester United to try to buy him back. I remember telling the chairman at the time that here was a player who fully intends to play every game and make a positive contribution in each one.

'It's a quality I look for when I'm assessing a player to work at Old Trafford, and Mark had it in abundance. You search for enthusiasm and I never regretted my decision to make him a United player again. Some people say you should never go back in life, and I know what they mean, but this particular return worked brilliantly for both the club and the player.

'Towards the end of his time with us, he brought a maturity to his game that enabled him to bring other people in to play more, and he contributed to the team in a much more forceful and consistent way. Perhaps the arrival of Eric Cantona helped him in this respect. The pair of them created a very potent partnership, which one season produced 47 goals between them, the best figures from a pair of strikers at United for many years. Their goals were a telling factor at the start of our trophy collection.

'Mark became an idol for many fans. They liked his commitment and saw in him a latter-day Denis Law, especially as a scorer of spectacular goals. For me, I liked the way he put injuries out of his mind. He barely missed a fixture, giving the impression of being armour-plated. His willingness to compete up the middle on his own when necessary, and his refusal to shrink from the most punishing markers, was like waving a flag of courage for the rest of the team.

Taking home the prize. Next target: win the league title.

'His team-mates knew that when they played the ball forward for him to hold while they got up the field, he was not going to lose it in a hurry. You take a lot of hard knocks playing at the sharp end, as I know to my cost as a one-time striker, and so I have always watched with particular interest to see how the front men react to punishment, and I have no hesitation saying that "Sparky" was the most courageous striker in the game.

'Centre-backs knew before they even went out that no matter how much they kicked him, he would come back for more. No matter how much punishment he took, it was all like water off a duck's back to Mark. His amazing durability gave him a tremendous advantage.

'Others would fold under the kind of hostility he came up against but he totally frustrated his markers by getting up, dusting himself down and carrying on with the job. I cannot speak too highly of his resilience.

'Mark Hughes always saved his goals for the right time. His speciality was to score the vital ones at important moments, none more so than his goals against Barcelona and later his super strike for our first double.'

Towards the end of season 1990-91, Alex Ferguson's new United were

beginning to gel impressively, as Gary Pallister, the rock in defence alongside Steve Bruce, explained: 'The season before we won the Cup-Winners' Cup, we had struggled in the league and the expensive newcomers – Neil Webb, Danny Wallace, Paul Ince and I – had taken plenty of stick, which had helped us come together in a tight unit.

'A lot of enjoyment had been expressed in some quarters because we were having such a bad time, and an "us and them" attitude grew up towards some of the pressmen. It all helped us to bond, to understand more about the club and the constant pressures, and I think we reaped the benefit in terms of team spirit.

'As for the Cup-Winners' Cup final, that was the biggest occasion of my career to date, the first time I'd come up against one of the true giants. It was a soggy night in Rotterdam, a really miserable Manchester-type night, and that suited us far better than it did Barcelona.

'The atmosphere was fantastic. Our fans filled about three-quarters of the stadium, and that gave us a terrific lift. We were very much the underdogs – I believe Barcelona were quoted at three-to-one on to win – and although they were missing Hristo Stoichkov, the brilliant Bulgarian, their side was packed with other top stars including Ronald Koeman and Michael Laudrup.

'But we were the better side for at least 90 per cent of the match, and when Sparky put us in front after 68 minutes, we really deserved it. Mind you, I don't think Brucie was too happy when Mark nicked his goal! He was certain that his header was going in but I don't think you could blame Mark for poking it over the line to make sure.

'At least there was no shadow of doubt about the second goal. No one who saw Sparky's strike will ever forget it. Apparently, the commentator had just said he'd taken it too wide when, typical of Mark, he lashed it into the back of the net with all his usual ferocity. Of course, the game had a special significance for him, returning to his old club, so it must have been a very sweet moment for him.

'Barcelona pulled a goal back when Les Sealey was beaten by a low shot from Koeman to make it 2–1. I'm sure Les was struggling a bit with the nasty leg injury he had picked up in the League Cup final defeat by Sheffield Wednesday, which meant he couldn't get across his line as quickly as usual, but fortunately it didn't cost us in the end.

'The main reason it didn't was a terrific goal-line clearance from Clayton Blackmore. I felt quite thankful to Clayton, but not as thankful as Brucie. He hadn't put a foot wrong all night but then he chested the ball down and tried to hit it back. Laudrup took advantage and when I saw his effort go past Les the horrible thought flashed across my mind that we were going to extra time after dominating so much of the play. Then Clayton popped up to save us, capping a season of magnificent performances at left-back.

'For Manchester United in particular, and for English football in general, in our first year back in European competition, we had proved we could still cut it with the best.'

United's team for the final was: Sealey, Irwin, Bruce, Pallister, Blackmore, Phelan, Robson, Sharpe, Ince, McClair, Hughes.

It was a great night for Gary Pallister, Mark Hughes and the rest of the team, but for Alex Ferguson, it was the turning point of his career at Manchester United. Beating the mighty Barcelona, as well as raising the team's game to finish fifth in the League, cemented Ferguson's position as a masterful manager who could meet the demands of the famous Red Devils.

United's Biggest Wins under Sir Alex Ferguson

BY SIX GOALS OR MORE

Result	Opponent	Venue	Competition	Date	Scorers
9–0	Ipswich T	H	Premier Lg	4/3/95	Cole 5, Hughes 2, Keane, Ince
8–1	Nottingham F	A	Premier Lg	6/2/99	Solskjaer 4, Yorke 2, Cole 2
7–0	Barnsley	H	Premier Lg	25/10/97	Cole 3, Giggs 2, Scholes, Poborsky
7–1	West Ham U	H	Premier Lg	1/4/00	Scholes 3, Irwin, Cole, Beckham, Solskjaer
7–1	AS Roma	H	Champions Lg	4/4/07	Carrick 2, Ronaldo 2, Evra, Rooney, Smith
7–1	Blackburn R	H	Premier Lg	27/11/10	Berbatov 5, Nani, Park
6–0	Bolton W	A	Premier Lg	25/2/96	Scholes 2, Beckham, Bruce, Cole, Butt
6–0	Bradford C	H	Premier Lg	5/9/00	Fortune 2, Sheringham 2, Cole, Beckham
6–0	West Ham U	H	FA Cup Rd 4	26/1/03	Giggs 2, van Nistelrooy 2, P.Neville, Solskjaer
6–0	Newcastle U	H	Premier Lg	12/1/08	Ronaldo 3, Tevez 2, Ferdinand

BY TOURNAMENT

Premier Lg (H and A) – see above

FA Cup (H) – see above

FA Cup (A/N) – 4–0 v Chelsea, 14/5/94 (final). Scorers: Cantona 2, Hughes, McClair
    – 4–0 v Southampton, 12/3/05 (Rd 6). Scorers: Scholes 2, Keane, Ronaldo
    – 4–0 v Fulham, 7/3/09 (Rd 6). Scorers: Tevez 2, Park, Rooney

League Cup (H) – 5–0 v Hull C, 23/9/87 (Rd 2). Scorers: McGrath, Davenport, Whiteside, Strachan, McClair
    – 5–0 v Rotherham, 12/10/88 (Rd 2). Scorers: McClair 3, Robson, Bruce

League Cup (A/N) – 6–2 v Arsenal, 28/11/90 (Rd 4). Scorers: Sharpe 3, Blackmore, Hughes, Wallace
    – 4-0 v Wigan, 26/2/06 (final). Scorers: Rooney 2, Ronaldo, Saha

Europe (H) – see above

Europe (A) – 6–2 Brondby, 21/10/98 (Gp). Scorers: Giggs 2, Cole, Keane, Yorke, Solskjaer

[9]

THE MAVERICK

THE CELEBRATIONS in Rotterdam had hardly died down before Alex Ferguson was throwing down the gauntlet and spelling out the next stage of his restless ambition. The day after the final, at his post-match conference, he told reporters, 'Now we will go on to win the championship.'

David Meek reports, 'I went up to him at the end of the conference and asked him why he was putting his head on the chopping block with such a bold prediction that could leave him with egg on his face, and his reply startled me. He said there comes a time when players must face up to their responsibilities and realise what is expected of them. He said they were good enough, as they had shown by winning the European Cup-Winners' Cup, and that they must now be prepared to make the effort required to win the league.'

Although never one to boast about his intentions, Ferguson had long been puzzled and frustrated by United's failure as a major club to make their mark in the league, and this was the wake-up call.

Change was in the air all round. Chairman Martin Edwards was floating the club as a public company and raising revenue to redevelop the Stretford End.

The players responded to their manager's clarion call with a great opening burst to the new season. In fact, they lost just one game in the first half of the season, but ran out of steam towards the end. Three defeats in the last four games meant they finished runners-up, four points behind Leeds. Consolation came in the form of the Rumbelows Cup, Brian McClair scoring in the 1–0 win against Nottingham Forest in the final.

They hadn't quite lived up to their manager's expectations, but it was nevertheless a serious declaration of intent and the following season they finally went all the way, winning the 1992-93 championship, their first league title for 26 years. Ferguson, always a shrewd psychologist, had provocatively challenged his men and it had done the trick. United were champions after so many managers and failed attempts since the days of Sir Matt Busby.

Ferguson had not just relied on inspiring his players. He had also brought in a new man, and that signing proved to be the most significant transfer buy of his career. Some might say that signing Eric Cantona from Leeds for a mere million pounds or so was either a wild gamble or a lucky fluke, but Ferguson is canny. He had seen something in the Frenchman that he realised would blossom on the Old Trafford stage – and so it proved.

To United supporters, Cantona was the god who came down from on high to lead their team out of the wilderness and into the promised land of the championship. What's more, he kept them in the lush pastures of success for a total of four Premiership titles and two FA Cup wins.

Cantona made an immediate impact. He arrived in November of 1992, came on as a substitute in a 2–1 derby win against Manchester City on 6 December and made his full debut a week later in a win against Norwich City, the leaders. One of football's favourite theories is that new players, especially foreign ones, need time to settle in, but Cantona was an instant catalyst, transforming the team, changing them from challengers to champions. He scored four goals in his first five games and proceeded to strike up a rapport with Mark Hughes, Paul Ince, Ryan Giggs and Lee Sharpe. United lost just twice between Cantona's arrival and the end of the season. It was neck and neck with Norwich and Aston Villa, who were well in the race, but Cantona was not only inspired himself, he lifted those around him. Something certainly got into Steve Bruce when he scored twice in injury time for a memorable 2–1 win against Sheffield Wednesday at Old Trafford.

With two games to go, United were four points in front and became champions when Villa lost at home to Oldham. So they took the title with two games to spare, 10 points ahead of their nearest rivals, their first league title since the days of Charlton, Law and Best in 1967. They had finally done it.

The success merely accelerated Ferguson's drive for more. That summer he bought Roy Keane from Nottingham Forest for £3.75 million, another tremendous investment, and like Cantona, a player with the temperament

Cantona salutes the United fans after scoring another goal, against Chelsea in April 1993, and a 26-year wait was nearly over.

Heading home against Spurs, January 1993. Eric Cantona galvanised United and gave the players the self-belief to know they could be champions again.

and experience to bring out the best from the FA Youth Cup winning team of '92, some of whom Sir Alex was almost ready to bring into his first team.

Ferguson, firmly in the driving seat as the new season approached, steered his players to a superb Premiership and FA Cup double in 1993-94. United joined Spurs, Arsenal and Liverpool as the only clubs to achieve the feat in modern football. The league was won by eight points to give them back-to-back championships for the first time since the days of the Busby Babes, Chelsea were beaten 4–0 in the final of the FA Cup and there would have been a treble but for a narrow 3–1 defeat by Aston Villa in the final of the Coca-Cola Cup, as the League Cup had become.

Tremendous sadness had descended on Old Trafford in January 1994 with the death of Sir Matt Busby, at the age of 84. The area below the Munich clock memorial became a sea of red and white as supporters laid their scarves, flags and flowers in memory of the grand old man of English football. Everton were the visitors that Saturday and to this day United have great affection for the Goodison Park fans because they stood so quietly during the one-minute's silence. Perhaps they were influenced by Ferguson's statesmanlike words when he said, 'The result of today's game is irrelevant. I want my players to go out and play the way Sir Matt would want them to. This game is for his memory and for what he did for football.'

However, the season's success was not achieved without Ferguson having to call on all his managerial skills to keep Cantona on the field and away from suspension. His patience was tested when Cantona returned to his maverick ways in an FA Cup-tie at Norwich and seemed to kick an opponent as he lay on the ground. Jimmy Hill described it on television as vicious, which drew an emphatic rebuttal from Ferguson. His response might not have been very statesmanlike, but it succeeded in taking the Frenchman out of the headlines in favour of himself, a situation with which Ferguson could easily live.

More diplomacy was needed a few weeks later at Swindon when Cantona was sent off for stamping on John Moncur, and the furore had hardly died down before Eric was sent off again for two bookable offences at Arsenal. The result was a five-week suspension, and the manager continued to juggle with the problem of restraining Cantona's wayward behaviour while giving him the freedom his personality demanded.

Cantona owed United in general and Alex Ferguson in particular every bit as much as the club and its supporters owed to him. He was the luckiest man in the game to land at the right club at the right time to work for the right manager surrounded by the right players.

He had been a professional for nearly nine years and his career prior to joining United had gone nowhere significant, except to achieve notoriety as the *enfant terrible* of French football. He had virtually had to flee his own country in order to find a club willing to take him on, and even in England it had proved difficult. It hadn't worked out at Sheffield Wednesday where he had a brief trial, and despite helping Leeds United win the championship, Howard Wilkinson clearly didn't rate his contribution very highly or he wouldn't have passed him on to Alex Ferguson for a beggarly £1 million fee.

Dramatically, the man's career changed almost overnight. Everything fell into place and Cantona found a manager who understood him. He must have been impressed when Ferguson told him that he could see nothing wrong with losing your temper provided you lost it for the right reasons. Now he had a mentor who could forgive his outbursts if they were triggered by passion and commitment to the team.

He must also have counted his blessings when, the following season, he found himself playing alongside a bunch of highly talented youngsters including Ryan Giggs, David Beckham, Paul Scholes, Gary Neville and Nicky Butt, who were full of running and prepared to give him the adoration that must have been more manna from heaven for a professional of no little ego.

Alex Ferguson parades the Premiership trophy round Old Trafford with assistant Brian Kidd on 8 May 1994. Six days later, United would win their first ever double.

Above all, he could not fail to realise that the club was a success waiting to happen, needing just one final piece of the jigsaw to create a truly marvellous picture – a situation that suited someone who liked to be regarded as the main man!

The Cantona bandwagon rolled merrily along as more youngsters were brought in to play acolyte to the man's godlike presence. Trouble was never too far away, though, and the following year, after two successive championship successes and an FA Cup victory, a flash of temper threatened to blow the whole thing sky high.

Cantona outdid anything he had ever done in France – such as the time he called a disciplinary committee stupid, or hitting one of his own teammates – by launching a flying kung-fu attack on Crystal Palace fan Matthew Simmons at Selhurst Park on the night of 25 January 1995. Pictures of his foot-first assault went round the world, triggering unprecedented debate and putting Ferguson under enormous pressure.

The player was suspended for the rest of the season, a ban later extended by the FA to cover the first 10 games of the following season. The incident was a police matter and when the case came to court, the Croydon magistrate gave him a two-week jail sentence for common assault, later

Cantona's influence over the younger players was to bring huge benefits to the club and to people such as David Beckham and Lee Sharpe as United moved towards a second double in 1996.

reduced on appeal to 120 hours of community service.

As enigmatic as ever after the court case, Eric puzzled the waiting media with his priceless quote: 'When the seagulls follow the trawler it's because they think sardines will be thrown into the sea.'

Ferguson handled the whole thing brilliantly, demonstrating yet again his ability as a manager, but at first even he thought that it would be impossible for the Frenchman to resume his career in England. When the player expressed interest in staying, though, the manager decided to support him. That was certainly a moment when Cantona should have counted his lucky stars. It was a remarkable act of faith by Ferguson in the face of the hysterical clamour at a time when the mood around the country was that he should follow in the footsteps of an even more famous countryman into exile on Elba.

Ferguson, not for the first or last time, got it right. Cantona stayed and remained a key player, sharing in two more championships, one a second Premiership and Cup double. His place among the Old Trafford legends was assured.

There is no doubt that Ferguson and Cantona enjoyed a special relationship that owed as much to Sir Alex's management psychology as it did to the player's ability.

It's perhaps not surprising, given the background of events, and despite signing Andy Cole early in the New Year, that season 1994-95 drew a blank in terms of trophies. They finished runners-up to Blackburn in the Premiership, and although they played well to reach the final of the FA Cup, they lost 1–0 to Everton.

It had been a testing season, but Ferguson quickly rallied his troops, saying, 'I am really proud of my players. It has been a fantastic effort by them. To amass 88 points in second place is a marvellous performance. They are down on the floor at the moment but they have battled against adversity before and they will bounce back. If you look at our record over the last four years, we have lost only 22 games out of 168 and never finished lower than runners-up, and that is remarkable. It takes a good team to beat us and, having got to 89 points, you cannot deny that Blackburn and Kenny Dalglish have done a great job taking the championship off us. We at United accepted the spirit of the challenge and congratulate them on their performance.'

Gracious and generous in defeat but still finding words of comfort for his own players – no wonder Alex Ferguson has lasted so long at the top. His was the reaction of a class managerial act, and already he was planning his next move, one step ahead of the press and even of his own supporters, as usual.

(10)

KIDS

FEW GUESSED what Alex Ferguson had in mind for the following season, other than a determination to win back the championship. Supporters could see for themselves that change was happening as builders moved in to start demolishing the North Stand in preparation for a grand three-tier construction that would take the capacity of Old Trafford up to 65,000. They didn't expect their manager to start his own demolition work by transferring three senior and popular players – Mark Hughes, Paul Ince and Andrei Kanchelskis.

In the case of Hughes, the manager had little choice because the player was at the end of his contract and hadn't signed a new agreement, so he was a free agent. Kanchelskis was thought to be angling for a move, and if Ferguson believes a player has lost interest in playing for Manchester United, he helps him on his way.

Ince was different. The fans had voted him their player of the year the previous season and he had played well, but the manager reckoned that he was getting too big for his boots, disregarding tactical instructions and generally bucking the system. When it comes to a player starting to call himself 'The Guv'nor' and having a personalised number plate bearing the letters 'GUV', Ferguson is not amused. There is only going to be one winner in that situation because there is only one boss at Old Trafford.

Hughes joined Chelsea, Ince moved to Inter Milan and, after a few fraught weeks, Kanchelskis was sold to Everton. That move left the Independent Manchester United Supporters' Association up in arms and calling for blood – the manager's!

Sir Alex's position was not helped by United losing 3–1 at Aston Villa on the opening day of the season, resulting in some critical headlines and

IMUSA talking about plans to bring Ince back.

Ferguson could easily have flipped with the fans, but he kept his cool and actually went out of his way to build bridges with the restless supporters. Reputations can be misleading. Many people thought that the rebel fans would be in for the hairdrying treatment, but it wasn't like that, as Johnny Flacks, a passionate United follower and chairman of IMUSA at that time, explained:

'The first time I met Alex Ferguson was at the funeral of Alan Gibson, the United director, and outside the church he came up to me and asked if I was Johnny Flacks. At the time we were perceived to be anti-Ferguson and anti the club, so I wondered what was coming next. He was very pleasant, though, and said he would like to come to the IMUSA meetings, which he did.

'We were very confused at the time over three major players going, especially as Paul Ince had told us that he didn't want to leave, but Alex Ferguson talked to us and was very open and honest, explaining things from his point of view. Sometimes he was telling us things he perhaps shouldn't have been, and we had to be careful the press weren't about.

'As a group, we established a good rapport with him and he was supportive of what we were trying to do for our members. I think he respects supporters and he made it clear that he wanted our support.

'Shortly after the treble, he gave me one of my most treasured memories. I had been to the Cliff training ground to interview him for one of the fanzines and afterwards he invited me up to his office and showed me a film of the last three minutes of the Champions League final in Barcelona shot from a camera behind the goal where United had scored the goals that won us the game.

'There was no commentary, just the film and the sound of the players shouting. For me, it was a unique experience and an absolute privilege I shall never forget.'

That was Ferguson the good guy, one of his many sides. He has never lost sight of how it feels to be a supporter, and has been known to stress to players that they should be aware of how it feels to go into work on a Monday morning after a bad performance by their team at the weekend.

Despite his occasional spats with the media, he has always wanted supporters to understand what he is trying to do. The big message he wanted to get across to IMUSA was that he was reshaping the team in the knowledge that a particularly outstanding crop of youngsters were waiting in the wings, and he was convinced they would become top players.

A moment of joint celebration: the Manager of the Year and the Young Eagle of the Year, Ferguson and Giggs, show off their trophies after a great season in 1992-93.

Alan Hansen said on television after the Villa game that you 'win nothing with kids', but Ferguson was right – as consistently successful managers have to be. Ryan Giggs led the way into the team, closely followed by Gary Neville, David Beckham, Paul Scholes, Nicky Butt, and, a little later, Phil Neville. These players provided not only Manchester United but England with the backbone of their teams.

Alex Ferguson had nurtured this group of players and had become a father figure to them as well as coach and manager. He looked after them off the field as well as on it. Ryan Giggs, the pathfinder as the first to break into the senior side, explained:

'When I arrived on the first-team scene, it coincided with a massive explosion in football with the launch of the Premiership, the impact of Sky Television and the introduction of the Champions League. The game expanded enormously and the players came under the spotlight. I came at the right time for marketing, but I was young and I think I was really helped by the manager sheltering me and limiting what I did with the media. I also felt that at the age of 22 people could easily get sick of seeing me and I didn't want that to happen because I was aiming for another 10 years at least. So I stepped back a bit. The incredible fascination of the media with David Beckham helped me to lead a quieter life, which suited me.

'I have only known one manager in my time at Old Trafford. Alex Ferguson brought me to Manchester United and steered me right the way through. He especially helped me in my younger days, involving me in training with the senior squad at just the right time, playing me in the first team at just the right time, and just as important, resting me at the right time. He is still doing it and I have implicit trust in him. Who wouldn't, as one of his players, after leading us to such sustained success?

'Every year seems to bring an even bigger challenge. The prizes get bigger and ambition is something in your blood. The manager makes sure it stays that way, because if he felt that you had lost your hunger for winning, I don't think you would stay at Old Trafford. He has lost none of his own commitment and passion for success and it filters down to the players.'

Inevitably, after losing three senior players and turning to his youngsters, season 1995-96 proved a rocky ride and it was a relief when Cantona returned to the fray after completing his suspension. Nobody quite knew what to expect but he scored a penalty in a 2–2 draw against Liverpool at Old Trafford on his return, and behaved impeccably for the rest of the

Alex Ferguson's handling of young superstar Ryan Giggs, seen here during a pre-season tour in summer 1993, is one of the reasons why Giggs still remains a formidable force almost two decades later.

season. Asked why he had decided to play on at United, he simply said, 'It's a love story, a love story.'

Even with Cantona back in action, United made hard work of it and title prospects looked grim as they fell further and further behind Newcastle. Manager Kevin Keegan and his Newcastle team celebrated Christmas with a huge 10-point lead. After losing at Tottenham on New Year's Day, however, United launched into a searing run that gradually whittled away Kevin Keegan's lead.

The youngsters made an increasingly important contribution, but it was Cantona who was the mainspring, embarking on a tremendous scoring run in both the league and FA Cup. He scored again in the key 1–0 win at Newcastle and the title race was neck and neck. Keegan famously flipped in a television interview, as he looked over his shoulder and found Ferguson playing mind games and wondering whether Leeds would play against Newcastle with the same fierce determination that they had produced against his own side.

It was a dramatic and exciting finish with United finally winning the championship by four points, a brilliant coup considering they had been 10 points behind at Christmas.

In the FA Cup, they knocked Chelsea out in the semi-final and then beat Liverpool at Wembley. Eric Cantona – who else? – smashed home a brilliantly volleyed goal for a 1–0 win.

From a worrying start, United had finished superbly to chalk up a Premiership and Cup double, a sensational achievement indeed for a manager who not many months before had been under heavy critical fire. Chairman Edwards summed up:

'At the beginning of the season, having let three very experienced players go, everybody wondered how the youngsters would do. I think that's what is so pleasing today. They told us we would win nothing with kids – I wonder what they are saying now?'

Alex Ferguson was rightly proud of his young men and had particularly warm words for Ryan Giggs. 'Any father would be proud to have a son like Ryan,' he said. There was certainly a strong family feel about the club at that time, and Ferguson went on, 'They have all been brought up the right way. They have been raised together, progressing through the various teams, and the process has given them key qualities, such as a shared work ethic and an ambition to be the best in their profession, as well as teaching them the way we think football should be played.

'Within this framework each has found his own identity and character.

One of the best sights in football – unless you're a defender – Ryan Giggs in full flight, as here during the 1996 FA Cup final.

They are individuals, not clones, which we also try to encourage, so that they have all found their own status with differing profiles.'

Although bust-ups with players can be spectacular – and there's only ever one winner – the caring side of Alex Ferguson is never far away, as Gary Bailey experienced when injury finished his career. Back home in South Africa, Gary is now a media star. He works for SuperSport TV, covering all England's Premiership games and broadcasting to 50 different countries. He puts it like this:

'I had come back from the 1986 World Cup in Mexico with a messed-up knee and was in rehabilitation when Alex Ferguson arrived at the club. Eventually, I played for him and it was a game I have never forgotten. We were a goal up at Luton but just before the interval they equalised and at half-time the manager wanted to know why. I explained how I saw it and he was very pleasant, but when it came to Colin Gibson, the full-back, to explain his part in giving away the goal, he obviously decided that he was the one to blame. He went nose to nose with Colin and as I watched the hair going back on Colin's head I realised what the lads had meant when they had warned me about the hairdryer treatment. As we were going out for the second half, I wondered if he was mad, but he looked at me, smiled and winked. I thought you clever so-and-so. He had decided that Colin needed a bollocking and so that's what he got.

'I played about five games for him before I realised that my playing days were over and went to tell him. He was kindness itself. He said he was absolutely gutted for me and immediately offered me a job to stay on as a goalkeeping coach. I explained I had been away from South Africa for 10 years and it was time to go home.

'Then he asked me to ride with him from the Cliff to his office at Old Trafford because he wanted a chat. He said I was no longer part of the dressing room, so would I tell him what I thought of the team and how they were playing. He may have ignored my opinions but he genuinely wanted to know. I would have really liked to play for the man. He has an ability to read people and a good balance to his management.

'Now I am enjoying my television work – no more Friday nights worry-ing whether I will be handling a greasy ball the next day or whether some centre-forward will be rearranging my face!'

Les Kershaw also knows Alex Ferguson from inside the club. Les is Ferguson's former chief scout and was, until recently, director of United's academy. Now he's a consultant.

'The press slaughter him at times,' says Les, 'and portray him as something he's not. Among many things for instance, so many people within the game seek his advice and he always does his best to help. He's also a massive earner for charity, not passively by just lending his name to causes, but as an active organiser.

'He falls out with the press because if they overplay their hand, he reacts. Players who upset the staff, well, it's the end for them. He has this loyalty to those who work for him. He's a loyal man, always supportive of the people who work for him. He never lets you down. In fact, he will go the extra mile for you. He has been brilliant for me. I have retired as director of the academy and I try not to get in Brian McClair's way.

'I joined United in 1988. I was established in a senior position, teaching chemistry at what was then Manchester Polytechnic, and very happy in what I was doing. I was always a football nut, though, coaching amateur teams and working for Bobby Charlton at his soccer school. I also did some scouting for Terry Venables and George Graham, but it was a hobby. Then I got a call from Alex Ferguson. We met at the Cliff and he said he wanted me to be his chief scout. I had a good job that I liked but this was Manchester United, so I took two years' unpaid leave of absence from the Poly to give it a go. It was a wonderful opportunity, and at the end of the two years he wouldn't let me go back to teaching. I stayed and have never regretted it. I live at Saddleworth and he's been to open our annual show. The people there think he's wonderful, but then, as I say, he is a very generous man with his time and supportive of those around him.'

11

PREDICTIONS, PROMISES AND A ROLLER-COASTER RIDE

DURING HIS DAYS in charge of Oldham Athletic, Joe Royle – a close friend of Alex Ferguson – would often make comparisons between his job and a theme-park ride. 'It's like sitting on a roller coaster. One minute you zoom up to dizzy heights, the next you come roaring down to earth. You can enjoy the experience but at times it can also leave you feeling pretty sick.'

Those words never had a truer ring for Manchester United than during the 1996-97 campaign. The ride began in the summer of 1996. Supporters were still celebrating the Wembley win over Liverpool that had meant United becoming the first English club to clinch the league and FA Cup double for a second time. To complete the double was a sign of greatness. To do it twice – the double double – was the stuff of dreams, but 48 hours after reaching Nirvana the roller coaster plunged rapidly downwards.

'Fergie: I'll quit in pay wrangle' screamed the front page of the *Manchester Evening News*. The story claimed the manager was ready to turn his back on the club following a contract dispute. Alex Ferguson wanted a six-year deal to take him beyond his 60th birthday and into retirement. United appeared unwilling to meet his demands.

To suggest Ferguson was even contemplating a walk-out was nothing short of sensational and the fans rallied to his side. Local radio phone-in programmes were swamped by irate callers protesting that the club should accede to the manager's demands. Others turned their wrath in the direction of chairman Martin Edwards, who was happy, as well as possibly a little relieved, to reveal they had got the wrong man.

'It might surprise a few people to know that I was not involved in contract negotiations with Alex Ferguson,' said Edwards. 'That was done by a committee of the board, and let me state categorically that the board were very anxious to keep Alex Ferguson.

'As in all negotiations, with players, staff or whoever it is, people have perceived ideas of what they are worth and the board has an idea of what they think somebody is worth. You negotiate it out. It doesn't help to have it in the public domain. Most people, when they are up for a salary review, go along to see their boss, it's debated, there is a bit of to-ing and fro-ing and the settlement is done.

'In football, because it has such a high profile, everybody wants to get involved and people start speculating about what is or isn't going on. The only ones who really know are those involved in the negotiation.'

Edwards was willing to speculate that the manager would not be leaving.

'I hope very much that Alex Ferguson will be manager of Manchester United in six years' time. Now whether you go to that in one contract, or it takes a couple of contracts to get there, is another matter.'

At 11 a.m. on Thursday, 16 May 1996, members of the remuneration committee of Manchester United plc gathered at Old Trafford for their annual meeting. Later they were joined by the manager's representative and it was 8.30 p.m. when the talking ended.

Maurice Watkins, the club's solicitor-director and a member of the committee, broke the news: 'We have agreed a new four-year contract with Alex Ferguson. We have had negotiations and these have come to very successful fruition. I am sure the manager is very delighted.'

He was.

'I'm happy it's all over,' he confessed the following morning. 'It's a new experience with the club having this remuneration committee, and it can be a bit frustrating, but at the end of the day you just have to be patient with it. It was a long time, and a long wait.'

These were the first managerial contract talks since the club went public, and a sharp contrast to the days when such matters would be sorted out in the chairman's office over a cup of tea.

'This is something I'm just going to have to live with, I suppose. It's not easy but it's such a big club now that we have to get on with it.'

Had he really been ready to resign?

'That was a bit dramatic that. There was certainly never any indication from me, quitting, but obviously there was a matter of principle involved and pride, too, comes into it. I hoped the club would recognise that. Fortunately, it's all settled now and I'm looking forward to being here for the next four years, and I hope they are as successful as the last four.'

According to the man who knows best, managing Manchester United is unique.

'Every day is a challenge. It's a very difficult job. There are 91 other managers who would like to manage this club – until they were in here for about three weeks, then they would probably need a break!

'It's a very difficult club to run, it's a very hard job, but I've been blessed with good energy and, pray the Lord, good health, and now I just have to see about maintaining the success the club has had over the last few years, which we have all enjoyed.'

Only six months away from the 10th anniversary of his appointment, and close to challenging Sir Matt Busby as United's most successful manager, Ferguson obviously had no thoughts of resting on his laurels.

'We have to improve the standard because we can't stand still at this place. We have to accept the challenge of Europe, we have to do better and that is where the standard has to be raised.'

His first task was to strengthen the squad but he made it clear that nothing would happen until after the UEFA European Championship – Euro '96 – had ended. Old Trafford was one of the venues, and the competition would provide him with the opportunity to browse for fresh talent. However, he had also set his sights on a player he already knew plenty about. Alan Shearer topped the wanted list and United offered Blackburn Rovers a record £15 million for the England striker.

Rovers refused to do business and Shearer turned his back on United for a second time, choosing to join his home-town club, Newcastle. Had he opted for Old Trafford, he would doubtless have added more winner's medals to his collection – switching to St James' meant he won nothing.

'I have no regrets. I have plenty of admiration for Sir Alex Ferguson and all that he has done for Manchester United, but once Newcastle came in for me, there was only one club I was going to join. I had supported them since I was a boy and my dream was always to play for them. As far as Manchester United was concerned, it was no contest,' Shearer revealed when he retired as a player a decade later.

Instead of Shearer, the United manager bought in bulk, taking advantage of a change in UEFA rules. The governing body had been forced to come into line with the European law that allows free passage of labour between EEC countries, meaning restrictions could be placed only on players from outside the commission's boundaries. If an English club wanted to field 11 players from EEC countries, it could, and United quickly took advantage of the new ruling.

Ten years on: Alex Ferguson during the November 1996 fixture against Arsenal. In his first decade he had picked up eight major trophies – as many as Sir Matt Busby in his entire career. And there was so much more still to come.

David Beckham announces his supreme talent to the world with a goal from inside his own half in August 1996.

Two Dutchmen – Barcelona's Jordi Cruyff, son of the legendary Johan, and goalkeeper Rai van der Gouw from Vitesse Arnhem – were joined by Norwegian duo Ronny Johnsen, a defender with Turkish club Besiktas, and Ole Gunnar Solskjaer, a young striker from Molde.

United also spent £3.5 million on a player from a non-EEC country, Karel Poborsky from Slavia Prague, after monitoring him during Euro '96. Poborsky's spectacular solo goal in the Czech Republic's win over Portugal was rated one of the best of the tournament, but the right-sided midfielder never reached the same heights during his time at Old Trafford.

That was mostly down to the emergence of David Beckham, who made it clear he was not going to be overshadowed as he opened the new season in sensational style with a goal still regularly screened by television 15 years later. Beckham hit a 55-yard shot from inside his own half, the ball dropping beyond the reach of Wimbledon goalkeeper Neil Sullivan, during a 3–0 win at Selhurst Park. It was hailed as the 'goal of the season' after only 88 minutes of the new campaign.

Things levelled out with a run of three draws before the second win of the season, against Leeds, and the defending champions had slid to seventh before a 4–1 home win over Nottingham Forest took them to the top. Three successive defeats – 0–5 at Newcastle, 3–6 at Southampton and 1–2 at home to Chelsea – plummeted them downwards and, to make matters worse, during the slump, Turkish side Fenerbahce won 1–0 at Old Trafford.

That was the first time in over 40 years of European competition that United had lost in Manchester, and hardly the way Alex Ferguson planned to mark the 10th anniversary of his appointment. When 6 November arrived, he put on a brave face.

'It's a tremendous achievement, 10 years as manager of Manchester United,' he said. 'It has been a fantastic experience and hopefully this is the start of another good decade.

'When I came, I never thought that I would still be here 10 years on. You never think that way. It's a long time. I was eight and a half years at Aberdeen, so eighteen and a half years with two clubs is quite extraordinary. Now I'm looking forward to the next 10.'

Ryan Giggs remembers Ferguson's arrival clearly.

'When he came here, I was on the books of Manchester City. I had been with them since I was 11 years old, and when I was 13, United asked me to come for a trial. It was around Christmas and I stayed in the university halls of residence for a week, after which United told me they wanted to sign me as soon as I had turned 14.

'That was when I first got to know the manager, although I had seen him a few times. He came to watch me playing for Salford Boys and when we trained at the Cliff. It was there I met him for the first time, in the canteen at the training ground.

'Even then he was brilliant, not just with me but with all the young lads. He took time out to talk to you and your parents. You always dream of being a footballer, but until you start playing for the first team you can't really imagine it. I have been with United for virtually the whole of the manager's career here and I know I owe him a lot.

'I suppose I have seen him change, but not much. His will to win is still there and his appetite for the game is the same as it was when he first came here. He has probably mellowed a bit. He still has a go at you after a game but it is a lot more mellow than it was a few years ago – but that isn't to say he doesn't still shout at you.

'As for him leaving, there's only one place for him, and that's here.'

Ten days into the 11th year of the Ferguson reign things took an upward turn again. United began a 16-match unbeaten run with a 1–0 win over Arsenal on the Highbury team's first visit to Old Trafford under new manager Arsene Wenger. Three months later, United remained unbeaten as they defeated the Gunners for a second time and stepped back into top spot.

A surprise defeat at Sunderland temporarily slowed the surge as the long run ended, but a week later Sheffield Wednesday were beaten at Old Trafford and the Reds were again league leaders.

For many, that game is remembered for the performance of Eric Cantona, creator of both goals, but there was another significant happening that afternoon. Director Mike Edelson invited along celebrity guests Mel C and Victoria Adams from the chart-topping singing group the Spice Girls. After the game they were taken to the players' lounge where 'Posh' met 'Becks' for the first time. The rest, as the saying goes, is history.

Despite the shaky start in the Champions League, United's challenge had gone well. They qualified from their group then beat FC Porto 4–0 in the quarter-finals before hopes of reaching the final were shattered. A 1–0 defeat by Borussia Dortmund in Germany was followed by a second-leg upset by the same scoreline, and the European dream was over once again.

However, it seemed nothing could stop United domestically. They virtually put paid to Liverpool's title hopes by beating them 3–1 at Anfield, and while experts predicted the outcome of the championship would hinge on Newcastle's visit to Old Trafford on Thursday, 8 May, in fact the race was over 48 hours earlier. United drew 3–3 with Middlesbrough on 5 May, and

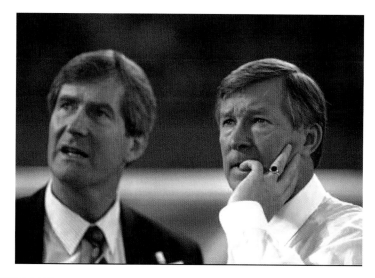

(Right) With Martin Edwards during the 1996-97 season. One of the reasons he had been so keen to recruit Alex Ferguson was to ensure the entire club performed well. That season, in May 1997, they showed the end result (below) as United won not only the Premiership title, but also the Pontin's Premier Reserve League, and the First and Second Divisions of the Lancashire League.

the following night Liverpool lost at Wimbledon and Newcastle drew at West Ham. The defending champions were out of reach.

Alex Ferguson had led his side to a fourth Premiership title in five seasons.

'It's a great feeling. People might say we would like to clinch the title in front of our own fans, which is true, but what you saw against Middlesbrough was just a typical United day, that roller-coaster emotional thing that anything is likely to happen at Old Trafford. The league is won over 38 games and we have managed to do it in 36, so we are very pleased.'

Five days and two games later – United had a run-in of four games in nine days – the Premiership trophy was paraded at Old Trafford following the 2–0 win over West Ham. Doubts about the progress made since the arrival of Alex Ferguson were all cast aside when not one but four championship trophies were handed out that afternoon.

As well as taking the Premiership crown, the club's other teams collected the Pontin's Premier Reserve League title and the championship trophies from the First and Second Divisions of the Lancashire League – top of the league at every level.

'I am a very proud man,' the manager declared afterwards. 'People talk about the motivation for a manager, but this is your motivation, when you see young players getting their rewards with 55,000 fans there to witness it. That is the way you want your seasons to end at this club. You don't forget these days. These are the ones you will always want to have and will always cherish. People talk about memories, and these are great memories for me.

'I think the achievement is being here 10 years. If you are here 10 years, then you have to be successful, and I have really enjoyed the success. I had great days at Aberdeen but this is a pinnacle. When you are in front of a full stadium every week with thousands more fans all over the world, you know you are working for a lot of people, and making a lot of people happy.'

The roller coaster had reached its summit, but seven days later down it came. On Sunday, 18 May, Eric Cantona, seen by many as the catalyst behind five seasons of success, surprisingly announced his retirement. Life would go on, but would it be the same without King Eric?

(12)

RING OUT THE OLD,
BRING IN THE NEW

WHETHER ERIC CANTONA planned to make such an impact by announcing the end of his playing days only he knows, but if the ploy was intentional, it was certainly successful. The football world went into a frenzy on that spring Sunday in 1997.

Most of the media turned up at United's hurriedly organised press conference at Old Trafford, expecting to witness the unveiling of a new player. For weeks, Middlesbrough's Brazilian midfielder Juninho had been linked to Old Trafford by newspaper speculation, but when a stony-faced Alex Ferguson and Martin Edwards walked into the room to take their seats behind a battery of microphones, it became abundantly clear the gathering was for a very different reason.

The task of dropping the bombshell fell to the chairman, Martin Edwards, and he read from an official club statement:

'Manchester United today announced that Eric Cantona had advised the chairman and manager that it is his wish to retire from football with immediate effect.

'I am extremely sorry Eric has arrived at this decision but understand and respect his reasons. Many of us believe Eric has been the catalyst for the most successful period in our history. It has truly been a magical time.'

The manager also paid his tribute:

'Eric was a wonderful, wonderful player and had a huge impact on the development of our younger players. He was a model professional in the way he conducted himself and I have to say he was a joy to manage. He is certainly one of the most gifted and dedicated players I have ever had the pleasure of working with and he will always be welcome at Old Trafford.

He gave us so many wonderful memories.'

On hearing the news, supporters began to head for Old Trafford. Groups gathered on the stadium forecourt, stunned by the unexpected announcement, looking on as others draped flags, shirts, scarves and posters of Cantona from the adjacent car-park railings. Soon the area was transformed into a shrine to the French star. No one had died, but it seemed Manchester United was in mourning.

United fans worshipped Cantona, but the love affair was far from one-sided. Eric regards the time spent at United as the highlight of his playing days.

'Everybody knows what I feel about Manchester United and about Alex Ferguson. He has been a great man and a great manager for me and for the team. For Manchester United.

'The four and a half years I was with Manchester United I enjoyed my best football and had a wonderful time. I had a marvellous relationship with the manager, coach, staff and players and, not least, the fans. I wish Manchester United even more success in the future.'

With Cantona out of the picture – or, to be totally accurate, now in it after giving up the game to try his hand as a film actor – life would go on, but there were many who felt this would be the biggest challenge Alex Ferguson had faced since the early days of his appointment.

The search for a new striker began with United being linked with Argentinean star Gabriel Batistuta, but any hopes of a deal collapsed when he was persuaded to stay with Fiorentina, even though the Italian club had appeared ready to accept an offer of £10 million.

There was a better reaction from Tottenham Hotspur when they were approached and persuaded to part with Teddy Sheringham. While Cantona would be a hard act to follow, the new boy quickly won his way into United hearts.

'I always wanted to play for a club like this. I heard that they had tried to sign me three years before I came, to play alongside Eric Cantona, and I would have liked that. I have to admit that I admired him from afar and thought he was a great player. Sadly, he had gone when I came so that wasn't to be, but like any professional footballer I came to Manchester United to win and be successful. I knew I had a better chance of doing that at Old Trafford than at any other club in the country.'

Sheringham, like his illustrious predecessor, went on to leave his mark, but things did not get off to the best of starts.

He was handed the Frenchman's mantle of penalty taker and helped win

With the 1997 Premiership trophy secured, Alex Ferguson had a problem: how to replace his iconic captain Eric Cantona?

the Charity Shield by scoring from the spot during a shoot-out against Chelsea. However, when it came to the serious stuff, he failed to convert a penalty in the opening game of the season, which just happened to be against his former club Tottenham Hotspur at White Hart Lane.

Despite the new player's personal misfortune, United won 2–0 to start an eight-match unbeaten run in the Premiership, which put Alex Ferguson on course to become the first manager to lead an English club to three successive league titles.

What many saw as the turning point came in the 84th minute of the game against Leeds at Elland Road. Roy Keane fell awkwardly while challenging Alfie Haaland as United pressed for an equaliser. Keane, Cantona's successor as captain, ruptured a cruciate knee ligament and was ruled out for the rest of the season. The battle for a fifth title in six seasons would now have to be fought without not just one influential player, but two.

The impact was gradual rather than instantaneous. A 7–0 win over Barnsley and a 6–1 victory against Sheffield Wednesday meant United had a four-point advantage when they faced Arsenal at Highbury in November. Although Sheringham scored twice against his old north London rivals, United lost and the season's second reversal meant their lead was cut to one point, and sent out a warning of things to come.

In Europe, United sailed through their group. They beat Holland's Feyenoord and Hungarian side Kosice both home and away as well as chalking up a 3–2 victory over Juventus at Old Trafford. Ryan Giggs scored a memorable 89th-minute goal against the Italian side, only to see it slightly overshadowed by Zinedine Zidane's strike seconds later.

Alex Ferguson had taken his side to the quarter-finals once again, but before facing French champions Monaco, the injury crisis deepened.

At the turn of the year things were going well. United led the table by seven points while in the FA Cup they played a sensational third-round tie at Stamford Bridge. At one stage they were 5–0 up against Chelsea and the Londoners eventually went out in a 5–3 thriller.

Slip-ups at Southampton then at home to Leicester took away some of the gloss, and there was a shock FA Cup exit in a fifth-round replay at Barnsley, yet by the end of February the lead had stretched to 12 points. Then the injuries began to bite.

The manager was forced to change his side several times and form became erratic. Rivals Arsenal kept on winning and when defeat at Sheffield Wednesday was followed by a draw at West Ham, all eyes turned on the meeting between the top two at Old Trafford. Marc Overmars scored the goal that gave the Gunners a 1–0 win.

The writing was on the wall, and an incident during the Arsenal game turned out to be one of major significance. Peter Schmeichel joined the ranks of absentees after injuring himself during a foray upfield. Possibly hoping to emulate his scoring success against Volgograd and grab the crucial equaliser, he was caught out of position and had to chase Dennis Bergkamp as the Dutch striker broke out of defence. Schmeichel lunged into a challenge and strained a hamstring.

The injury ruled him out of the return leg against Monaco, where he joined Ryan Giggs, Gary Pallister, David May, Jordi Cruyff and long-term absentee Roy Keane in the grandstand to see David Trezeguet score with a speculative power drive after only eight minutes. Both Gary Neville and Paul Scholes limped off injured before half-time.

Ole Gunnar Solskjaer scored a 53rd-minute equaliser but the game ended 1–1 and Monaco went through on the away goals rule, a result that stunned chairman Edwards.

'It smacked of the previous season and the semi-final against Dortmund,' he said. 'It was the same sort of situation. The crowd was up for it, everybody was up for it and suddenly we lost an early goal and were left chasing the game. We had high hopes of Europe. We had played very well in the competition in the group stage. Winning those first five games got everybody's hopes up and I thought the away leg against Monaco was a good result.

'I suppose if you analyse it, with all the injuries, it caught up with us really. We had missed Keane all season, but even without him we were playing reasonably well in the league. Then Pallister was a miss, Giggs obviously a miss, as well as Peter Schmeichel, who is one of the best, if not the best, goalkeepers in the world. Those players were key to our earlier success.'

The European dream had ended but the title race was still on, if only for a short while. Wins over Wimbledon at Old Trafford and Blackburn at Ewood Park kept United on top until 10 April, when a home draw against Liverpool brought the change round. Arsenal won again and led the table, clinching the title a week later, the day before United's closing home game against Leeds.

Alex Ferguson was already planning for the next season and made his intentions clear by investing a record £10.75 million in Dutch defender Jaap Stam from PSV Eindhoven. The player would face the media 24 hours after the Leeds game but found himself the centre of attention after watching his future club in action from the comfort of the director's box.

Besieged by journalists following the 3–0 win, Stam turned oracle as well as observer.

'I have never been here before. I had only seen it on television or read about it in the newspapers, but when you are here it is a fantastic atmosphere and the crowd is great. This is the club I have always been a fan of from my younger years. That is why I chose Manchester United, and I hope I can have some good years of football here. They are one of the biggest clubs in the world and in Holland everybody looks up to Manchester United.

'I am not looking forward to playing with any particular players, but with the whole team, and my ambition is to win trophies in England and in Europe.

'United have a great team and they have proved that. They did well in the Champions League this year and it's a shame they didn't win the championship of course, but we'll do it next year. I think that maybe next year United will be champions and we will do well in the Champions League. I am very confident of that.'

His words went down well with his future manager as Alex Ferguson's 11th full season in charge ended without a major trophy, and he too saw hope on the horizon.

'Next season I will have another new player – Roy Keane. He is fit again and ready to pick up where he left off,' said Ferguson, as he reflected on a campaign during which United had scored 101 goals in all competitions.

Once the title was beyond reach, Ferguson had given some of his younger players first-team experience. Teenager Wes Brown played 30 minutes against Leeds, then the whole game at Barnsley on the season's closing day. John Curtis, Danny Higginbotham, Michael Clegg and Phil Mulryne also featured against Barnsley.

'It's been unusual for us really. It's usually gone right to the wire for some reason or another, but it has been a good season for us in some ways. We have finished top goalscorers in the league, and that applies to all our teams in all their leagues. That tells you something about how Manchester United try to entertain. I think we have tried to do that all the time.

'While it's disappointing not to win anything, there are a lot of good things for the club as a whole. There is a good structure and we have got everything in place. We aren't searching for anything, pulling rabbits out of the hat or anything like that. We have a formula and we are quite happy with that. We just have to get a pool of players who can stay fit all the time and I think we have a great chance next year.'

13

THEY COME AND GO ON THE ROAD TO GLORY

To class Manchester United as failures after their 1997-98 campaign was perhaps a little harsh, but that was the opinion reached by many critics as Alex Ferguson closed the doors on an empty trophy cabinet.

Some took things a step further by forecasting that the resurgence of Arsenal under Arsene Wenger would signal the end of the Scot's reign of supremacy, but time would prove that theory to be nothing more than wishful thinking. Martin Edwards put things in perspective with a chairman's view of the situation:

'You can't expect to win the double every year. I judge success as being there or thereabouts every year and we have done that. We have not been far off winning the championship for the last seven years. That is tremendous success.'

His words were based on the evidence of United's performances since missing out on the old Football League title in 1992 – champions, following the launch of the Premiership in 1993, double winners a year later, second again in 1995, another double in 1996, champions again in 1997, then pipped in the title race of 1998. No other club had come close to maintaining that kind of form and Alex Ferguson was determined no one was going to push him aside without a fight.

He knew he had to strengthen his squad and planned to use the summer of '98 to that effect. An assault on the Champions League had become the prime target. It was the one prize that had eluded him during his managerial career but a change in UEFA's rules the previous year presented him with an opportunity to tilt at the game's top prize.

Before that, qualification was for champion clubs only, but in a bid to increase the attraction of the competition, runners-up were given the chance to take part, provided they could win their way through the early knock-out rounds. It would be a longer journey to the final, but a gamble Alex Ferguson was ready to take.

The arrival of Jaap Stam was the first move towards the formation of a group of players he felt would be capable of handling the challenges of domestic football as well as Europe's increased demands, but the Dutchman's arrival was offset by the departure of a popular member of the senior squad.

Middlesbrough manager Bryan Robson seized the opportunity to make a move for Gary Pallister, a fee was agreed and the central defender moved back to Teesside.

'At the time I had mixed emotions,' Pallister recalls. 'The club accepted the bid but the manager told me it was up to me to decide. I still had another year on my contract and he said, "If you want to stay, all well and good, but if you want to go to Middlesbrough, then it's your choice."

'I was in two minds, but I had seen players of the calibre of Robbo and Brucie being moved on, and the heartache they suffered, and I felt that if the club had accepted a bid, it was my time to go.

'I was not going to stick around and maybe not play, so I made the decision to leave. It was tough but the Gaffer was honest in his thoughts. He had brought in Stam and had Wes Brown coming through and it could have turned a bit sour for me. Who knows what might have happened? It was a difficult situation at the time but, as I had always said, when my time came I would leave and not try to hang onto something that wasn't going to be as good as it had been, which would sour my memories.'

Pallister went back to his former club after 317 league appearances for United, during which he had played a major part in all those early successes of the Ferguson era.

'When I arrived, there was a lot of optimism because we had just signed Neil Webb and Micky Phelan. Danny Wallace came shortly afterwards and Paul Ince, who had taken his medical at the same time as me but signed a couple of weeks later. There was this feeling that the players who had been brought in were going to get us back on track, but that wasn't the case.

'Three weeks after I arrived we were walloped 5–1 by Manchester City, and there was a lot of conjecture about the manager's future. The players were taking a slaughtering in the press. Images of a cracked club crest appeared in some of the papers with headlines such as "United in Disarray".

'They were difficult times because a lot of money had been spent and a lot of people expected results to be achieved overnight and that just wasn't going to happen. We won the FA Cup at the end of that first season and I suppose that was the turning point.

'I remember the Gaffer saying after that game, "You've had a taste of it now and this can be the catalyst for something good as long as you retain your hunger and your willingness to work at the game." And so it proved.'

These were, allegedly, the difficult years of the Ferguson regime but according to former England international Pallister, there was no sign that any of the pressure was getting to the manager – nor, when the winning started, was there any transformation of attitude or approach to the job from the Gaffer.

'I don't recall noticing any change in the manager. If there was any pressure, he handled that himself and tried to keep it away from the players. When things weren't going so great it was, "Look, we aren't going to get any help from outside, it's all about what's in the dressing room. We are the only ones who can shape our destiny. We can't control the media and what is going to be said, so you just have to try and take what you want from that and prove people wrong." '

All the success in which Pallister shared might have triggered a change of tack from the manager, but there was none according to the former defender.

'He still gave out the rollickings, he still gave out the pats on the back, but I didn't really see any visible change. Only he will know what was going on inside. I'm sure he enjoyed the success a lot more than when people were putting his neck on the block, but there was certainly no variation in what he was doing day to day with the football club.

'Everybody realised he had been trying to alter everything there, especially the scouting system and the youth policy. He wanted to bring a lot of young kids through and I think everybody at the club, and certainly the chairman and the directors, even in the dark days, could see that he was working towards an end.

'He had a plan and ultimately that is why they backed him when things weren't going so well. They knew the club needed to be overhauled and I believe they could see that what he was doing would have long-term benefits. That's why they stood by him.'

Gary Pallister has fond memories of his time as a United player but when asked to single out the ultimate moment, surprisingly, he rates his single taste of European success in the Cup-Winners' Cup of 1991 above all other achievements.

Gary Pallister (centre) with Mark Hughes and Bryan Robson after winning the 1994 title. He believes that Alex Ferguson did a superb job keeping the pressure from the players during the days when trophies were more elusive.

Dwight Yorke is welcomed to United by Alex Ferguson in August 1998. Yorke was in prolific form in his first season to prove himself another superb buy for the club.

'For all the Premiership titles and FA Cups we won, the best night I had was in Rotterdam. The whole atmosphere, the whole occasion was unbelievable. I will never forget it. It was like a Manchester evening in Holland. It was a rainy, misty kind of night and we were playing a team that was supposed to be going to have no problems beating us, but we produced a great performance.

'I remember seeing the stadium still three-quarters full of Manchester United fans when we did the lap of honour, and the party afterwards was probably the best I have ever been to. The next day, when we got back home, we had a trip around the town parading the trophy and the lads just didn't want the experience to end.

'We partied and partied and partied. That is the abiding memory I have from my time at Old Trafford and if you ask any of the lads from that era, they will all say the same. It was the best night ever.'

There were close-season departures. Brian McClair ended his 11-year spell at Old Trafford and joined Motherwell, while Ben Thornley, one of the successful youth side of the early 90s and a player at the opposite end of football's ladder, moved to Huddersfield Town.

Ferguson sought new blood by mixing business with pleasure and taking in some of the World Cup games in France while enjoying his annual break. However, he made his opening move for one player before the competition got under way and Cameroon midfielder Marc-Vivien Foe seemed to be on his way to Old Trafford. Unluckily, he broke his leg during the build-up and the transfer from French club Lens was called off.

United were linked with many players involved in the tournament but the summer was mainly filled with speculation about one closer to home – Aston Villa's Dwight Yorke. The striker's name hit the headlines when the Midlands club announced that they had rejected United's £8 million offer, which their chairman Doug Ellis regarded as 'an insult'.

The spotlight switched to Holland's Patrick Kluivert and a deal was struck with his club, AC Milan, but the Dutchman appeared reluctant to move to Manchester, hinted he was on his way to Arsenal, and then signed for Barcelona.

The new season had already started and, more importantly, the Champions League transfer deadline was just hours away when, on 20 August, Ferguson finally got his man. Yorke was prised from Villa's grasp thanks to a record £12.6 million cheque changing hands.

The Trinidad and Tobago striker quickly realised the difference between the two clubs. When he spoke about his first recollection of life at Old

Trafford, he said, 'Wow! I was amazed. I didn't expect anything like it. There were television cameras everywhere, microphones piled up in front of me and faces as far as I could see. I had never seen anything to match that.

'I suppose the media hype had built up the transfer, and I knew it was big because I couldn't help reading about it. Obviously, when the biggest club in the world is interested in a player and that player is you, you are bound to have a few sleepless nights, and I did.

'I had no regrets about leaving Villa Park. The nine years I spent there were fantastic and it was very difficult for me to drop all that, but I went to Old Trafford to fulfil my dream and I didn't want anything to get in the way.

'I was just delighted the manager saw me as the final piece of the jigsaw in the team he was putting together to try to bring some silverware back to Old Trafford. My aim was to try to give Manchester United another dimension, and hopefully excite a lot of people at the same time.'

Was that record price tag a burden?

'There were a lot of people out there scrutinising every move and every touch I made, but that had nothing to do with me. I always believed in my own ability, and if I'd had any doubts that I wasn't up for the job, then I wouldn't have wanted to go there in the first place.'

No sooner was the Yorke deal tied up than United accepted a £5 million offer from Tottenham for Ole Gunnar Solskjaer. As with Pallister, the manager left it to the player, who was still under contract, to make the final decision about whether or not to accept the move, and the Norwegian declared that he would prefer life as a squad player at Old Trafford. That was all Alex Ferguson needed to hear. The decision proved to be one of greater significance than anyone might have predicted at that time.

Solskjaer stayed at Old Trafford and was soon joined by another Scandinavian as a £4.5 million investment brought Sweden's Jesper Blomqvist from Italian club Parma, and the Ferguson summer spending reached an all-time high of almost £28 million. However, it was money matters off the field that were about to make big news.

Manchester United plc became the target of a £623 million bid from satellite broadcasting company B-Sky-B. Takeover talk continued for months before the deal was called off, following the intervention of the Monopolies and Mergers Commission.

During that period Peter Schmeichel caused a stir by revealing plans to retire from English football at the end of the season. The goalkeeper chose

to bring things into the open to end mounting speculation about his future.

'For me, it was important to keep it quiet until everybody knew at the same time and they got the right explanation. If I had gone out speaking to clubs, more rumours would have been thrown about and it would have come out in the wrong way. It was important to be able to concentrate on playing and end all the speculation. I told the chairman and the manager, and they could sense that I had given it a lot of thought and it wasn't something I had come up with because I was tired or had had a late night. They knew it was a final decision and couldn't be reversed, and they respected me for that. The way they treated me was fantastic and they helped me a lot. They also knew it was better to support my decision rather than try to reverse it.

'I have said before that Manchester United is the ultimate place to play football and I still mean that. It's a fantastic club and it has a fantastic manager. It has the best and the most supporters and, by miles, the best stadium. It is a fantastic place and I knew it would be a sad day when I walked out of it.

'Alex Ferguson is probably the best manager around. I cannot see anybody who has the same sort of determination, the same kind of drive that he has, and he has a way of transferring that into the players.

'We had an attitude, and we had it from the moment I first came to the club, that "we are going to win this game, and nothing can stop us." That came from the manager and was one of the things that gave us so many good results. The drive he has is fantastic. He will not accept not winning.

'He is also a decent person, an honest person, and somebody that, if you have a problem, his door is always open and he will help you. Coming from abroad like I did, you will always get problems that need to be solved. I knocked on his door plenty of times and he always helped. He is a very special person to me.'

Shortly before Christmas came another surprise. Assistant manager Brian Kidd, Alex Ferguson's right-hand man, accepted an offer to take charge at Blackburn Rovers. The search for a replacement stretched early into the new year when the relatively unknown Steve McClaren, deputy to Jim Smith at Derby County, became Old Trafford's number two. The appointment brought to an end the comings and goings of that season, but by then Manchester United were heading for the pinnacle.

Peter Schmeichel, arguably one of Ferguson's greatest ever signings, makes another save, against Inter in the Champions League quarter-finals, March 1999. Having announced his retirement for the end of the campaign, he was looking for a special way to go out.

14

TREBLE VISION FOR
THE COMEBACK KINGS

ALEX FERGUSON HAS childhood memories of the moment Sir Edmund Hillary and Sherpa Tensing reached Everest's summit, and during his playing days, man took his first steps on the moon. However, throughout the years that had taken him to the peak of his managerial career, one major challenge had eluded not only him, but all those who had gone before. Despite more than 40 years of trying, no English club had won the game's three major tournaments in the same season. The grand slam of European Cup, league championship and FA Cup remained the unreachable star. Some had come close, but the ultimate treble was unconquered territory.

In May 1977, in what turned out to be Tommy Docherty's swan song at Old Trafford, United beat Liverpool at Wembley and in doing so prevented them from taking the three top prizes. United's second double-winning year of 1996 took them close to the sun but in Europe's intense heat, like Icarus, they lost the use of their wings just when they needed them most.

As Alex Ferguson celebrated his 57th birthday in December 1998, his team was still in the chase for the clean sweep, but only the most patriotic, or perhaps the most blinkered, supporter would have risked a wager on the dream being attained that season. True, the treble was possible but with 18 Premiership games remaining, Inter Milan waiting in the quarter-finals of the Champions League and an opening FA Cup-tie against Middlesbrough five days away, little mention was made of it being achieved.

There were certainly no predictions from the manager as he looked back on the year about to end.

'It was disappointing not winning the league and we all felt that. We are not taking anything away from Arsenal but the injuries in March cost us very dearly. But for them, I think we would have done better, even in the Champions League.

'This season has been reasonable. We have achieved what we set out to achieve and that was to qualify from a very tough section of the Champions League. They called it "The Group of Death" and it wasn't far short of that. To knock out a good team like Barcelona says a lot for our club. We have also managed to be up there at the top end of the league, challenging, and coming into the new year it's up to us to put the foot down on the throttle and get going.

'There have been a lot of changes and in the modern game you can expect that. Pally and Choccy McClair left in the summer and that was sad to see them go because they were fantastic players for us, great servants and loyal to me. That was sad, but you get on with the job of making sure that Manchester United always stay top.'

Losing Brian Kidd in early December was unexpected, according to Ferguson's description of the parting of their ways in his autobiography *Managing My Life*. He paid tribute to his former right-hand man:

Naturally, the first-team players were sorry to see him go. He had proved himself an outstanding coach who was meticulous in his preparation for training. I had always recognised, and made a point of acknowledging, the important role he played in getting the team ready for games.

The seven years we spent working together was a golden time for Manchester United. His forte was training players and with us he revealed a gift for getting close to them. Each individual in the squad came to feel that Kiddo wanted him in the team. In fact, when I gave Brian his say about who should play, naturally he had his favourites. Not surprisingly, they were mainly lads he had brought to the club when he was Youth Development Officer. Just as his predecessor, Archie Knox, gave me splendid backing while I was laying the foundations in my first five years at Old Trafford, so Brian was an integral part of the success that came in a flood afterwards. Along with his achievements as a player, his excellent contribution as my assistant assured him of an honoured place in the history of the club.

United were second in the table when Kidd left and, following his departure, form dipped slightly with three successive Premiership draws at Aston Villa and Tottenham, and then at home to Chelsea. However, a 1–1 stalemate against Bayern Munich on 9 December, falling between the Villa and

Solskjaer scores one of his four goals against Nottingham Forest in
February 1999, after coming on as a substitute in the 74th minute.

Paul Scholes, David Beckham, Roy Keane, Ole Gunnar Solskjaer, Andy Cole and Ryan Giggs celebrate scoring a late winner against Liverpool in the fourth round of the FA Cup, January 1999.

Spurs games, was enough to see both teams through to the knock-out stage at the expense of Barcelona and Brondby.

After the shock of a 3–2 home defeat in the Premiership against Middlesbrough on 19 December, few in the 55,152 who witnessed the upset could have realised they had seen Manchester United's last defeat in any game that season.

The transformation turned out to be sensational. After the 'Boro reversal, Nottingham Forest were beaten 3–0 and United picked up a creditable point from Gianluca Vialli's Chelsea at Stamford Bridge. In the new year, Middlesbrough were beaten 3–1 in the third round of the FA Cup and Ferguson's mean machine rolled on, winning 4–1 against West Ham at Old Trafford and beating Leicester 6–2 at Filbert Street.

Liverpool came next, spectacularly knocked out of the Cup as United demonstrated their fight-to-the-death attitude. The Merseysiders were preparing to celebrate victory after leading from the third minute through a Michael Owen strike, when goals from Dwight Yorke (88) and Ole Gunnar Solskjaer (89) swept United through.

Two more league wins took United back to the top and after the second of those fixtures, a 1–0 victory over Derby County, Kidd's replacement took up his new post. If Steve McClaren's final game as Jim Smith's deputy at Pride Park was a disappointment, his first as United's new assistant manager made up for it.

Derby's closest rivals, Nottingham Forest, temporarily managed by Ron Atkinson, provided the opposition and United won 8–1 at the City Ground. Solskjaer stole the show, coming on as a 74th-minute substitute and promptly scoring four times before the final whistle.

'I told Steve that was the standard we expected from him now he has come to Old Trafford,' the jubilant manager joked as United sat four points clear. 'He is certainly going to have to go some to better that.'

McClaren will never forget that introduction to his new club.

'They played really well and after a few minutes we were 2–1 up. I said to the staff, "Is it like this every week?" By the end of it, I was thinking, "This is so easy."

'Normally, at Derby, I would be up and down and panicking in the last 20 minutes, holding on to a lead, or trying to get a goal back, but it was different sitting there 8–1 up, nice and comfortable and enjoying the occasion. I said to the boys afterwards, "At least you've kept me in the job another week!"'

He confessed to arriving in his new post with no preconceived ideas.

'After the success United had had, it was a case of if it ain't broke, don't fix it. I just went in, had a look at the routines, saw how things were done and kept the players on their toes. I made sure the training and practice sessions were good.

'I took a watching brief and got to know the players, their habits, the little extra things they liked doing and what they disliked. You could say I was learning about them. They were obviously wary, looking and learning about me as well.

'You can always improve. You can always get better. It's like me in my career, and everybody else. You can't stand still. There has got to be progress, and if we could improve the players even by two, three, five per cent, we would still make them better players. If you make them better players individually, you will make them into a better team.'

No one knows whether events would have followed the same pattern had Jim Ryan continued to fill his temporary role as Alex Ferguson's number two, but United found the golden touch as Steve McClaren settled into his new post. They could not stop winning.

In the FA Cup, Fulham were beaten in round five, and Chelsea overcome 2–0 at Stamford Bridge in a replayed quarter-final. Arsenal were next up, but before that, all eyes were on the Champions League quarter-final against Inter Milan. A 2–0 first leg at Old Trafford set things up perfectly for the trip to Italy. Paul Scholes scored two minutes from time for a 1–1 draw and United were through.

In the next round, another late goal, this time a last-minute strike from Ryan Giggs, prevented a 1–0 home defeat by Juventus. A week later Giggs was again the hero in the FA Cup semi-final against Arsenal as he took United to Wembley with a goal described by his manager as, 'The best there has ever been scored in any FA Cup-tie.' Few would accuse him of overstatement.

It needed a replay at Villa Park to settle the issue and the game was packed with high drama. Beckham scored after 17 minutes, Bergkamp equalised in the 69th. Arsenal were awarded a penalty almost on full-time but Schmeichel saved and the tie went into extra time. With 19 minutes gone, Giggs ran more than half the length of the field, leaving defenders sprawling, before cutting inside and shooting high into the net.

'I just kept going until I saw Dave Seaman in front of me, then hit the ball as hard as I could,' was the modest way in which Giggs described his goal – the perfect combination of speed, skill and spectacular finishing.

In the league, Chelsea slipped out of contention, leaving United and

One of the greatest goals of recent years: Ryan Giggs' solo effort to win the FA Cup semi-final replay against rivals Arsenal helped keep the treble dream alive.

Jesper Blomqvist, Steve McClaren and Dwight Yorke celebrate qualifying for the Champions League final.

Roy Keane powers past Davids and Pessotto of Juventus in the Champions League semi-final. His towering performance that night saw United through to the final.

Arsenal to fight it out. Many predicted the pending fixture pile-up would cost Ferguson his fifth title. As things turned out, this was not the case, but suspensions did provide an unwanted burden as United closed in on the Holy Grail.

The treble was on, but talk about it was declared taboo at Old Trafford. No player, or any of the management team, responded to media questions when back-page headlines yelled about the possibility of United taking all three prizes from football's top shelf.

'Juventus will feel they are now the favourites and rightly so. It was a great result for them but they may live to regret us scoring our late goal. I have a gut feeling that we can reproduce the form we showed in the second half when we created three or four chances. Something tells me that we are going to win,' was the closest it got, when Alex Ferguson summed up the opening game against the Italians.

In Turin it seemed United had been right to keep quiet. After six minutes, they trailed 2–0. Filippo Inzaghi had scored twice, leaving a battered United on the ropes, 3–1 down on aggregate and battling to stay upright. Everything pointed to a sad exit, but Roy Keane had other ideas.

The Irish skipper was an inspiration. Leading from the front, he pulled a goal back with a header from a David Beckham corner in the 24th minute, but his joy was short-lived. A few minutes later he brought down Zidane and was shown a yellow card. Coupled with a booking from the first leg against Inter, that meant if United got to the final, Keane would miss it. Keane's response was to make sure his team-mates got there.

United poured forward and in the 34th minute Yorke dived in to head home a cross from Cole and suddenly the visitors were in the driving seat. If the score remained the same, United would go through to the final in Barcelona thanks to their two away goals.

As the game went on, United twice hit the framework but the Italians also had their moments with Inzaghi denied a hat-trick by the agile Schmeichel. Paul Scholes came on as a substitute and within eight minutes was booked, a punishment that, like Keane's, ruled him out of the final.

Heartache was quickly forgotten as seven minutes from time Yorke burst into the Juventus box only to be pulled down by the 'keeper. The referee was about to award a penalty but before he could stop play the alert Cole nipped in to slide the ball home for a memorable 3–2 victory.

Martin Edwards, chairman of the football club, summed things up after witnessing the drama:

'I was nervous at 2–2 because it needed just one break by Juventus and they would be in the final, and when we hit the post twice I began to think, is it really going to happen? In the end, we did it with style and now we wonder about the treble. Obviously, it would be fantastic if it happened, but I still think it would be a miracle.'

Whatever might happen, United's season was heading for an amazing climax, and when Arsenal lost at Leeds the miracle was on.

United's remaining league games were at Blackburn then at home to Tottenham. They drew at Ewood Park to relegate Brian Kidd's Rovers, who four years earlier had been champions, and the destiny of the title hinged on United beating Spurs on the season's closing day.

For the first time since 1965 they clinched the championship in a game watched by their home support, but they could not have got off to a worse start. Tottenham had to win to give Arsenal any chance of retaining their title, and scored in the 25th minute.

United fought back. Beckham scored with a fierce shot from the right wing, and two minutes into the second half, Cole lobbed the ball over Ian Walker for the final goal of the game. Part one of the treble was completed, and the chairman's miracle was closer to becoming a reality.

Part two was a formality. Newcastle were United's Wembley opponents in the FA Cup. Even without regular left-back Denis Irwin, a suspension victim following a ludicrous sending off at Anfield during the Premiership run-in, Ferguson's side looked in a different class.

There was a worry early on when Keane was injured and replaced by Sheringham after only nine minutes, but the substitute made the perfect entrance by scoring within a minute. Scholes tied things up in the second half, leaving Alex Ferguson's side one win away from completing the dream. The prize at stake was the biggest of all.

Bayern Munich, fellow qualifiers from 'The Group of Death', were United's opponents in the final, having eliminated fellow countrymen Kaiserslautern then Dynamo Kiev to get there. As far as the United manager was concerned, he was hoping it would be a case of third time lucky. His side had drawn both earlier meetings with the Germans.

The showdown in Barcelona's Nou Camp was a nail-biting affair. United got off to the worst possible start, conceding a simple goal after just five minutes when Mario Basler slammed a free kick through their defensive wall. It seemed the enormity of the occasion was having an effect on Ferguson's young players.

Robbed of Keane's leadership and the creativity of Scholes, United started the game with Beckham in centre midfield alongside Butt, and

Goalscorer Teddy Sheringham heads on to set up Ole Gunnar Solskjaer to score the winning goal in added time during the Champions League final against Bayern Munich, 1999.

The United team celebrates a fabulous comeback that completed a unique treble of Premiership, FA Cup and Champions League victories.

Giggs and Blomqvist filling the wide positions, but the team seemed to be struggling to establish a comfortable pattern of play. Bayern were firmly in control.

Even when United did settle down, they could not breach the German defence and Ferguson decided it was time to switch things around. With 23 minutes to go, Sheringham replaced Blomqvist and the transformation was instantaneous.

Cole almost equalised with a spectacular overhead kick and United began to dominate play, but in their eagerness to push forward, they left their defence exposed. It took a tremendous save by Schmeichel to keep out a chip from Stefan Effenberg. Bayern sub Mehmet Scholl hit a post and with less than 10 minutes remaining, the United boss made another switch, Solskjaer for Cole, as the accent went on total attack.

This left more gaps and again Schmeichel, handed the captain's armband for his final game, thwarted Scholl, diving full length to push his shot round a post. Two minutes later when Carsten Jancker rammed the ball against the bar, Alex Ferguson admitted he was ready to accept defeat.

'I started to adjust to losing the game. I was reminding myself that the important thing in defeat would be to keep my dignity and accept that it was just not our year.'

The final whistle approached and in one last desperate effort United pushed forward and won a corner. Schmeichel ran from his goal and into the Bayern box, hoping to get on the end of Beckham's cross, or at least cause confusion. With seconds to go, Giggs helped the ball on, Sheringham swept it in and United were level.

Extra time loomed but Italian referee Pierluigi Collina kept things going. There was stoppage time to use up and three minutes of it had gone when United forced another corner.

It was the last throw of the dice. Beckham crossed, Sheringham eased the ball across goal and Solskjaer, running in on the far post, flicked it with the outside of his right boot into the roof of the net – Manchester United 2 Bayern Munich 1, and the Germans had neither the time nor the spirit for any kind of fight-back. The whistle went. The Nou Camp erupted.

Alex Ferguson had taken his side to the summit. 'We were trying to attack all the time. Nobody can deny that our team plays with a spirit to attack and will to win. We were prepared to take risks and, in football, when you are prepared to be like that, you deserve to succeed.'

The ultimate treble was his.

Alex Ferguson takes a moment with the Champions League trophy in the changing room at the Nou Camp – the pinnacle of any club manager's ambitions.

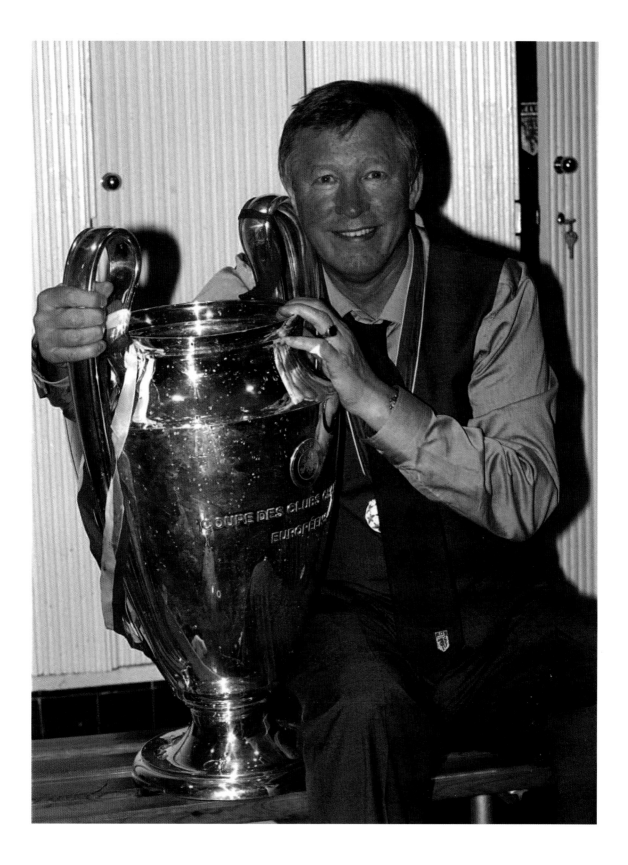

15

THE HONOURS KEEP COMING FOR SIR ALEX

DOUBTLESS IT HAD BEEN the talk of the Ferguson household for several days, but on Saturday, 12 June 1999, the rest of the country learned the family's secret when the morning newspapers declared, 'Arise Sir Alex!'

The name of Alex Ferguson was included on the Queen's Birthday Honours list. He was awarded a knighthood for his services to football, proving correct the speculation that had circulated since the Champions League was won 17 days earlier – the Manchester United manager would soon follow in the footsteps of his legendary predecessor Sir Matt Busby.

Sir Alex was modest in his response.

'This is a great honour for Manchester United, my family and for me.'

He was a little more forthcoming in his soon-to-be-published autobiography *Managing My Life*:

Until my dying day, I shall be grateful to Manchester United for all that my association with the club has given me. For somebody who loves football as much as I do, there is no better place to be. When I learned during the summer that I was to receive a knighthood, I had to smile at the thought of how far football had brought me since the time in my Govan childhood when I had to wait for a neighbour to give me a pair of hand-me-down boots before I could turn out for the street team.

I am thrilled about the knighthood but I hope it can be seen as honouring my family and my friends and everybody who ever worked with me. In particular, I hope it can be seen as honouring Manchester United and all the people, from great players to canteen ladies, who have helped me there over the years.

While the team display all three trophies during a race day at Haydock Park, Sir Alex Ferguson and his wife Cathy went to the Palace to receive his knighthood – yet another award to help make 1999 a perfect year.

It was the perfect ending to what had been an astonishing 12 months for the man who was now the most successful manager in the history of Manchester United. Club Chairman Martin Edwards was among the first to offer his congratulations:

'I think Alex getting his knighthood is an honour for the club and for everyone involved with it. Clearly, the honour came about with him being the manager of Manchester United and the success Manchester United has had, so everybody in the club takes a bit of pleasure out of it.'

However, there was another way of looking at things. The newly elevated manager had made it clear he had no intention of continuing in the job once he had reached his 60th birthday, and doubts were cast about Sir Alex's future.

Interviewed by Tom Tyrrell for United's official magazine, Edwards revealed his thoughts about what lay ahead when the Ferguson era ended. Asked if the manager would 'move upstairs', his answer caused a stir:

'That's a difficult one because there are a number of things to consider. First of all you will remember when Sir Matt retired and somebody else came in… If Sir Alex is still there in the background, with all the success he has had, is that going to be a comfort or a hindrance to his successor? Secondly, is that something Sir Alex wants?

'It would be very difficult for him to be there without actually feeling a need to get involved. You know the way he is, he likes to be involved. He is a hands-on person and I think it would be difficult for him to resist that.

'As for finding a possible replacement, it's a bit premature at the moment, but clearly we have got it in mind. Sir Alex has said this is going to be his last contract and I think it will be. He will be 60 years of age by then. I think we have to have a successor in mind in three years' time, so we are fortunate in that we have time to look at it and plan for the succession.'

Finding a new manager was something for the future. More immediate matters had arisen for the club supremo to deal with during the summer of 1999, and Edwards stunned football by announcing United's withdrawal from the forthcoming season's FA Cup.

The reason? United had been invited to take part in a new FIFA-organised tournament in Brazil and the club had decided the only course of action to take was to accept. The decision followed pleas from the Football Association and the then Minister for Sport, Tony Banks, who felt if the European champions did not go to South America, it might seriously affect England's chances of staging the 2006 World Cup.

United found themselves under fire from all quarters.

'Quite clearly, it was put to us that if Manchester United did not compete in the tournament in Brazil, that would severely damage the chances of England winning the 2006 World Cup bid. It was purely on that basis that we withdrew from the FA Cup and agreed to play in Brazil. It was made quite plain to us that it would enhance the chances of the 2006 World Cup bid if we played in Brazil, and it was put even more strongly than that – we could jeopardise England's chances if we didn't,' says Edwards.

It was a no-win situation. By withdrawing, United were snubbing tradition, but if they snubbed FIFA's invitation, they would have to shoulder the blame for missing out on the World Cup.

Wisely the manager left the talking to others and kept himself busy in the transfer market, where his main priority was to strengthen his goal-keeping pool. He was looking for a player capable of filling the void left by Peter Schmeichel.

First, he signed Aston Villa's Mark Bosnich, taking the Australian back to the club where he had started his career as a fresh-faced teenager. Then, as the new season started, he landed another goalkeeper, handing over £4.5 million to Serie A club Venezia for their Sicilian star Massimo Taibi, whose passage into English football was far from smooth.

Taibi signed four days after United lost the UEFA Super Cup 1–0 to Lazio in Monaco, and a mix-up with his European registration meant he was ineligible for the first of the two group phases of the Champions League. He made a thrilling debut at Liverpool, where his heroics earned a 3–2 win, but then the costly mistakes began.

A blunder against Southampton allowed a Matt Le Tissier mishit to trickle under his body, and after an October humiliation at Chelsea, where the treble winners were beaten 5–0, he faded into the background before eventually returning to Italy.

The Chelsea upset could easily have taken some of the shine off Sir Alex's testimonial game, but the charity showpiece attracted a crowd of 54,842. A World XI, including Eric Cantona, Cafu, Rio Ferdinand, Paul Gascoigne, Gianluca Vialli and Peter Schmeichel, took part in an evening of high entertainment.

It was the first opportunity Old Trafford had to show its appreciation of Schmeichel's contribution to the club's successes, although the sight of the former 'keeper ending the game playing centre-forward as Steve Bruce kept goal may have come as a surprise.

Peter Schmeichel with Alex Ferguson, early in his time at United. The Danish keeper proved hard to replace.

Roy Keane and Alex Ferguson prepare to fly out to Brazil for the Club World Championship in January 2000. The previous month, Keane had given his manager a boost by signing a new contract.

'When I announced that I was going to leave the English game, I said that I would do my best to see that United finished on a high, and to have the Champions League final as the last game was exactly what I set out to do.

'I know that may sound a bit arrogant but everybody, me included, worked really hard on it. In the past we have been so close yet so far away, but then we had that little bit of extra luck and I really felt we deserved to be in that final. To have it as my last game was just another happy occasion for me.

'I felt that in Europe we were more positive in our approach in that final campaign than in previous seasons. We set out to score goals. That is very rare for teams in Europe to do, but it was our natural game and the manager did the right thing to let us go out and do that and not be too tactical about the thing.

'Now and again, if you are too tactical, it can mess things up and confuse matters more. If you play as close as possible to what is in your nature, then you will always get the best results. We did that, in Europe especially, and I think we did everybody proud. We entertained, we scored goals and we made history along the way by beating an Italian side in Italy for the first time, and that was down to our positive approach.

'I will never forget my time at Old Trafford, and certainly not that final season,' said Schmeichel, who had joined Sporting Lisbon and was on the way to helping them win the Portuguese title in his first season.

More honours came Sir Alex's way the following month as he was handed the Freedom of Glasgow to make it, in true football style, a hat-trick of such recognition. The city of his birth followed Manchester's tribute four months earlier and that of Aberdeen in 1983.

'When I was given the Freedom of Manchester, I felt greatly honoured. I was following in the footsteps of Sir Matt, who was rewarded in the same way, and realised what a part of my life the city had become after 13 years living down here.'

By the end of the month, Sir Alex had every reason to feel on top of the world. United became the first British side to win the notorious Inter-Continental Cup, the meeting between the European and South American champions, which in its 40-year existence had hosted some controversial confrontations.

The game was staged in the Olympic Stadium in Tokyo. Roy Keane scored the only goal as Brazilian side Palmeiras were defeated, and Ryan Giggs was given a new car as man of the match. The manager reflected on this latest achievement:

'It was a fantastic trip for us, a really good experience. The whole organisation and preparation and the excitement of the game were fantastic. Team spirit was brilliant and it was a really great exercise. It was a massive game for the Brazilians – they had prepared for it for a month. They played two friendlies in Japan during the build-up and were there for 12 days. They had the Brazilian flag draped around their dressing room and were singing their national anthem before they went out. It was a really good atmosphere and a big match for them.

'Did we feel like world champions? Well, when you win the European Cup, then go and play the best team in South America, obviously it is as near as you can possibly get to being the world champions, and it's well deserved. I thought it was a great achievement for the lads.'

There was little time to bask in the glory but any fears that the trip to Japan might have taken its toll on the squad were quickly dismissed. Four days later Everton were beaten 5–1 at Old Trafford and United were heading for the new millennium at the top of the Premiership.

A further boost to the club's chances of more success that season came before the next game, a Champions League second group match against Valencia, when it was announced before kick-off that Roy Keane had finally put pen to paper on a contract extension, ending months of speculation he might leave the club. Keane later admitted that he came close.

'I won't lie. Three days before I signed we were quite a bit apart in terms of my contract, and I had to look at my options, which were to go abroad. I felt I couldn't go to another English club. I was flattered and embarrassed by the interest from abroad, and the money being mentioned was frightening, because I was on a free transfer. But if it had been about money, I wouldn't have been at United in the first place.

'There was a lot of speculation about where I might go, although my priority from day one was to stay, but United weren't coming up with the contract. As it got closer to 1 January [when he would have been free to talk to other clubs] that was it. They came up with the deal and I signed it.'

In keeping with the occasion, Keane scored the first goal of the night as Valencia were beaten 3–0, a win that propelled United towards the quarter-finals once again. Sir Alex was both relieved and delighted to hold on to such an influential player.

'I had a few chats with Roy over the months and made sure he knew how much we wanted him. The night he signed, it was absolutely brilliant. The news of Roy staying lifted everyone and it was a night that he will remember, I'm sure. He was my captain and such an influence for the team. He had a determination to win and a hunger about his whole life that spread throughout the team.'

United saw out the century with a 2–2 draw at Sunderland before leaving for Rio de Janeiro and the inaugural FIFA Club World Championship, which turned out to be an event filled with controversy. David Beckham was sent off in the opening draw against Mexico's Rayos Del Necaxa, host side Vasco Da Gama beat them 3–0 and interest ended with a 2–0 win over South Melbourne.

Even so, Gary Neville was left wondering if United had been pioneers in a competition that might one day replace the World Cup.

'I think that could be the case because it is FIFA's tournament and they have got the power to do whatever they want. If they make it into a massive tournament, there's no reason why that shouldn't happen. People in this country laughed at the European Cup 40 or 50 years ago and now it's the biggest thing there is. Who is to say that, in another 15 or 20 years, this is not going to be the biggest competition you can play in? We were pioneers and it would have been fantastic to have put our name on the trophy.'

Gary's theory may have gone down well with his manager, whose own views on club-versus-country issues are well known.

The gap in United's domestic fixture list lasted 28 days. The first game after their return from Rio was a Premiership clash with Arsenal, who, like leaders Leeds, had failed to put any light between themselves and the defending champions in the absence of their rivals.

United had slipped to second place but, by the end of January, they had regained top spot, where they were to stay until the end of the season. There was disappointment in Europe, though. A creditable 0–0 draw at the Bernabeu in the quarter-final with Real Madrid was followed by a second-leg defeat, when they were beaten 3–2 at Old Trafford. Seven days later, with five games of the season remaining, the championship was secured with a 3–1 win at Southampton.

Already Sir Alex was planning for the new season. When Chelsea were beaten 3–2 at Old Trafford, the game was watched by Dutch striker Ruud van Nistelrooy, but the plan to sign him from PSV Eindhoven collapsed. There were problems with his medical and the player returned to Holland where, in a bid to attain full fitness, he ruptured a cruciate knee ligament. The £18.5 million deal was put on hold as Sir Alex made it clear he was prepared to wait for van Nistelrooy to recover fully.

So ended a most remarkable season. United had scored more Premiership goals (97) than the previous best, with a goal difference of plus

52, and had won more points (91) than had been achieved in any other 38-game campaign. Old Trafford established a new British average league attendance of 58,017, a record destined to be short-lived as ground capacity rose to 67,500, and Sir Alex Ferguson remained the most successful manager in the game.

'Winning the Premiership is special, no matter how many times you do it. Winning the first one was special because it opened the door for us, but to continue the success has been remarkable, and it's great credit to the players we have had over that period. Over the years we have developed an attacking purpose. It's the philosophy of the club.

'It's hard to win the league and nobody can take it for granted. Over the last few years the Premiership has become harder and harder. A lot of teams have spent a lot of money reinforcing their squads and bringing better players in, so that is the challenge. We know Arsenal and Chelsea, Leeds and Liverpool are going to be ready for us, and that is what makes it such an interesting competition.

'I think we are getting better and I hope to improve things next year, particularly in Europe, where we can perhaps realise our full potential.'

16

THE MAGNIFICENT SEVENTH

SIMPLY THE BEST – that is how Sir Alex Ferguson viewed his Manchester United squad as he looked forward to the 2000-01 campaign. Ahead lay the possibility of becoming the first manager in English football to lead a club to three successive league championships, behind him another season on which United had stamped their domination of the domestic game.

'Ability-wise, they are the best, and they are improving. It is always very difficult to compare with older players but in my mind they are the best,' he said, explaining why he had gone out of his way publicly to thank the squad when handed the Old Trafford stadium announcer's microphone during the parade of the latest Premiership trophy.

'They deserved that. They know what I think of them anyway but I felt it was right to do it in front of our fans, who themselves had made a great contribution, as have my staff. These are the important people and they deserved to be recognised and I think that it should have come from me.'

United supporters were understandably on a high. They had just seen a sixth title won in eight seasons as the club followed the pattern set in 1994 when one successful campaign was followed by another – two in a row in '93 and '94, again in '96 and '97, then in '99 and 2000. Good things apparently come in twos. Yet regardless of the success, a feeling of apprehension still hung over Old Trafford.

Sir Alex had made it clear he did not plan to continue in the job beyond the summer of 2002, so just two seasons were left before his retirement and speculation had started to simmer about the search for a possible replacement.

Some claimed it to be a sign of things to come during the close season when United splashed out a record £7.8 million on World Cup winning goal-keeper Fabien Barthez. When the Frenchman was unveiled to the media on Wednesday, 31 May, Sir Alex was nowhere to be seen. He had started his summer holiday. As Barthez told the world, 'I'm so happy to sign for United and come here for six years because everybody knows Manchester is a big club, a big team, with big players. I am here to play football and win many things with Manchester United. My ambition is, like all the players, to win, to win, to win,' the manager was sunning himself in the South of France.

The collapse of the van Nistelrooy deal meant no more incomings that summer, but there were departures. Jordi Cruyff left to join Spanish club Alaves, having completed his four-year contract. His one regret was not being able to prove himself at Old Trafford.

'I enjoyed my days at Manchester United. There is no doubt about that and I have no axe to grind with anyone. The manager was always fair with me, but the problem was I was injured a lot while I was there. Also because of the style of play he adopted, I don't think he ever had the chance to see me play in what I regarded as my best position, coming in from behind the main strikers. I couldn't expect him to change things for me, and I have no regrets about any of my time spent in England. When I left United, I left behind many friends.'

Henning Berg also moved on, returning to Blackburn Rovers, where he teamed up with United youngsters John Curtis and Keith Gillespie and the now veteran Mark Hughes.

Gillespie was a member of United's Class of '92, the FA Youth Cup winning side that included David Beckham, Paul Scholes, Nicky Butt and Gary Neville, all now established first-team regulars. In eight years, boys had become men, but according to the elder of the Neville brothers, little had changed.

'I suppose we have been expected to perform at our peaks for the last five years. There was a lot talked about age and, to be honest, you feel the same at 19 or 20 years of age as you do when you are 25. The only thing is you have probably been there a few times before, but I don't think there was any added expectancy. We knew we just had to go out and perform to our standards. We had set ourselves a high standard and we had to maintain it.

'We had just had a successful season, winning the league and the Inter-Continental Cup, but despite winning the league in the style that we did, we wanted to go into the next year and improve again. We had set ourselves a standard by winning the three trophies in one season in 1999 and while the next season was a fantastic one, our performance maybe dropped a

United stalwart Gary Neville in action against Aston Villa on Boxing Day 2000: 'We had to step it up a gear again.'

little lower. We went into 2000-01 knowing we had to step it up a gear again and really grind teams into the ground.'

The Manchester United chequebook remained closed for most of that summer but that was not the case for many of the other Premiership contenders. There was frantic dealing in the transfer market but Neville viewed the approach taken by his own club as another example of Sir Alex Ferguson's shrewd management.

'The buying was a sign that clubs had to change their styles and adapt a lot, but the manager had developed something here, so the squad didn't need wholesale changes. He brought in one or two players every year. Change was continual, but it happened as a slow transition rather than making massive turnarounds each year, which some other clubs seemed to have done.

'I don't see how big changes can be the way forward. If you want to maintain success over a long period of time, you have got to have continuity and stability, and that's what we had got at this club.

'You expected Chelsea, Leeds and Liverpool to go out and spend money because they had just seen us win the title by 18 points, and they wouldn't have enjoyed that. They had to try to catch us up. All we could concentrate on was trying to carry on moving forward, but it didn't surprise me that other clubs spent large amounts of money.'

United were given an early opportunity to test the quality of Chelsea's investment in Jimmy Floyd Hasselbaink and Eidur Gudjohnsen when the clubs met in the season's curtain-raiser. Hasselbaink scored one of the goals as Chelsea won 2–0 in the last Charity (now the Community) Shield to be staged at Wembley before redevelopment began.

Few would have imagined, as Sir Alex led out his side before the start of his 14th full season in charge at Old Trafford, that work on the national stadium would still be ongoing as his 20th anniversary as manager approached.

The Wembley upset, during which Roy Keane was sent off, gave no real indication of what was to follow when the season got under way. Chelsea challenged but in early October a new name topped the Premiership and United went to Filbert Street to face leaders Leicester City.

Many back pages predicted the end of United's reign as they took on Leicester on the back of a 1–0 defeat by Arsenal. United had other ideas. Sheringham scored twice and Solskjaer added a third. The defending champions reclaimed top spot and began a run of seven successive Premiership wins.

Sir Alex found himself the centre of attention when speculation claimed he might be offered the opportunity to take over as England manager. He refused to play any part in the debate but England regular Gary Neville did have an opinion:

'I think the manager is happy here and while it would be great for the United lads in the England squad if he was to do it, I don't really think it's on the cards.'

He was right. The job was eventually given not to a Scot but a Swede – Sven Goran Eriksson.

Sir Alex's 14th anniversary came on the eve of the season's first major crossroads, a decisive Champions League clash with Dynamo Kiev.

United had suffered mixed fortunes in the first group round of the competition. They met Anderlecht, winning 5–1 at Old Trafford then losing 2–1 in Belgium, and PSV Eindhoven, who won 3–1 in Holland but were beaten by the same score in the return. The game in Kiev ended goalless and progress to the second group phase hung in the balance.

'It's a massive game that we have to win. That's straightforward, and in that situation I feel the players have got the capabilities. We have seen it many times before. They have got the experience and they have the nerve. It is going to require some nerve because these games can become nervous occasions. I think the players have the temperament to handle it.

'We've come a long way in 14 years but even when I started, my first game at Oxford was an important one because the nature of this club is to win matches. We have an expectancy, which means you have to deliver, and I have been proud of what the players have achieved over the years. This is another test for them, which I hope they will relish. I know they will.'

In sharp contrast to that first game of the Ferguson regime, the one due to take place was worth around £5.5 million to the club if they could reach the quarter-finals.

'There has been a dramatic change in the game since 1986,' said Sir Alex. 'The money factor is nothing to do with the players at the end of the day, and I would never place that sort of pressure on a player's head. The money is the concern of the plc side of the club. Money is important because we are a plc but the most important thing is winning and, to be honest, I would gladly win this game even if it meant not making another penny out of the Champions League.'

Sir Alex had come under fire for his team selection during the early stages of the competition, when he rested players because important Premiership games loomed. He knew he would face more flak if things went wrong against the Ukrainians.

'In some respects, we have only ourselves to blame for being in this position. I take some of the criticism in the sense that I played a weakened team against PSV, but that was for the best reasons. When you manage a club, and considering the number of games we have, you have to have another outlook about your next game. You have to look at the big picture, and the situation we were in at that moment was that we had a game at Arsenal on the Sunday, and I felt that was important. Had we won that game we would have been sitting in a very good position, and at the end of the season that could be justified.'

A single Teddy Sheringham goal was enough to see United through against Dynamo Kiev, but skipper Roy Keane was far from pleased with some sections of the Old Trafford support – not the dyed-in-the-wool home and away followers of the club, but those occupying the corporate hospitality sections, who have since become known as 'the prawn sandwich brigade'.

'Our fans away from home are as good as any, but at home, sometimes you must wonder, "Do they understand the game of football?" We are 1–0 up and there are one or two stray passes, so they start getting on players' backs. It's just not on. At the end of the day, they need to get behind the team, like those fans away from home who are fantastic. I would call them the hard-core fans. At home, they have their few drinks and probably their prawn sandwiches and don't realise what is going on out on the pitch.'

The impetus of the victory carried over into the Premiership where Middlesbrough, Manchester City, Derby and Tottenham were beaten. United had opened an eight-point lead at the top of the table by early December and were on course for their third title in a row, but Sir Alex was looking beyond the end of the campaign.

The club announced that talks had opened with the manager about a role he might take on when he stepped down at the end of the next season, which he remained committed to do. Sir Alex was happy to stay on in some capacity, not on the playing side, that would satisfy both him and the club.

An official statement said: 'Peter Kenyon, the chief executive, has reiterated his desire to keep Sir Alex at the club and he is happy to stay. Nothing has been decided yet but talks are on-going.'

January ended with a 1–0 win over Sunderland, taking United into a 15-point lead as Liverpool, Arsenal, Sunderland and Leeds battled for second place. Even with four months of the season remaining, it looked to be a case of when, rather than if, Sir Alex would clinch that third successive title.

*A hat-trick of
Premiership trophies
is completed in April
2001 – and the
celebrations feel just
as good.*

*Sir Alex Ferguson
drinks a toast to
celebrate becoming
the first manager
ever to win three
successive league titles.*

Any talk of a repeat of the 1999 treble success was played down within the confines of the club, and the chance of it happening disappeared when West Ham won 1–0 at Old Trafford in the FA Cup fourth round, and European hopes were dashed in the Champions League quarter-finals by Bayern Munich.

By 14 April, with five games to spare, United clinched their seventh Premiership title in nine seasons. It was yet another record for Sir Alex and his players, their task completed eight days and one game earlier than the previous season. They did it on the day United fielded the club's oldest debutant as they beat Coventry City 4–2 at Old Trafford.

A few weeks earlier there was a scare when Barthez was injured during the pre-match warm-up against Leicester. With Rai van der Gouw recovering from a knee operation, the manager was forced to turn to 20-year-old stand-in Paul Rachubka, who performed well in the 2–0 victory. Feeling it was too big a risk to rely on the youngster, Sir Alex signed former Scottish international Andy Goram on loan from Motherwell. On the day after his 37th birthday, Goram faced Coventry. The game kicked off at noon and less than five hours later United were champions as Arsenal were surprisingly beaten 3–0 by Middlesbrough at Highbury.

Sir Alex became the first manager in the history of English football to lead a club to three successive championships. Before him, the legendary Herbert Chapman had seen Huddersfield Town secure the title in 1924 and 1925, then moved to Arsenal before the Yorkshire club won the championship for a third season in a row. At Highbury, he was in charge when Arsenal were crowned champions in 1933 and 1934 but died before their third success in 1935.

Liverpool's Bob Paisley came close, winning the title in 1982 and 1983, but had handed over to Joe Fagan before the Merseysiders' third successive championship.

Sir Alex was unquestionably Manchester United's most successful manager, and while too modest to claim it himself, regarded by many as the best the game had seen.

17

THE GAFFER DOES A U TURN

IF THE 2001–02 SEASON was to be Sir Alex Ferguson's last in charge of Manchester United, he made it clear long before the campaign got under way that he would not go out with a whimper. There were certainly no signs that he was ready to spend his winter days by the fireside with slippers and pipe, nor slip silently into the background to make way for the new man. His approach to his last campaign was, as always, full of Ferguson fervour.

The plan was to hand his successor a squad of players who were capable of continuing the run of success that had started with that FA Cup win over Crystal Palace a decade earlier. He demonstrated this intent less than a fortnight after tying up the seventh Premiership title when the delayed deal for Holland striker Ruud van Nistelrooy was completed.

Sir Alex is a man of his word. When the original transfer fell through and van Nistelrooy needed cruciate ligament surgery to save his career, the United manager had declared he would stand by the player, even though there was every reason to turn his back on PSV Eindhoven and look elsewhere. As soon as van Nistelrooy was ready to play top-level football once again, United re-opened negotiations, and on 23 April 2001 they got their man. During the 12-month delay, the fee had swollen to a record £19 million.

Van Nistelrooy claims he will never forget the support shown by the Manchester United manager during the time he fought his way back.

'For me, it was great. He came to visit me in Eindhoven 10 days after my injury and that was very special to me. We talked about the players who had had the same injury and the way they had worked in order to come back.

I was able to think along the same lines about the way I wanted my reha-bilitation to go.

'It was very important to remember how much I wanted it, and the way we talked then was good to think about during my recovery.

'When you have support from people like that, it makes you hungrier to get back. It gives you a good feeling. I had so much support, from fans of PSV and people from the UK, and that was nice for me.'

United were not the only club chasing his signature. Real Madrid were also interested.

'Yes, but for me it wasn't a choice to make. It was easy. I had been at United a year earlier and it was perfect for me. To give myself the opportu-nity to come back was my biggest goal and when you get support from the club and from the people of the club, it was big for my spirit to fight and come back stronger. It really helped me. I had such a good feeling with the club that I wanted to come back strong. That was my biggest goal.'

He signed a five-year deal, committing himself to football at Old Trafford until 2006, claiming his one regret was that Sir Alex would not be in charge to see him through that period. Asked if he might be tempted into a change of heart, Sir Alex's reply was short and to the point, but avoid-ed the issue: 'I'm not going into that.' If he was having second thoughts, he was keeping them to himself.

The United manager was, however, willing to speak about the way he had broken the club transfer record to buy the Dutchman. Had he imag-ined 20 years earlier that one day he would spend £19 million on a player?

'It has been coming for ages. I suppose you can't stop the moving train. There is evidence of how the market goes in certain periods. It goes quiet and then accelerates again, another transfer record is broken, and that's just the way it is. There are a lot of things you could have told me 20 years ago that I might not have believed – they have taken down the Berlin Wall, haven't they?'

It is also doubtful whether he would have agreed had anyone suggested he would be manager of Manchester United longer than Ruud van Nistelrooy would play for the club. He also outlasted the four other sign-ings he made that season, one of whom made the investment in van Nistelrooy look like small change.

Eighty days after the Dutchman's arrival, an incredible £28 million changed hands as Juan Sebastian Veron moved to Old Trafford from Italian club Lazio. Sir Alex appeared to regard Veron as the final piece of what every-one believed to be his final jigsaw, and he felt able to justify the expenditure.

Ruud van Nistelrooy, £19 million worth of goalscoring power, made an immediate return on Sir Alex's investment when he scored twice on his Premier League debut against Fulham, August 2001.

'I have always felt there have been players who can make a difference. Cantona, Roy Keane, Barthez – three great instances of how a player can make a difference. Obviously, over the years, names have tripped off my tongue many times because my dream was always to make us the best. Now Peter Kenyon's determination has made it possible and I think he and David Gill did a fantastic job to make the Veron transfer happen, because it was the kind of thing Manchester United should do. Not always, because the market can be ridiculous, but from time to time a major signing lifts everyone around the club.'

According to Kenyon, the chief executive, the fee was 'money well spent. Now everyone at Old Trafford, the players, the staff and the fans can't wait for the start of the next season.'

Before then, a summer tour took Sir Alex and the players to the Far East, where games in Kuala Lumpur, Singapore and Bangkok drew crowds of over 200,000. Back home, a further crowd of 66,957 turned up for Ryan Giggs' testimonial. Van Nistelrooy and Veron played in every one of those games, and van Nistelrooy scored his first goal for his new club in the opening tour game in Malaysia. Veron scored his first in the Giggs match against Celtic.

Sir Alex insisted he would retire as planned the following summer and terminated all public discussion on the issue. Journalists were advised to steer clear of the subject or else, but this did not prevent speculation continuing about who would be next in line to the Old Trafford throne. The search was under way.

'It's a huge turning point,' said Martin Edwards, 'a huge transition coming up. Sir Alex has been our most successful manager – you only have to look at the last nine years and seven titles to see that. It's going to be a huge void to fill, and a very brave man who takes on that mantle. We are looking very closely, very carefully at the moment, and hopefully we will pick the right man to succeed Sir Alex, but it will not be an easy task.'

During the summer two major figures had left the club. Teddy Sheringham returned to Tottenham Hotspur and Steve McClaren stepped into his first managerial post, taking over the vacancy at Middlesbrough created by the departure of Bryan Robson.

McClaren's record at Old Trafford could well remain unsurpassed. United ended each of his three seasons as Sir Alex's deputy as champions, his first campaign culminating in the treble. Apparently, he had moved on because of the uncertainty that would surround his own future when the manager stood down.

The arrival of Veron increased speculation that England boss Sven Goran Eriksson – the Argentinean's former coach at Lazio – was favourite to move to Old Trafford, and the Swede fanned the flames by claiming during one international press conference that he missed the day-to-day involvement with players that club management provided.

As the season got under way, it was the departure of a player for Lazio, rather than anyone arriving via the Rome club, that caused a major stir. Only months into a new three-year contract, Jaap Stam was sold to the Italians for £14.7 million in a move that was reportedly sparked off by disclosures in the player's autobiography.

'Some say I didn't fit into Ferguson's plans, others say it was because of the book, but no player can sit on the bench at 29. I wanted to play every game, and at a very high level, as well. I wasn't happy with the situation. I played there for three years and did well – then within two weeks I was not wanted any more.

'I don't think there is any better club in England than United, so I did not want to go to any other club in England. It's hard to say if selling me was a mistake. It was their choice. They made that choice and the obvious thing then was to go.'

In the months that followed, Sir Alex revealed that concerns about Stam's long-term fitness following Achilles tendon surgery led to the decision to sell, not the contents of his life story.

Stam's replacement was Laurent Blanc, signed 24 hours before the Champions League deadline. The 35-year-old, who had long been admired by the United manager, moved from Inter Milan, but this time no record fee was involved. He came on a free transfer and went straight into the side for a win over Everton.

Even with the injection of new blood, United made a sluggish start to the season. By December, they had slipped to an uncustomary ninth in the table. They were through to the second phase of the Champions League, but there was little evidence that this might be another all-conquering season.

As the manager passed his 60th birthday, things were improving, and a run of nine straight wins swept United into top spot. They reached the fourth round of the FA Cup thanks to a rip-roaring 3–2 win at Villa Park.

During UEFA's winter transfer window, Sir Alex signed Uruguayan international Diego Forlan to bolster his strike force, depleted by the £7 million transfer of Andy Cole to Blackburn shortly before the new year. Then, the first signs of another major change began to surface – a change of mind.

Around Christmas, Sir Alex's family had apparently asked him to re-think his retirement plans and by the end of January, rumours started to circulate. Whispers reached a climax with the truth finally coming out when, in an innocent pre-match interview, Mikael Silvestre told the world the manager was staying.

'It was a big surprise. We didn't expect to know who was coming in before the end of the season. Now we know. It was announced by the coaching staff this morning after training when Sir Alex told us, "It won't be a secret any more, so I have to tell you that I'm staying on as manager."'

The club issued a statement on the Stock Exchange:

'The board of Manchester United plc confirms that it was recently approached by Sir Alex Ferguson with regard to him remaining as manager of the club beyond this season. The board has entered into discussions with Sir Alex and his advisors on a new contract. These discussions are continuing.'

Three weeks later, football's worst-kept secret became public. Peter Kenyon made the official announcement:

'When I became chief executive, one of my first meetings on the morning I took up the appointment was with Alex, who'd already announced he was retiring. I genuinely wanted to meet him because I felt he was too young to retire. He was fit, he was healthy, and we had an awful lot still to achieve at Manchester United.

Sir Alex relaxes in his Carrington office, just after he announced in February 2002 that he was going to stay on as manager. As his wife Cathy had said: 'Retire when you're tired'.

'On that occasion, I couldn't get him to change his mind but for the next 12 months it certainly kept the print going in a lot of newspapers as to who was going to follow him, and we went a long way down that road. We said right from the onset that it wouldn't start in earnest until after Christmas because quite clearly it was going to be a big season for us and it was going to be made even bigger by the fact that Sir Alex had announced that he was going to retire.

'The pressure was enormous but shortly after Christmas we became aware that Sir Alex wanted to re-think his position. I had said from day one I was confident we would have a manager in place for the next season, and that we would have the best manager in place. I am delighted we achieved both those things.'

Sir Alex agreed a new three-year deal, to the delight of Sir Bobby Charlton. He and his fellow directors had not been looking forward to the task of appointing a replacement.

'It was a problem solved for us. Not a major problem because we would have handled it, but we believed him when he said he wanted to finish because he felt he wanted to give more time to his family and his wife.

'We all thought, and many people must have said this to him, what was he going to do at the end? What would he do when he had nothing to do? He decided to stay, and his wife decided to let him stay a little bit longer, which was no problem to us whatsoever. We were delighted and there was no embarrassment of having disappointed anyone else.

'We were at the stage when we were talking about who should replace him, and in the process of doing it, but in the end it wasn't necessary, which was first-class news.'

Sir Alex seemed both relieved and delighted to be carrying on as manager:

'It was a big U turn, and it only came about following the intervention of my wife and my sons. They colluded with each other to make me stay on, but it was the thing I wanted to hear anyway, because I was worrying about what I was going to do.

'I couldn't see myself riding into the sunset, not just yet, and as my wife Cathy said, "Retire when you're tired," and that's a good point.

'The word retirement is an unfortunate one in our lives. It doesn't apply in places like America. Here, you have this sort of time cap on you about when you retire because you know you have to, while in the States there's no such thing.

'But I feel strong, I feel young, I feel fit and, hopefully, my health will continue to be good and I can go on and enjoy the next three years, because we can get better. I feel there is a great future for Manchester United. There are some areas to address, to make improvements, but what is encouraging is that we still have a vibrant youth system and a fantastic medical and coaching staff. That is a great platform for any player coming to Manchester United, particularly the young people.

'I'm delighted to remain with Manchester United, which is a difficult club to leave as any player will tell you. It's engrained in the fabric of your life and you don't only get into personal relationships with people you work with but those who come to training and watch you play, with supporters, and that becomes personal and very bonding. It's a difficult club to leave and I found that in the last few months.'

Stay he did but, sadly, there was no dream ending to the season. Sir Alex had set his sights on reaching the Champions League final, staged in his native Glasgow, but United fell at the penultimate hurdle, beaten under the away goals rule in the semi-final by Bayer Leverkusen.

They bowed out of the FA Cup in the fifth round, beaten at the

Riverside by Steve McClaren's Middlesbrough, and there was an equally disappointing ending to the Premiership campaign when a winning run by Arsenal allowed them to overhaul United and clinch the title in front of a subdued Old Trafford.

Liverpool were runners-up as United finished in third place, the first time since the launch of the Premiership that they had ended a campaign lower than second. Sir Alex was remaining at the helm, but it looked as though stormy waters lay ahead.

United's League Results under Sir Alex Ferguson

Season	P	W	D	L	F	A	Pts	Posn
1986-87	42	14	14	14	52	45	56	11th
1987-88	40	23	12	5	71	38	81	2nd
1988-89	38	13	12	13	45	35	51	11th
1989-90	38	13	9	16	46	47	48	13th
1990-91	38	16	12	10	58	45	59	6th
1991-92	42	21	15	6	63	33	78	2nd
1992-93	42	24	12	6	67	31	84	1st
1993-94	42	27	11	4	80	38	92	1st
1994-95	42	26	10	6	77	28	88	2nd
1995-96	38	25	7	6	73	35	82	1st
1996-97	38	21	12	5	76	44	75	1st
1997-98	38	23	8	7	73	26	77	2nd
1998-99	38	22	13	3	80	37	79	1st
1999-2000	38	28	7	3	97	45	91	1st
2000-01	38	24	8	6	79	31	80	1st
2001-02	38	24	5	9	87	45	77	3rd
2002-03	38	25	8	5	74	34	83	1st
2003-04	38	23	6	9	64	35	75	3rd
2004-05	38	22	11	5	58	26	77	3rd
2005-06	38	25	8	5	72	34	83	2nd
2006-07	38	28	5	5	83	27	89	1st
2007-08	38	27	6	5	80	22	87	1st
2008-09	38	28	6	4	68	24	90	1st
2009-10	38	27	4	7	86	28	85	2nd
2010-11	38	23	11	4	78	37	80	1st

Alex Ferguson managed United for only part of 1986-87, and the results during his period in charge were as follows:

| | 29 | 11 | 10 | 8 | 36 | 29 | 41 | |

18

ANOTHER SEASON, ANOTHER RECORD, ANOTHER TITLE

IF SUCH A PUBLICATION as the *Encyclopaedia of Football Clichés* existed, David Beckham would not have had to delve deep into its volumes to come up with the words he chose to describe feelings in the Manchester United dressing room when the players learned Sir Alex was staying on as manager.

'I was over the moon. We all were,' he said. 'We had heard the rumours but nobody believed them, and when he told us we were delighted. He said his wife had persuaded him to stay, and we all know about wives making the important decisions, don't we?'

Whether the change of heart influenced Beckham's own decision to remain at the club is something only the player himself knows, but the midfielder, whose future had hung in the balance during most of the 2001-02 season, signed a new contract once the manager's future seemed secured.

Supporters attending the closing home game of the campaign saw football's most successful manager and the world's best-known player meet in the centre of the Old Trafford pitch and exchange handshakes and hugs. All seemed well, but Sir Alex openly declared his frustration when the talking ended, pointing an accusing finger at Beckham's representatives.

'It was going on and on and you start to wonder what the hell *is* going on. To be honest, I think David always wanted to sign, and that's important, but there were always concerns, the demands agents put on and things like that. The most important person was the player.'

Beckham, who had tied himself to United until 2005, ended the season recovering from a broken metatarsal, an unwanted souvenir of United's

David Beckham was delighted when his manager decided to stay on, and in May 2002 was signing a new contract to stay at Old Trafford.

Champions League run-in, but recovered in time to take part in the World Cup in Japan and South Korea.

While Beckham would stay – or so everyone thought – others left. Dwight Yorke was reunited with former striking partner Andy Cole at Blackburn, and Ronny Johnsen, Rai van der Gouw and the long-serving Denis Irwin were released at the end of their contracts, along with young midfielder Ronnie Wallwork, who joined West Bromwich Albion.

Irwin left after winning more honours than anyone before him at Old Trafford, and went on to end his career with Wolves. He was always held in high regard by Sir Alex, who referred to him as the 'model professional', and the full-back has a mutually respectful view of his former manager.

'I was lucky that, throughout the whole of my senior career, I played under two of the best managers in the game – Joe Royle at Oldham Athletic and Sir Alex at Old Trafford. They both influenced my life. I had a very stable life as far as managers were concerned and that helped.

'Joe Royle and Willie Donachie picked me up and got me going at Oldham and Sir Alex did the rest after taking me to Old Trafford. That's where I won my first trophy.

'I have to say when I went to Old Trafford I never in my wildest dreams thought that I would win as much as I did. You can never think of what might happen that far ahead. When I arrived, they had just won the FA Cup and the club was beginning to go places. The manager had settled in and all the time I was at United, we seemed to win trophies, a couple of doubles and a treble, so it was a great 12 years for me.'

Irwin is another who saw little change in the manager's attitude while he was with United.

'It was always the same whenever a season started. We set out to win trophies and worked hard to do it. We always had a lot of talent at the club and set our standards high, which is why United have stayed at the top for so long. I thought it was a fantastic gesture, and typical of the man, when Sir Alex handed me the captaincy for my final game. We had a great relationship and while he let go at me a few times, he's let go at nearly everybody in the dressing room. That's part and parcel of being a footballer at Old Trafford. You expect high standards at United because the manager demands it, and if you fall short, he certainly lets you know.

'When I look back, there are so many highlights, but I suppose the one that tops the lot has to be the last couple of minutes in Barcelona.

'That was a great night both professionally and personally. My family were there – my wife and little boy, my mum, sisters and uncle – and that

Denis Irwin takes his leave at Old Trafford for the last time as a player after 529 appearances for Ferguson. Only Ryan Giggs, Paul Scholes and Gary Neville have made more appearances for the manager.

win against Bayern finished off the treble as well, so it was a great end to the season.

'Before that, winning the first Premiership was also something special because it lifted a lot of pressure off the club, and you always remember your first medal. Mine was in the Cup-Winners' Cup in Rotterdam, but that's a bit of a blur, too! As I got older and wiser, I enjoyed every success we had and took in a bit more.'

In a bid to maintain the high standards that Irwin referred to, Sir Alex appointed a new assistant, but the choice was a surprise. Since the departure of Steve McClaren, coaches Jim Ryan and Mike Phelan had filled the role, but in June 2002, Carlos Queiroz, a man virtually unknown to those outside professional football, arrived.

Queiroz had an excellent pedigree. He had been manager of Portugal, South Africa and the Arab Emirates at international level, and in charge of America's MetroStars and Grampus Eight from Japan's J League. According to Sir Alex, while the search was on, the name Queiroz kept cropping up.

'I spoke to two or three players who had worked under him, and they said he was fantastic to work with. Then I spoke to Luis Figo and two or three other Portuguese players, and they absolutely raved about him. The portfolio was building up quite nicely, so I decided to have a chat with him and was very impressed.'

The Mozambique-born Queiroz settled in quickly.

'I personally feel very proud to be part of the biggest and best football family in the world, and to be surrounded by so many great professionals and so many quality people. I couldn't be happier.'

Was he happy to play second fiddle to Sir Alex?

'I may have been in charge in some of my previous roles, but it was a great challenge for me the way Sir Alex invited me to be his assistant. When you work in this team, you don't feel like a secondary person. It is a case of just working hard, performing well, and thinking about Manchester United. I don't think about myself.

'Of course, it was a bit different because in the last 17 years I had been in the position of full responsibility, but I committed myself to the job because when you have an opportunity to work with a man like Sir Alex, and the opportunity to work for Manchester United, then you don't lose it.

'I saw it as an opportunity to learn, and I based my decision on that main principle. I came gratefully, because I had an opportunity to learn as well as being in such a fantastic club.'

There was another new arrival during the summer but this was

In June 2002, Carlos Queiroz joined United as Sir Alex's assistant and helped him plot their way to an eighth Premiership title that season.

Alex Ferguson welcomes Rio Ferdinand to United, July 2002. Rio has been the bedrock of the defence ever since.

someone supporters knew plenty about. Shortly after the appointment of the new deputy, United again smashed the British transfer record as Rio Ferdinand crossed the Pennines from Leeds in a deal worth a total of £33.5 million.

On Monday, 22 July the tall England defender found himself in a press conference, sitting alongside his new manager, and Sir Alex was wearing the expression of an angler who had just landed a prize catch. Sir Alex told the press conference that Ferdinand was indeed a big fish.

'You can identify a potentially great player but then you have to try to think how you could possibly get him here. That wasn't going to be easy. I knew the pitfalls, it was going to be a hard road, but we got to the end of it and we're so delighted.

'We knew Rio was going to be a fantastic player and the board wanted him as much as I did. His talents are obvious and who wouldn't want him at Old Trafford? Everyone wanted him, so that made it easy for me. In fact, Peter Kenyon and David Gill did all the running, believe me.'

There was plenty of running for Ferdinand in that first season, some of it uphill. United wobbled slightly in their opening European qualifier in Hungary, losing 1–0 to the unknown and virtually unpronounceable Zalaegerszeg, but a 5–0 win in the return ushered them safely into the first phase of the Champions League. Successive victories over Maccabi Haifa (5–2), Bayer Leverkusen (2–1) and Olympiakos (4–0) raised hopes of another successful campaign, and there was an added incentive to do well after UEFA chose Old Trafford as the venue for the final in 2003.

No wonder Sir Alex confessed, 'I have to admit that I really enjoy the European scene. It's good to travel in Europe because there is a different atmosphere. You are always cautious about what tricks you are going to have to face. There is far more cunning about the game abroad and your preparation has got to be right, and I think that's good.

'I enjoyed last season. I thought we did really well in Europe last year and we hope we can have as good a campaign this season. Obviously, we hope we can get to the final at Old Trafford.'

Few people expected United to do well because they were handicapped from the start. Gary Neville had followed the trend set by soulmate Beckham by breaking a metatarsal and Fabien Barthez missed the start of the season, as did Ferdinand, whose Premiership debut for United was delayed until the third game, an eventful 1–1 draw against Sunderland at the Stadium of Light.

During that game Roy Keane was sent off after a clash with Jason

McAteer, a member of Mick McCarthy's Republic of Ireland side. So was Keane – or, at least, he had been until he walked out of their World Cup camp prior to the start of the tournament. Keane wrote about the row in his autobiography, which had just been published, and, like Stam before him, he found himself in the headlines, but it had little to do with the World Cup bust-up.

Keane admitted that he made his red-card challenge on Alfie Haaland during the derby game at Old Trafford in 2001 as a direct result of comments made by the Manchester City midfielder, who had formerly played for Leeds, when the United skipper lay injured with cruciate ligament damage at Elland Road in 1997. The FA took exception. Keane was fined £150,000 and banned for five matches, but it was 27 games later before he reappeared. Keane had been having hip problems and United seized the opportunity for him to have surgery while suspended. By the time he came back, things looked bleak.

United lacked consistency in the Premiership and, by November, three defeats left them trailing in fifth place. Two more coincided with Keane's return. The second of these was a 3–1 Boxing Day upset at Middlesbrough, where Steve McClaren was proving to be a thorn in his old boss's side. Replacement Queiroz remained optimistic.

'We don't panic. If we don't get the three points in a game, we are not happy, but it happens. Some games you lose or draw. Of course, Manchester United is all about winning and we like to win all games, but we know we can't do it. If you take into consideration the situation of the team since the beginning of the season, think how many times we have been forced to change the defensive line-up, the midfield, the forwards, using different combinations. Remember that sometimes we have had three days only from one game to another to prepare almost a new team, a different team. I think they are doing OK.'

He was as philosophical about claims that his coaching methods were contributing to the slump in form, and showed he could handle the brickbats.

'That is why we are here, that is why we are professionals. We accept criticism and learn to respect all opinions, but I am sure that everybody knows nobody is perfect. I am also sure that everybody knows that nobody can be right all the time.

'I have always said I respect all opinions, and I also respect the intentions, but I am not saying they are right. I have an open mind to learn from criticism because every time I see something positive that can help in my life. If I could ring and thank them, I would pick up my phone and do so because they have helped me.'

United's luck began to change. As in 1998 when United lost at home to Middlesbrough, the defeat at the Riverside turned out to be the last Premiership game they would lose that season.

At one stage, not the treble but the quadruple, a clean sweep of all three domestic competitions and the Champions League, was on the cards, but it was not to be. Arsenal ended their FA Cup run, they lost in the League Cup final to Liverpool and Real Madrid ruined all hope of playing a Champions League final on their home ground. Madrid won 3–1 in the first leg of the quarter-final in Spain and, although United staged a tremendous fight-back to clinch a 4–3 victory at Old Trafford, it was not enough. That night David Beckham came off the bench and scored twice, catching Spanish eyes.

So four possible prizes were reduced to one. A winning run swept United to the top of the Premiership and they claimed another title on Sunday, 4 May as Arsenal, the only threat following Liverpool's dramatic slump in form, lost 3–2 at home to Leeds.

A week later, United were presented with their eighth Premiership trophy after the closing game of the season at Goodison Park, with the last goal of the campaign scored by David Beckham – and the opposing side that afternoon included a precocious teenager named Wayne Rooney.

19

ALL CHANGE ON THE BIG RED BUS

SIR ALEX FERGUSON was relaxed as he reflected on the campaign just finished. Manchester United had won another trophy, he had been proclaimed the most successful manager English football had known, but as far as he was concerned, basking in any glory was definitely out.

'It is no personal satisfaction now for me. When I first won the league, I could have gone to heaven. Now it's just a case of maintaining this club all the time, and making sure we are there. That has to be my job and I cannot be looking at personal things.

'I achieved everything I wanted to achieve when we won that first league. All the rest is bonus time, but the club has to go on. If I can't do it, then somebody will be there ready to take my place, and the one thing time has given me is the experience and the understanding of what the needs of this club are.

'That is why I am talking this way, because we have to maintain this big beast of a club. It's a bit of an obligation, but more of a duty in the sense that you become part of the club. It's very easy to get entrapped in this club and think like a supporter, because it does tend to get you a bit romantic about some of the things you would like to do here.

'As far as I'm concerned, I feel great. There's nothing in me that says the decision I made to stay on has been wrong. Without question, it was the correct decision, and I have felt really good since I made it. I am fit anyway. I have no plans to retire. No plans at all. I could go on for another few years, albeit if they want me. I have got two years left from this June and I'm definitely not making any statements about what I'm going to do – ever again!'

So there were no predictions about what might lie ahead, although it is doubtful if even Sir Alex could have forecast all the headline-making events that unfolded during his 17th summer in charge at Old Trafford.

For months, speculation surrounded David Beckham, who was being linked with a move to Spanish football. The rumours began shortly before United played Real Madrid in the Champions League but were dismissed by Sir Alex as nothing more than mind games from the opposing camp.

'We expected that. We were not surprised. It only came out when the draw was made, and we were playing them. You know what they are up to. There has certainly been no approach from Real Madrid and I can assure everyone of that. I'm not saying that is the reason this has come about, but it is coincidental to say the least. When did it arise? When we got the draw for the quarter-finals.'

Beckham was not the only target of the Spanish giants. Reports claimed they also wanted Ruud van Nistelrooy and this brought a swift 'hands off' from the manager.

'In my time at Manchester United I have never had a player snatched away. For any player who has left here, it has been our decision.'

Those words were never of greater significance than on Tuesday, 17 June 2003 when United announced that David Beckham had been transferred to Real Madrid for £25 million. Supporters were stunned, while the player himself commented:

'It probably won't be clear until I meet up with the rest of the lads and get back training and meet the people in Madrid. It is starting to hit me now that I'm not a Manchester United player any more, but it won't really sink in until I'm walking out at the Bernabeu with the Real Madrid kit on,' Beckham declared in his first interview as a Madrid player.

He left with 'mixed emotions'.

'I spent 13 to 14 years at Manchester United. I've always been a United supporter and will always follow Manchester United. It has been a massive part of my life and will always remain a big part of it.

'People always said that the manager and me had our ups and downs, and of course we did. That's part and parcel of life in general, but to be honest, me and the manager always had a good relationship. He was the reason I joined Manchester United, apart from it being the club I supported. He is the reason I'm the player I am today.

'He would not have put me in the team at 17 if he didn't have a good feeling about me. I have to thank the manager for that. OK, the relationship had its ups and downs but he was always a father figure to me and I will never forget that.'

Newspapers speculated that things soured because of the change in Beckham's lifestyle – from quiet London boy dedicated to becoming a top professional footballer to celebrity perched on the 'A' list summit whose every move was monitored by the media. Hardly a day passed when he or his show-business wife were not news, something Sir Alex regarded as a distraction.

When Madrid came knocking, he was happy to agree to Beckham leaving. Beckham himself commented:

'I can look back at my time at Old Trafford as so many great, great memories. So many things happened to me and I will always have a special place in my heart for people connected with the club.

'There was my debut against Brighton, my first goal against Galatasaray at Old Trafford, being in the same team as Eric Cantona, talking face to face with Bryan Robson – a very nervous but exciting moment because he was my idol – being put in the team and winning the league year after year with the friends I have grown up with. Sometimes people don't realise how much winning means to players when you do it so many times, but believe me those players loved it.'

So Beckham went to Madrid and a week after his departure came another shock – Carlos Queiroz was joining him at the Bernabeu. The United number two had so impressed during his first season as Sir Alex's assistant that when the Spaniards sacked coach Vicente del Bosque, they turned to Old Trafford to fill the gap.

The exodus had not finished, but a week after Queiroz's exit an arrival elsewhere caused a stir. Chelsea had a new owner. A young Russian billionaire named Roman Abramovich had bought the club for £140 million, pledging to take it to the top. Only time would tell.

One of Abramovich's first moves was to bankroll a £15 million deal to take Juan Sebastian Veron to Stamford Bridge shortly before the new season began, while to bolster his squad, Sir Alex invested in five new players. He bought American goalkeeper Tim Howard from MetroStars, David Bellion from Sunderland and Eric Djemba-Djemba from French club Nantes.

Two days after United won the newly named Community Shield by beating Arsenal 4–2 on penalties, Brazilian World Cup winner Kleberson was signed from Atletico Paranaense, and £12.5 million – half the fee received for Beckham – was handed to Sporting Lisbon for teenager Cristiano Ronaldo, who had impressed his future team-mates during a pre-season friendly against the Portuguese club.

New signing Cristiano Ronaldo is introduced to Gary Neville by Sir Alex. The young Portuguese star had greatly impressed the team during a pre-season friendly.

Did the start of a new season hold as much excitement for Sir Alex?

'Yes. Perhaps I'm more concerned than excited – concerned that we are going to do well. Is my team right? Is the atmosphere right? Is the camaraderie good? Have I got the player profile I need? The character? I always have those concerns.'

Were there any worries about the latest intake of new players?

Ronaldo skips past the Newcastle defence, August 2003, to show that in their new No 7 United have a very different style of player compared with David Beckham.

'Not worry. There is a difference between concern and worry. When you concern yourself, you can do something about it. When you worry, you can put yourself in the grave. I don't worry.'

So what had that eighth title success done for him?

'Exactly what it did for the players. It goes back to the fact that we are good at winning. It showed all the great attributes we have shown before over the decade. When the chips were down, we produced. That was missing the season before last. Mistakes were made, individual errors. There was a relaxation in some people's minds. They thought that because I was going they were going to have an easy life. I'm not going to let anyone have an easy life, am I?

'A lot of players had signed new contracts, I had said I was leaving, there was something missing, and I think everyone recognised that. They got it back last season and I think they knew themselves what winning really means. Only when you lose like we did the previous season can you feel the real taste of winning in the right way.'

During the summer, Chelsea blew the top off the transfer market as Abramovich's wealth funded deals worth close to £100 million. Not even Real Madrid could compete at that level but there was no envy from Sir Alex.

'We are a different club. We base a lot on young players. The last four or five buys Real Madrid have made have been the biggest signings in history, money-wise – Zidane, Figo, Ronaldo. Massive. Now David Beckham at £25 million.

'We would look for a player who might make a difference to our team, but also look for players coming through, such as Fletcher, John O'Shea and Wes Brown. We will always do that and place great store on that. It makes Manchester United different from the rest and we have a rapport with the fans through young players. We have probably got some of the best young players in the country now at 16 and 17 years old. We have some fantastic young players but we have to balance the two things up. If that was to vanish, then we would be wasting a lot of money on youth.

'What we have to do here is always try to improve ourselves. If you stand still in this game, you go back, and we don't want to go back. We always refer to this club as "the Bus"– if you miss the bus, sorry! You're left behind and we can't have people who are left behind. We want them all on the bus in order to move forward. Particularly when we have been successful, we have to try to improve and create a more competitive element in the club, which we should have done in 1994 but didn't. We want to do that this year. That is a lesson without question.'

The Bus began its journey into the new season in sensational style, with three straight wins. Ronaldo was introduced to Old Trafford in the first of those as Bolton were beaten 4–0, but by the turn of the year, the Bus had lost its way.

Before that, Chelsea struck another significant transfer deal with United, but this time it did not involve a player. Six weeks into the new campaign, Peter Kenyon announced that he was moving to fill a similar role at Stamford Bridge and David Gill replaced him as chief executive at Old Trafford.

'It was a surprise,' said Sir Alex, 'but you get surprises at this club all the time. We always say there's never a dull moment here. I get on well with Peter and we had a good relationship. David Gill is a young man who came here six years ago and has been working closely with Peter on a lot of the projects that have materialised over that period. He will do well and we will have the same working relationship because the important thing at this club is to go on. We can't stand still and weep and cry when somebody leaves. We have had Bryan Robson retiring, sold Paul Ince, David Beckham, everybody leaves here at some point. We cannot just stop dead. We have to go on, but I was surprised because no one had an inkling, that was the thing. There were no rumours going about, nobody knew.'

Meanwhile, his new-look side struggled to find consistency, injuries took their toll and when Rio Ferdinand was banned for eight months for failing to turn up for a random drugs test, the possibility of winning a ninth Premiership title began to wane.

Even though United were top of the table going into the new year, after Ferdinand's last game, things started to slide. He limped off injured during a league game at Wolves to begin his punishment, which included a £50,000 fine, and United lost 1–0 in what was a top versus bottom clash. Arsenal took advantage and began a run that ended with them taking the title.

Sir Alex strengthened his squad, not with a defender but another striker. Frenchman Louis Saha was bought from Fulham for £12.8 million. He made an instant impact by scoring on his debut against Aston Villa, then twice more in a 4–3 win at Everton in his second outing. Sadly, Saha soon became another injury victim and, as the Premiership campaign faded, Europe was also a disappointment.

United had confidently won their way through the qualifying group and into a newly introduced knock-out round ahead of the quarter-finals, but it was there they came up against FC Porto and their young manager, Jose Mourinho.

The coach, who had learned his football under Sir Bobby Robson at Barcelona, made it clear that the prospect of crossing swords with an eminent figure such as Sir Alex held no fears. After the first game, which Porto won 2–1, the United manager had accused the opposition of time-wasting, and using gamesmanship to influence the referee to get Roy Keane sent off. Mourinho's response was interesting.

'I believed there were a lot of mind games going on and that is something I didn't understand. The match in Porto was for my team a wonderful match. It didn't hurt me when I heard the things Sir Alex is supposed to have said. I understand that for one side a manager or a player can have emotional reactions after a match, or can also make some statements before a match to try to create a special atmosphere.

'But I thought with the power United have as a club, and with the individual players they have, they didn't need to do that. This sort of thing goes on in Portuguese football and I suppose I can't really say anything against it because I do it myself.'

Ahead of the return, he warned that Porto would fight to the death and they did precisely that, cashing in on a last-minute mistake by Tim Howard to draw 1–1 and reach the next round.

So there was to be no Premiership and no Champions League for United, but one prize was left for Sir Alex as the season ended. They won the FA Cup for the 11th time, beating Millwall 3–0 in a one-sided final at Cardiff's Millennium Stadium. Cristiano Ronaldo and Ruud van Nistelrooy (2) were the scorers.

The critics came down hard on United. The big prizes had gone to others, Arsenal taking the title without losing a game all season, Mourinho's Porto winning the Champions League. Then Mourinho announced his appointment as the new manager of runners-up Chelsea. Sir Alex refused to view the season as a failure, though.

Sir Alex with three of his new generation of players: Darren Fletcher, Cristiano Ronaldo and John O'Shea. New faces, but the FA Cup was in familiar hands in 2004 – it was a record fifth success for Fergie.

'I don't think consolation is a word that should apply to the FA Cup. I always say every year that I hope we can win a trophy. It is very competitive in this country, and a lot of history and tradition is associated with the FA Cup. Only one team can win it. We did.'

The Big Red Bus was ready for another journey.

Sir Alex Ferguson's Complete Career Record

Competition	Played	Won	Drawn	Lost	Goals For	Goals Against
Premiership	734	472	158	104	1452	627
Division One	225	97	70	58	319	227
League	959	569	228	162	1771	854
FA Cup	112	76	20	16	215	82
League Cup	92	59	10	23	165	99
Champions Lg	188	104	48	36	330	169
UEFA Cup	4	0	4	0	2	2
Cup-Winners'	13	8	4	1	20	8
Europe	205	112	56	37	352	179
Other	24	8	8	8	32	30
Total	**1392**	**824**	**322**	**246**	**2535**	**1244**

Sir Matt Busby was in charge of United for 1141 games; Sir Alex Ferguson overtook that total in April 2007.

20

FERGUSON'S FIFTH AMENDMENT

FROM THE MOMENT he first walked through the door at Old Trafford, Sir Alex Ferguson was a man with a mission – to re-establish Manchester United as a leading power within the game.

As he approached 20 years at the club, few would have disputed that he had reached that goal. But, like Oliver Twist, he wanted more. The hunger to add to an already impressive collection of trophies remained the same, and he had no intention of handing over the keys to the display cabinet just yet or, perhaps more importantly, those to his office.

He continued to lay the foundations for the future in a bid to extend United's run of success.

New young talent was brought to the club, some in big money deals, others in less publicised transactions, like those which saw Giuseppe Rossi and Gerard Pique arrive from Parma and Barcelona.

The prospect of unveiling another truly successful side made him want to prolong his managerial career and a Fifth Generation of Ferguson's Manchester United was not so far away. Speaking in 2006, he said:

'Being here 19 years – 20 in November – probably gives me the best view of the standards we have had, so I therefore take it seriously when people say, "It's not like the great days and the great players we brought through like Giggs and all the others [Beckham, Scholes, Butt, the Nevilles]."

'That was a one-off miracle. I suppose it wasn't a miracle in one sense because of the work that we put into it. We worked our socks off. We were working harder than any other club in the country at scouting, trialling, making decisions, with me going to see parents everywhere. We were speaking to parents, having them over here and taking them to dinner on Friday nights.

'I was never out of bloody hotels. I would go for dinner with them, getting them right for the weekend, and then head down to London. That is how David Beckham arrived.

'Our scouting is always judged because of those players from 1996 but that is not quite fair. It was a one-off. What we have done over the years is develop a consistent stream of young players who have done well in the game, not necessarily always playing for Man United.

'In the present squad we've got John O'Shea, Wes Brown, Darren Fletcher, Pique, Rossi. We've got the two Jones boys, Ritchie and David, Chris Eagles, Lee Martin. We are a very vibrant club in terms of getting young players and the squad, quite rightly, is as good as we have had.'

Some of the next generation had already found their way into the senior side; others were waiting for their moment, with the rebuilding taking a giant stride before the start of the 2004-05 campaign when United persuaded Everton to part with their prize asset, Wayne Rooney.

The biggest teenage prospect the game had seen in years arrived at Old Trafford for a transfer fee of £20 million and with the hope of fulfilling a dream.

'Obviously when I was a kid I was always an Everton supporter but Man United were winning all the trophies, and I thought to myself that one day I would like to go there and play in front of all those people and win things, and here I am.'

Rooney admitted that the opportunity of working under Sir Alex influenced his decision:

'Over the last few years I have seen how he has worked with the young players he has here and how he has got the best out of them. I hope he can do the same with me. I want to do my best and win things. The spotlight is going to be on me a bit more but I feel I am big enough and strong enough to handle that.'

United now not only had Rooney, but also Cristiano Ronaldo, two players coveted by all their rivals, and Sir Alex considered them the cornerstone of his next big side, predicting either of them could one day captain Manchester United.

'Cristiano and Wayne are only kids but they are leaders too. Those two are leaders. Absolutely. You take my word for it: Cristiano Ronaldo is a leader, an absolute leader. He is a magnificent personality. Intelligent, powerful, strong, courageous. He is a leader; him and Rooney are the leaders of the new team.'

Rooney was one of those missing from the side on the first day of the 2004-05 season. He had joined United while recovering from a broken metatarsal, an injury picked up during England's exit from the European Championships, and also absent was another summer signing, Argentinean full-back Gabriel Heinze from Paris St Germain.

He and Cristiano Ronaldo were involved in the football tournament at the Olympic Games in Athens while Rio Ferdinand was still five weeks away from the end of the suspension imposed the previous season. Ruud van Nistelrooy was recovering from hernia surgery, and other injury victims included Louis Saha, Wes Brown, Jose Kleberson and Ole Gunnar Solskjaer.

There were new faces on show in striker Alan Smith, an instant hit with United fans following his move from Leeds, and Liam Miller signed from Celtic at the end of his contract, and a familiar one too. A few weeks earlier Carlos Queiroz had returned to Old Trafford, reappointed assistant manager on a three-year contract following another change round at Real Madrid. The reunited management team looked on as their players battled bravely but lost 1–0, and according to Sir Alex that was that.

'We lost the title on day one,' he reflected at the end of a season which saw Jose Mourinho's Chelsea become champions for the first time in 50 years.

There were some bright moments.

Rooney's debut was pure Roy of the Rovers as he blasted home a hat-trick during a 6–2 win over Fenerbahce in the Champions League. Then Arsenal's unbeaten league record, stretching back more than a year, was shattered 2–0 at Old Trafford with Rooney hammering in the final nail in stoppage time, and the Gunners were beaten for a second time, 4–2 at Highbury four months later, when Ronaldo scored twice and John O'Shea sealed the win.

The young ones had stamped their mark but at the end of a season when European hopes were dashed by AC Milan, United finished third in the Premiership and their one realistic chance of winning a trophy faded when, in the words of the manager, they 'battered Arsenal' in the FA Cup final but were beaten 5–4 in a penalty shoot-out.

It was events off the field which made big news as Sir Alex's 18th full season ended and Manchester United became the target of a takeover. After 14 years as a public limited company, the club was bought by an organisation run by American tycoon Malcolm Glazer and his family.

Some supporters staged protest marches and demonstrations, others

Wayne Rooney scores again, making one of the most spectacular United debuts imaginable when he hit a hat-trick against Fenerbahce in September 2004.

Rooney and fellow new recruit Alan Smith celebrate a goal that helped secure United's famous 2–0 victory over Arsenal in October 2004, thus bringing to an end the Gunners' long unbeaten run.

wondered what the future held as uncertainty hung over their heads but once the next campaign was under way Sir Alex eased many minds.

'Nothing has changed. I can only judge people on how I deal with them and the Glazers have been terrific. They have never interfered in any shape or form with anything. They have just let us get on with it because they know we can manage. I am more than happy with the way things have gone and they have respected our position very well.'

Life went on.

Holland's international goalkeeper Edwin van der Sar was signed from Fulham and Sir Alex added spice to the squad by bringing in South Korean star Ji-sung Park from PSV Eindhoven.

Phil Neville left, opting for a move to Everton in search of regular first-team football and United got off to a good start, winning their first five games before being struck a major blow when Gabriel Heinze was ruled out for the season with cruciate ligament damage.

On 6 November, they marked Sir Alex's 19th anniversary as manager by ending Chelsea's long, unbeaten record – just as they had done with Arsenal's the year before – but fittingly, this time it was a Scot, Darren Fletcher, another of the new generation, who scored the crucial goal.

Two weeks later Roy Keane parted company with the club, his days ending when his contract was terminated. He went with a glowing testimony from Sir Alex.

'When I talk about Roy I always say he is the best player I have had, but he wasn't the best footballer. He wasn't the best goalscorer, he wasn't the quickest player, he wasn't the best in the air, he wasn't the best tackler. He was the best at everything which evolved into making a player. His concentration, his attitude, his winning mentality was as big an influence on the team as anybody, as any player,' is how Sir Alex remembers the man who contributed to seven of United's eight title-winning campaigns to that point, as well as all the other achievements since his arrival in 1993.

Keane was granted a testimonial and six months later returned for what turned out to be his swansong. He played for both his new club Celtic and United during the showpiece then a few weeks later announced his retirement from football. Perfect timing from a man who was quick to play down rumours he had left because of a rift with his manager.

'It was bad timing when I left in the sense that I was injured, it was November and I couldn't sign for another club until January. But I agreed with the manager it had come to an end. There is never a nice way to leave a club, especially one like United when I had been there for so long, but we both knew it was for the best and there is no doubt in my mind that is true. It was all very amicable and I certainly did not lose any sleep about it.'

Nor it seemed would Sir Alex.

'I always remember Jock Stein saying, "Remember one thing. You fall in love with players and we all do, you maybe have one particular favourite or something like that, but you can't let the favouritism detract from you doing your job."

'But you have favourites, we all have favourites. We have great players and you do tend to fall in love with them but when you have a group of players for a long time like we had in the 1999 side and it built up to that great success, then they get old and it changes.

'Denis Irwin got old, Roy got old, Ronny Johnsen got old and got some injuries, Peter Schmeichel retired, Andy Cole got into his 30s and we got a great offer for him from Blackburn. Teddy got old but is still playing!

'You have to then look ahead to see where you can be in two or three years' time and that is the hard part at this club because as you do that you have still got to be successful. The hard thing is to change, to evolve the team and still be successful while having an eye for the future.'

The new generation tasted success in the 2006 Carling Cup final when a side which included a rejuvenated Louis Saha, back from long-term injury problems, overcame Wigan Athletic 4–0. Sir Alex used the final to give January signings Nemanja Vidic and Patrice Evra the opportunity to pick up a winner's medal just weeks after their arrival, while the squad dedicated the victory to Alan 'Smudger' Smith who had broken his leg during United's FA Cup exit at Anfield.

The League Cup in its many guises has never topped Manchester United's list of priorities, but that is not the Ferguson viewpoint. To him a trophy, any trophy, can be the first step:

'We want to win finals and because we took that attitude it proved correct in the sense that it galvanised our whole season, the players' confidence came through and you could see maturity in the team.

'I will always remember Ryan Giggs saying when we beat Nottingham Forest in the League Cup final in 1992 and went on to win the league for the first time in 26 years the following season that it was the "launch pad" and there is every reason to see that again because of the group of players we have got here, the young players all maturing. This could be a great team again in the not too distant future.'

And what might that future hold for the United manager?

According to another of his players from the past, nothing too dissimi-

The backroom team celebrate after beating Wigan 4–0 to win the Carling Cup in 2006. Valter di Salvo, Carlos Queiroz, Sir Alex, Tony Coton and Mike Phelan share in the joy of winning Fergie's 17th major trophy for United.

Paul Scholes in action against Celtic in the Champions League in September 2006. His dynamic performance inspired United to a fifth straight win at the start of the season. For Sir Alex it was a trip down memory lane taking on one of the Old Firm.

lar to anything that has gone before.

Gary Pallister, who was in at the beginning of the Ferguson reign of success, has kept in step with events at his former club in his role as a media pundit. He knew that big names would continue to arrive, as was the case when the £14 million Michael Carrick was bought from Tottenham Hotspur during the summer of 2006, while others would move on – like record-scorer Ruud van Nistelrooy who was sold to Real Madrid.

'Sir Alex has never been afraid of making big decisions. I suppose he is from the old school. He doesn't really pamper his players and that's for sure. He is very blunt and forthright in his management style. He's got no room for people who don't share the same desire to go and win things and if you don't pull your weight, you are not going to be on his Christmas card list!

'He is very forthright, very passionate but it lets you know how desperate he is to win and what he is ready to do to achieve it. You either go along with that and go with the flow or you bail out. He asks questions of you as a footballer and if you don't match up to it then you won't last very long.

'It is difficult to try to guess what he will do. He has tried to retire once and realised that while he is still fit enough and has that will, he just couldn't walk away from the game.

'I can't really see that changing. I should imagine that he now has that desire to go out at the top because some people have written him off.

'Some have said he is no longer the manager he used to be, his team is nowhere near as good as those teams from the past, but I think they are getting closer.

'Sir Alex is building this "fifth team", as he calls it, and while it is going to be difficult for him, I am sure the desire is there to go out as a winner.'

21

CLOUD NINE

AT THE TIME, SIR Alex Ferguson reckoned that his ninth Premiership success as manager of Manchester United was his best ever. Certainly the season 2006-07 title was won against all the odds and was the least expected. For two or three years previously, the club had been out of the title hunt, playing second fiddle to Chelsea with some critics questioning what challenge United would be able to make in the coming season.

Supporters had just experienced three seasons without winning the Premiership – a long time for Manchester United fans in recent years – and they could see few signs that things were going to improve before the campaign got under way.

In fact before the start of the season there was a feeling from some pessimists that things were going to be difficult again, with little sign of transfer activity while the supporters looked enviously at moneybags Chelsea who had celebrated their title victory by going out and spending even more on Andriy Shevchenko and Michael Ballack.

To make matters worse in the eyes of many fans, Sir Alex had sold their leading goalscorer, Ruud van Nistelrooy, to Real Madrid during the summer, though others felt he had been sold at the right time. He had already decided that there was no longer any room for the influential Roy Keane, a player he once described as the heartbeat of the side.

On top of that, his most recent signings were still settling into the team. Things were grim on the injury front, too, with Alan Smith slow to recover from a badly broken ankle. There was also concern about Paul Scholes, who had missed half the season with a worrying eye complaint.

There was certainly excitement about young stars Wayne Rooney and

Cristiano Ronaldo, and there was confidence in Rio Ferdinand and goal-keeper Edwin van der Sar, too. But Ferguson clearly had faith in his squad as the only major reinforcement was to buy Michael Carrick from Spurs to bolster the midfield, though some fans had hoped that there would be more new faces.

So, for many critics, there were still questions as to whether United would be able to regain the title, and few journalists predicted them to do so at the start of the campaign. But when the going gets tough that's when the tough get going and Sir Alex Ferguson, as dynamic as ever, kept his cool and slowly but surely we saw a football miracle come to pass.

United got away to a good start and eventually nosed ahead of Chelsea to crush their rivals on the last lap of the season and beat them to the title by six points with a couple of games to spare.

Even Ferguson was a little surprised by the team's success. He had been working hard to rebuild, bringing in younger players to lower the average age of the squad. As he pointed out, it had been a transitional, rebuilding period for the club. He thought it would take longer because it was the new team's first season together as a unit and he thought it would need more time to settle and prosper.

So in that sense he rated the 2006-07 Premiership as his most impressive and says: 'I think it is the club's greatest achievement because it is a relative-ly new team who have won the league at their first attempt.

'I did think it was going to be a difficult task, given Chelsea's spending power. They have been the opponents recently with the most resilience. We had to make important decisions about how we changed the team and it wasn't easy. You grow a familiarity with players like Phil Neville and Nicky Butt, and it's sad when you have to let them go. Roy Keane was certainly difficult because he had been such a big influence on the club.

'But that's what decision making is all about. You have to try and con-struct a team that is fresh all the time.'

Ferguson clearly got his decisions right. He confounded the critics and he had launched a squad capable of maintaining success. As he said: 'This team is young. They can grow together. They have ability and they have the right spirit.

'There is a good spirit in the dressing room and it stood us in good stead as we approached the finishing line with the tanks running low! Everyone has contributed, ranging from senior players like Ryan Giggs and Paul Scholes to newcomers like Michael Carrick and Nemanja Vidic and includ-ing youngsters like Darren Fletcher and John O'Shea. Some folk forget how

Michael Carrick, United's big sum-mer signing in 2006, brings his influence to bear during the Champions League fixture against Celtic in September.

young they were when they started coming into the side, and we still haven't seen them in full bloom yet because they are only just starting to mature.

'Indeed, I would go as far as saying that if they stay together the whole team is going to get better. They have already proved themselves by winning the Premiership and hopefully we can take it on from there.'

Europe remained a frustration. After devastating Roma 7–1 in the Champions League quarter-final at Old Trafford, hopes were high that they could go all the way, especially when they won the semi-final first leg 3–2 against AC Milan at Old Trafford.

But the Reds were shattered when they crashed to a 3–0 defeat in the San Siro Stadium. Ferguson remained upbeat, though, and told us: 'We were downhearted after Milan but don't believe the doomsters who suggest that Milan's brilliant win means we will never catch them. You must keep things in perspective. Just as our super victory against Roma didn't make us world-beaters, so Milan's performance doesn't make them light years better than us. The fans shouldn't worry, success in Europe will come because we have the potential to go to great heights again.'

Many followers will tell you that they rate the breakthrough of 1993, when Sir Alex won his first league title and ended 26 years for the club without the championship, as the most significant success in the history of the club. It was certainly a strong side with players like the maverick Frenchman Eric Cantona, Mark Hughes and Steve Bruce.

But if you talked to Sir Alex Ferguson at that time, he would tell you that this Premiership success was the best, perhaps because he had bounced back off the ropes and given himself a new lease of life with the chance of even better things to come. For us, it was the moment the manager showed he had not lost his touch and that the future was still Red!

It was certainly a tense last lap, like the end of a boxing match with both fighters spent, but still doggedly punching away as they struggled to the end. Both Manchester United and Chelsea showed signs of distress in the closing stages, with major injury lists that meant that they had to field more or less the same players match after match without the chance to rest key personnel and no let-up because both clubs were so heavily involved in three different competitions.

United and Chelsea battled through to the last four of the Champions League and then faced each other at Wembley in the final of the FA Cup. Chelsea triumphed in the Cup, but United came out on top in the Premier League while Chelsea faltered, and perhaps the significant factor was that

Cristiano Ronaldo slots home United's fifth goal against Roma on a magnificent night at Old Trafford in April 2007.

Sir Alex and Carlos Queiroz celebrate after United's 7–1 triumph over Roma, which was the biggest Champions League victory under Sir Alex.

the Reds enjoyed a lead to put their rivals under pressure.

Sir Alex admitted he was concerned about the mental and physical fatigue, and said: 'Those last few matches were highly demanding. Injuries seriously depleted our squad and in the latter stages we were down to 14 senior players so there was little scope for bringing in fresh legs.

'I think this was evident when we played the second leg of our Champions League semi-final against Milan in the San Siro. The Italians were much fresher and sharper, and I felt we had left something on the field at Everton in our previous league game.

'Then when we squeezed home 1–0 at Manchester City in what turned out to be the fixture that clinched the title for us, I thought the team were running on empty. As you would expect in a Manchester derby, it was a tough game but the boys dredged something up from somewhere to see us home.'

The United manager believed it was the team effort that swung the title his way for his ninth Premiership in his 21 years in the hot seat at Old Trafford. 'We have a lot of major stars and strong personalities at the club these days but we don't have any inflated egos,' he explained.

The FA Cup final was frankly a disappointment, not just the result but also the performance. We have seen it so often that when a match is being billed as a potential classic and expectations soar it simply fails to live up to expectation. And what was expected to be the FA Cup final to end all finals between United and Chelsea turned out to be a let-down.

This was a game between the two best teams, the Premiership champions and the runners-up. It was hailed as just the right kind of confrontation to do justice to the brand-new Wembley, which on the day simply did not materialise.

Chelsea are a good side of course and it was always a strong possibility that having beaten them for the Premier League that United might have to concede the Cup. It was just sad that they didn't go down with all flags flying, and Chelsea were no better. They scored for a 1–0 win, but we had to wait until five minutes from the end of extra time for that.

The problem was that there were two teams both playing 'no risk' football; two teams with so much respect for each other that they felt they couldn't afford to take chances and play with the kind of attacking abandon that ironically got them to the top of the tree in the first place. They cancelled each other out, and frankly the first half was a bit of a bore. Most of the critics were kind. I imagine they didn't want to spoil what in theory should have been a great occasion.

Edwin van der Sar saves a late penalty from Darius Vassell to secure a nervy 1–0 victory over Manchester City which would guarantee that United were Premiership champions again.

The moment of controversy, as Petr Cech carries the ball over the line under challenge from Ryan Giggs during the FA Cup final.

That's the trouble with football; there is no guarantee that the participants will follow the script that everyone had clear in their minds. The game improved in the second half but it didn't reach any great heights. United thought they had gone ahead when Ryan Giggs slid into Petr Cech and carried both the goalkeeper and the ball over the line. Referee Steve Bennett failed to spot that the ball had gone over the line but without television replays it was impossible to see and a referee can't give something he hasn't seen.

Sir Alex Ferguson reckoned United should have had a penalty for the way Michael Essien had tackled Giggs from behind and there is logic in that, but really United didn't look like winners. To be fair, Chelsea didn't either, except they produced a great goal thanks to Frank Lampard and goal machine Didier Drogba. In that sense Chelsea deserved to win and United could console themselves with the championship – and that's not a bad consolation.

As Ferguson said: 'Our boys have already proved themselves by winning the championship and we can take it on from there.'

He was rejuvenated by that Premiership success: 'I just don't feel tired any more,' he said, and to prove it he was soon building for the next season, with Owen Hargreaves finally recruited from Bayern Munich for a fee of around £18 million.

Hargreaves, playing as an anchor man in midfield to allow Paul Scholes and Michael Carrick more forward roles, was signed to take United to a higher level, especially as he was joined by winger Nani from Sporting Lisbon, Anderson the midfielder from Porto and Carlos Tevez from West Ham. It was one of Sir Alex's most hectic summers in the transfer market.

The significance lay not just in the addition of some very useful players, but the message of intent the transfers sent out; the fact that Sir Alex Ferguson was as ambitious and bold as ever, as well as clearly enjoying the confidence of the Glazer family, who released the money and demonstrated their own faith in the future.

Sir Alex celebrates at Old Trafford after picking up his ninth Premier League title with United.

22

PROPHECIES AND PROMISES

FOOTBALL THRIVES on predictions. A lucrative pools industry was founded on the fact that fans cannot resist trying to guess the outcome of games. Ex-footballers spend match days broadcasting opinions on who will win, and who won't. Some get it right, some are very wrong. Will Alan Hansen ever be allowed to forget that legendary prognostication of 1995 (see Chapter 10) when he told the world – and Sir Alex in particular: 'You'll win nothing with kids'? Weatherman Michael Fish must cringe when he sees the much-played recording of his biggest gaffe, as he assures viewers there is no chance of hurricanes hitting the south of England, hours before devastation struck.

And on the subject of devastation, as this is being written, an American preacher has forecast that the end of the world is imminent. If you are reading these words you know he too was wrong!

Predicting the future can be a dangerous game, but it is one Sir Alex has always been willing to play and never more so than at the start of the 2007-08 season when he was asked how he expected the campaign to pan out. His vision appeared to be of a closer battle for honours than previous years, with the race going 'down to the wire', and he got it spot on.

'My experience is that when it gets to the end of January, there are usually just two or three teams who break away. I don't think there has been a year where the top four have all been battling it out in the final stages of the season, but it could happen this time. Others could challenge too. Portsmouth have spent big. This is Martin O'Neill's first full season at Aston Villa and they'll be difficult to beat. Roy Keane will have Sunderland really determined (in his first season as a manager he had won promotion), they will be flying out the blocks. Newcastle could improve under Sam Allardyce; David Moyes has done a lot of signing at Everton by lengthening the contracts of his present players. I expect to see some strong challenges.'

He had high expectations of his own players too: United had spent big, agreeing deals for three players before the close of the 2006-07 season as Portugal international Nani, England midfielder Owen Hargreaves and Brazilian youngster Anderson were tied up. Then on the eve of the new season a fourth new boy waited to make his entrance.

Speculation that Carlos Tevez, the Argentinean fireball who sparked life into West Ham during his short spell at Upton Park, was a Ferguson target, turned out to be true. Tevez signed on Friday 10 August, just too late for him to be available for the big kick-off, but his new manager was delighted with the acquisition.

'Tevez has proved in his year at West Ham that he is an absolutely top player. Whenever I saw him playing, I said to myself that I wished we had done it last season when we had the opportunity, but there were too many complications surrounding him at the time. We have bought to forge the future in Nani and Anderson, and that's the right thing to do. Bringing in Hargreaves gives us the kind of ingredients we need in our midfield, particularly in big European games. Those signings will be good ones.'

Pre-season preparations had gone well. A four-game tour of Asia satisfied the appetite of the club's vast army of Far Eastern followers, with the players mobbed like pop stars wherever they went. They responded by scoring 15 goals in four games and played to full houses in Japan, South Korea, Macau and China.

Like his manager, Wayne Rooney was another looking ahead, but would life be any harder going into the new campaign as defending champions?

'I don't think there is any more pressure on us because we won the league last season, it's just the same as always. The mood is really good in the squad and hopefully we can do well again and try to win the title again.'

Would there be more concentration on the Champions League this time?

'I'm not sure. To be honest, I'd take any trophy at the start of the season. The Premier League is the competition you play in week in, week out. For me, it's more important. Nevertheless, the Champions League is a massive tournament and I'd love to win it. It was particularly disappointing to get knocked out in the semi-finals last season, having gone into the game in Milan with a lead. Hopefully we can do well again throughout the whole campaign, especially in the Champions League.'

He did not have long to wait for his next trophy. It was won before the season officially started, but when the Community Shield saw United clinch victory over Chelsea in a Wembley penalty shoot-out, few realised it was a sign of things to come. The closely contested game ended 1–1 after normal play, before Edwin van der Sar thwarted Chelsea and United won the shoot out 3–0, leaving Sir Alex in optimistic mood.

'What I've seen this summer is that in the training there's been a far better stability and continuity. That's a good sign. I also feel there could be an improvement in some players this season, but it's always difficult to improve as a team – don't forget we had 89 points last year. Possibly where we can get better is when we get to the final stages of the cup tournaments, but the young players are hungry for more success.'

It was clear his own appetite had not diminished between seasons.

'When you come to this club, it's not a matter of whether the fire dies down in the summer, because there is always something happening. This summer is possibly the first time I've had a holiday when I didn't need to worry about signing a player. The only problem with being on holiday is when you get the new fixture list, and as soon as you look at it you are starting to plan ahead.'

No amount of forward planning could have prepared him for what happened in the first week. On day one United faced Reading at Old Trafford. Steve Coppell's side held out gallantly to draw 0–0, but during the first half Wayne Rooney was injured and a scan later revealed he had broken a metatarsal in his left foot. It was the third time in as many years he had suffered such an injury and he would be out for seven weeks.

In came Tevez, as United faced Portsmouth at Fratton Park in the second game. Another draw – this time 1–1 – and another twist, when Ronaldo was sent off late on. He was suspended for two games, so when the first Manchester derby of the season took United to Eastlands for game three, there was no Rooney, no Ronaldo and no joy.

City were outplayed but won 1–0, giving the league table a new look. City were top, Chelsea second and Wigan Athletic third, with Everton, Portsmouth and Newcastle all above Arsenal who were seventh. United were trailing in 16th place and already seven points off the pace.

It was the kind of start that would have caused ructions in some boardrooms and threatened many a manager's job, but not at Manchester United. Even Sir Alex's biggest critics were not ready to start campaigning for his head, but that was not the case at other clubs.

Nani and Owen Hargreaves join Sir Alex Ferguson at the Carrington press conference in July 2007 to announce their signing for United.

Louis Saha scores United's second goal in their 2–0 Premier League win against Chelsea in September 2007, Avram Grant's first game in charge of the Blues.

Tottenham Hotspur were due at Old Trafford and, according to newspaper reports, this was a club in turmoil. After two defeats, the rumblings were getting louder, with manager Martin Jol said to be fighting to stay in his job. Sir Alex was bemused.

'I suppose there have been managers sacked after four or five games at the start of a season but you say to yourself: "What are they doing?" I know enough about Martin's work to recognise him as a good manager. I interviewed him for the job here as my assistant when Carlos left, and I know the work he did in Holland was outstanding. He doesn't really need me to trumpet his abilities, everyone is aware of them, it is just sad that there is such a knee-jerk reaction in football today.'

He gave an insight into the pressures managers come under – and that included himself.

'There are similarities to the Tottenham situation and when I came here back in 1986. They haven't won the league for 45 years, and it is a club with a fantastic football history and a reputation for producing fantastic football players. That creates an expectation. This is only Martin's second full season and I don't think he has had time. He needs time to win a championship at a massive club like that.

'I don't know how many times over the years I have sat here and supported managers who are under pressure. You know it isn't fair, but it doesn't change. I suppose it happens here from time to time. When I have a bad spell, I hear people saying that I should have retired six years ago, that I am too old and all that nonsense, but there is a quick route to criticism in our football today.

'When I first came here, there was a group of people they called the "Second Board". They used to meet on a Monday in the Grill Room at Old Trafford and discuss everything that had happened on the Saturday, making their opinions known. That happens at football clubs and that is perhaps where the seed is sown.'

Sympathy with the Jol cause, perhaps, but he made it clear where his priorities lay: 'You can say every game is a must win game…but we will win on Sunday.'

No prophecy, this was a promise.

There had been enough evidence during the City defeat to convince him the poor start was nothing more than – to use one of his favourite expressions – 'a blip'. United had been in a similar position before and come out on top, and he was confident they could do it again.

'At City everyone played with great intensity and commitment. The concentration of passing was terrific; it was just that the finishing let us down, so you have just got to ride along with it. It is no point in me deserting that. It's because they are not winning games that it puts a different slant on everything, but it won't derail us. We are quite content about how we are going to approach this. Winning is the name of the game and I am definitely aware of that.

'The bad start is the complete opposite of last year, so that makes it more coloured than it should be. That must have been the most bizarre derby game in the history of football. Has there ever been a derby game anywhere in the world where the home team never got a corner kick?'

The corner count was United 11 City 0, but if fate had favoured his neighbours in that game, it was United's turn a week later. Who can say how events might have evolved if Robbie Keane's first-minute strike had gone into the United net rather than bouncing to safety off the crossbar?

Would this have put added pressure on Sir Alex? Would Jol have silenced his critics? Who knows? As it was United got their first win, Jol's position worsened, and by mid-October he was sacked.

He was not alone. Before the turn of the year, seven Premier League managers would be out of work, and Jol was not even the first to go. Instead, it was a man whose career, year for year, was even more successful than Sir Alex's.

When the news broke it was a sensation. Chelsea's most successful boss, Jose Mourinho, seemed to have job security for years to come, but on 20 September the club issued a statement announcing it had parted company with its manager 'by mutual consent'. The 'Special One' had gone, and days later Sir Alex again found himself speaking in support of a fellow manager as he prepared his side to face a Mourinho-less Chelsea at Old Trafford.

'The issues surrounding Jose leaving are a disappointment for the game. I feel he was terrific for football and terrific for Chelsea. I enjoyed the competition with him. He was something fresh and new and he has been fantastic, an unparalleled success without question. I wish him well. He has been good for the game, but that is as far as I want to go into it. It is now a test for whoever replaces him.'

The Ferguson focus was firmly on Manchester United. 'We are looking at ourselves. We have enough on our plate right now and I am not looking at Chelsea. What it does to them doesn't matter to me. We're still playing Chelsea and it is still the same players and that in itself is a challenge for us.'

Enough on his plate? Did those words mean he had problems?

A wry smile, a shake of the head, then a serious answer. 'Managing this club is important. We have got to win every game. That is the challenge that has always beset us and it is never going to change. At the moment we are gradually getting towards something like our better form and we have achieved quite a bit in the last few games. That has given us a reasonable platform to go into this game.'

Avram Grant, Chelsea's newly appointed director of football, was the man in charge and his side faced a rapidly reviving United. Following the Tottenham win there had been further victories at home to Sunderland then away to Everton. They had also beaten Sporting Lisbon in Portugal in the opening game of their Champions League group and a 2–0 win over Chelsea gave the league table a more familiar appearance.

Arsenal were now top with United second, three points behind; Manchester City lay third and Liverpool fourth. Chelsea had slipped to sixth. In the weeks that followed, the Carling Cup campaign ended abruptly when Sir Alex fielded a young side which lost 2–0 to Coventry City at Old Trafford, but that was the only setback between August and November.

After Spurs, a run of nine unbeaten games, eight of them wins, kept United in second place and secured an early qualification for the knockout phase of the Champions League. Supporters began talking about a possible trip to Moscow, where the European final was being staged and Patrice Evra revealed his thoughts too:

'How much do I want to win the Champions League? Lots! It was my first target when I came to sign for Manchester United. I don't just want to go to the final, I want to win it. That is why I changed clubs. I don't know whether it will be this year or next, but I want to win this cup.'

A much shorter trip than Manchester to Moscow brought the second league defeat, as United lost 1-0 at Bolton, whose new boss Gary Megson was one of those who had been involved in an unusual session of managerial musical chairs. After Mourinho's departure from Chelsea, Megson left his job at Leicester City and took over from Sammy Lee at The Reebok, while at Tottenham Juande Ramos was brought from Seville to replace Martin Jol.

Then on 5 November, the day before Sir Alex celebrated 21 years at Old Trafford, Chris Hutchings was sacked by Wigan Athletic and Steve Bruce was persuaded to leave Birmingham City to fill the vacancy, before another Ferguson protégé, Alex McLeish, one of his successful side at Aberdeen, replaced Bruce at St Andrew's.

While that was happening, bottom club Derby County sacked Billy Davies, and Paul Jewell, who had been manager of Wigan before

PROPHECIES AND PROMISES **199**

Hutchings, took over. Crazy? The game's longest-serving and most successful manager could only scratch his head in bewilderment: 'I have said it time and time again. There is no evidence that sacking the manager gets you success.'

The Bolton defeat was quickly forgotten. Three days later, Sporting Lisbon were beaten 2–1 at Old Trafford bringing a philosophical reaction from Sir Alex: 'That's what you have to do when you are a good team, recover from a defeat and get on with it.'

He was ready for what lay ahead.

'December is a crucial month. By the end of December, we are going to know for certain who is going to be challenging for this league. There may be some points dropped here and there, but the important thing is to be at the top or round about there on New Year's Day, then the second part of the season can be a really progressive step to get the title.'

The progressive step was a massive stride. After Lisbon, Fulham were beaten 2–0 at Old Trafford, with the result possibly contributing to another manager losing his job, this time Lawrie Sanchez, who two weeks later was replaced at Craven Cottage by Roy Hodgson.

Next, Derby County were hammered 4–1 on a day United hopes were boosted when Arsenal surprisingly lost at Middlesbrough; then at Liverpool Carlos Tevez scored the only goal in a tense but satisfying win; finally on Boxing Day, United went top after a 4–0 win at Sunderland.

It was the season's halfway stage and the big four were back together. United led with 45 points, Arsenal had 44, Chelsea's resurgence saw them third with 38 points, two ahead of Liverpool. There was every reason for seasonal joy in the United camp, but as the year ended it all turned sour.

Two days before Sir Alex's 66th birthday, West Ham, who must have a strong claim to being his bogey club, became party poopers yet again. 'They beat us twice last year and that win at Old Trafford ensured their survival in the Premier League, so we can expect a toughish game, and I'm sure we'll get one,' Sir Alex warned before kick-off.

After it, nothing went right. United led through Ronaldo's 18th goal of the season, but when he missed a second-half penalty it seemed to inspire West Ham and they fought back to win 2–1. In January the seesaw tipped again.

United won every game, while Arsenal surprisingly dropped points, the crucial weekend coming when Newcastle were beaten 6–0 at Old Trafford three days after sacking manager Sam Allardyce, and the Gunners could only draw at home to Birmingham City. United were top on goal difference bringing this quip from the manager: 'You never know how useful that will be, but if we can get to the end of the season with a seven-goal difference and three points more than Arsenal that'll do me!'

Little did he know, but that would not have been enough to win the title. As for the departure of his close friend Allardyce he added: 'It seems to me that Newcastle, as soon as they lose a game, their manager's career is threatened. How many managers have they had in my time here? The thing with Newcastle fans is that they think they should be winning games 5–0 all the time. They have got to say to themselves that time is the thing. I'm convinced that of all the managers they've had, Sam was capable of doing better than most.'

In the FA Cup there were wins at Aston Villa then over Tottenham at Old Trafford, before United were given an intriguing home tie in round five. They would face Arsenal and if there was to be a psychological turning point of the season, then surely this would be it.

A week before the cup tie the club commemorated the 50th anniversary of the Munich Air Disaster. Although only a teenager at the time, Sir Alex clearly remembers the tragedy and acknowledged the significance of marking the event: 'Fifty years is a long time, but the memory is never erased because that particular team, with all those young players who lost their lives, started the origins of the romance of Manchester United. The great thing about what happened through that, is they built a team to win the European Cup 10 years later.

'It is a fantastic story. In that team of 1968 only two players were bought, the rest were produced by the club. It really mirrors what the club is about and how we develop young players. It's a never-ending search for us to produce our own young players.'

The anniversary game against Manchester City ended in a 2–1 defeat, leaving United five points behind Arsenal, but the cup tie produced the first indication that one of their rivals might cave in. It finished United 4 Arsenal 0. Did the manager feel this was a sign of things to come?

'I hope so. Only time will tell, of course, but when Arsenal come here in April, hopefully there is a different picture and we will be in a better position points-wise. I wasn't surprised by the result. I know the expectations of this club and I know what my expectation of my team is and they reached their highest level. When they do that they can beat anyone.'

The Ferguson forecast of a battle of the big four was on. In the Champions League, United reached the quarter-finals where they joined Chelsea, Liverpool and Arsenal. In the Premier League an incredible run of

Sir Alex Ferguson and the rest of the United bench celebrate at the final whistle at Wigan after United had secured the Premier League title in 2008.

Paul Scholes scores a terrific goal in the second leg of the Champions League semi-final against Barcelona. It was enough to send the Reds through to the final in Moscow.

wins saw them storm through March scoring 18 goals without conceding, but any thoughts of a repeat of 1999's treble vanished when they were knocked out of the FA Cup by Portsmouth, one of the sides Sir Alex had singled out at the start of the campaign.

The March run saw them beat Liverpool 3–0 on the afternoon Chelsea overcame Arsenal at Stamford Bridge and moved into second place. According to Sir Alex, the pendulum had swung. The big challenge would now come from Stamford Bridge.

'I have always said you don't dismiss Chelsea because of the size, strength and experience of their squad. They are back on song with that victory, they've a big chance of the league title. I see them as the main threat now. It's a selfish situation, but we hope that Arsenal keep on dropping points and we keep on winning. It's a competitive league; we have to remember that. I made this point early in the season. I felt the games the top four had against each other would be more significant this season than ever before, because other teams would be taking points off us and that has been the case.'

Arsenal folded. Knocked out of Europe by Liverpool, they began April in third place, six points behind United. By the time the sides met at Old Trafford, Sir Alex's post-cup tie words had come true. United were in a better position and improved it with a 2–1 win.

With four games remaining, they were nine points ahead of the Gunners and five in front of Chelsea, who were paired with Liverpool in the semi-final of the Champions League. United would meet Barcelona in the other game, with the possibility of Russia staging the first all-English Champions League final.

Domestically the top two wobbled. Chelsea drew at Wigan, United did likewise at Blackburn. In the next game, when they met at Stamford Bridge, a controversial penalty gave Chelsea a 2–1 win. With two games to go United topped the table only on goal difference; it could not have been closer.

Chelsea's remaining fixtures were away to Newcastle and at home to Bolton, while United faced West Ham at Old Trafford and had to travel to Wigan on the final day. The Ferguson pre-season prediction was coming true. It was going 'down to the wire', not only in the Premier League but in Europe too, where United beat Barcelona over two legs thanks to a single goal. Paul Scholes was the scorer and his manager felt the midfielder was the chosen one:

'Maybe that's God's way of repaying him after he missed the 1999 final because of suspension,' Sir Alex said after the 1–0 win at Old Trafford. 'Fate is fate and I believe in fate, plus the fact that he has been with us since he was 14 years of age and he knows what it means to the club. He'll be the first name on that team sheet in Moscow because he deserves to be.'

In Moscow United would face Chelsea, who had ended Liverpool's hopes after a thrilling 4–3 aggregate win. It was United versus Chelsea for the Champions League, United versus Chelsea for the Premier League. All or nothing?

With a superior goal difference (+53 to Chelsea's +37), provided they could win their remaining games United would retain the championship, and with West Ham beaten 4–1 as Chelsea won 2–0 on Tyneside the contest went down to the final day of the season Sunday, 11 May.

If Wigan could chalk up their first win against United, and if Chelsea beat Bolton the trophy presentation would be at Stamford Bridge; if not the celebrations would take place at the JJB Stadium, 10 miles down the road from Old Trafford.

If – the biggest word in football.

Steve Bruce's Wigan fought with spirit, but the issue was put beyond doubt through a penalty from Cristiano Ronaldo and a late strike from Ryan Giggs, who was brought into the game as a second-half substitute and stepped straight into the history books. As he took the field, Giggs equalled Sir Bobby Charlton's 758-game appearance record for United and, with Chelsea and Bolton drawing 1–1 and the Premier League race over, became the first player to win 10 championship medals.

'I can't ask for anything more than that, can I?' was his reaction. 'The most important thing today was getting that win and that title, because the lads have worked hard all season as a squad and it's fully deserved.'

Was this any better than the other nine?

'They are all special. The first one was important because we had waited 26 years to win it, but after that they have all been brilliant. I said last year what it meant to me to win nine titles and overtake Phil Neal and Alan Hansen's record, but to get to double figures…you don't even dream of that when you set off playing. But I have been lucky, I have played in some great teams, with some great players and been lucky enough to have been in the position to win 10.

'The thing about this one is we have won it on the day, which we haven't done too often. Normally it is done and dusted before that, but you wouldn't always want to do it that way.'

Sir Alex was a proud man: 'We're all proud. I'm proud of the players and the staff. The team spirit was excellent, the support was fantastic. It was a difficult day, the last day, you make a mistake and anything can happen. After a minute people behind me were shouting "Chelsea are winning 2–0!", but you have to put all that aside and let the players concentrate on their job and they made certain nothing untoward was going to happen. Where do I put them along with my other teams? Well, if they win the European Cup you will have to put them right at the top.'

Elated as his players paraded the trophy around Wigan's compact stadium, his thoughts were on what lay ahead. In the week that followed, he revealed what he considers to be the worst side of his job. He had to name 18 players to represent Manchester United in the first all-English Champions League final, 11 starters, seven substitutes from a squad of 25 – delight for some, disappointment for others.

'I'm not going to enjoy it. I know my team, but naming the substitutes is the biggest problem because some very good players are going to be left out. The consolation for anyone who is not playing in the final is to be on the bench, because then they feel part of it. I just hope that at some point in the future the Champions League extends the substitutes' bench to 11 outfield players as they do for World Cup games.

'That would be justified for the final, because the dilemma I have is deciding who is not going to be on the bench and having to tell them. That should be taken from me. I know I have done it many times, but it doesn't get easier; in fact it is more difficult because this team is starting to blend together and mature and you get to know them better.

'They all know they have contributed a lot to the season, so for them to be left out, and be told by me..? It doesn't matter what I tell them, I don't think it resonates with them at all. The disappointment is deep and it's understandable.'

Gary Neville, Louis Saha, Ji-sung Park, rising star Gerard Pique the Spanish defender who scored twice during the group stage, and goalkeeper Ben Foster were among those who would watch from the wings.

The final was perhaps an anti-climax, but not its outcome. United led after 26 minutes when Ronaldo scored his 42nd goal of the season. Chelsea equalised through Frank Lampard and eventually the tussle went into extra time, during which Didier Drogba was sent off. Like that pre-season clash at Wembley in the Community Shield it ended 1–1.

The story was back where it started, it was déjà vu all over again! The destiny of the Champions League would be settled in a penalty shoot-out, but when Ronaldo's shot was saved by Petr Cech, it seemed to be slipping away from United. Chelsea were one kick away from winning the trophy,

Cristiano Ronaldo scores with a towering header to give United the lead in the Champions League final against Chelsea. It was his 42nd goal in a stunning season.

Sir Alex becomes one of only a few managers ever to lift the Champions League trophy for a second time, after United's penalty shoot-out victory.

and skipper John Terry confidently stepped up. He placed the ball and ran forward, but his standing foot slipped in the Moscow mud; his shot flew beyond Edwin van der Sar but hit a post.

With the scores level at 5–5, Ryan Giggs fittingly scored United's next, then Nicolas Anelka stepped up. He had to score to keep Chelsea in the contest, but his shot was tame and the hero of Wembley all those months earlier became king of Luzhniki Stadium. Edwin van der Sar saved confidently and was mobbed by his team-mates. United were champions of Europe for a third time.

Fate decreed that 50 years after Munich, 40 since that first victory of 1968, the Champions League trophy should find its way back to Old Trafford. The young men of 2008 earned their place in Manchester United folklore and the partying went on into the night.

From the celebrations emerged Sir Alex Ferguson, who was already looking to the future. He had enjoyed the moment but commented: 'I won't be manager here when I'm 70 and I won't be managing any more than another three years at the very most. You have to think about time for yourself and my wife's getting older, and you have to think about that. She deserves a bit of my time. The older you get, you get guilty about it. The big fear is what you would do with yourself. There's too many examples of people who retire and are in their box soon after because you're taking away the very thing that makes you alive, that keeps you alive.'

Prediction, prophecy or promise? Sir Alex will be 70 on 31 December 2011.

23

NECK AND NECK

ONE TOPIC filled the sporting headlines more than any other during the summer of 2008 – Cristiano Ronaldo's future. Speculation claimed the most feted footballer in the game was wanted by Real Madrid, with rumour turning to fact when the Spanish club's president, Ramon Calderon, openly declared he was going to sign the World Player of the Year.

If the story had bones, then Ronaldo added the flesh when, while on international duty, he said in an interview: 'Yes, I want to play for Real Madrid, but only if it is true they are eager to pay me and Manchester United what they have been saying they will.'

According to reports, Ronaldo could expect a salary of around £15 million a year from Madrid if he agreed to a £70 million move, but the player added: 'It does not depend on me, but it is important to send a message.'

United responded to all of this by pointing out that Ronaldo was on a long-term contract, was not for sale and would not be leaving Old Trafford. Sir Alex added that if Ronaldo no longer wanted to play for United, then the man with the Golden Boot could spend the coming season 'in the reserves'.

Angered by Real Madrid's way of doing business, Sir Alex re-emphasised the position: 'Ronaldo has four years left on his contract. He is a Manchester United player and will still be a Manchester United player next season.'

Ronaldo had spoken out while taking part in Euro 2008 with Portugal, but when their interest in the tournament ended, it was revealed he needed ankle surgery and would be out of action for three months. By the time he had recovered, the issue was settled. Madrid had stepped back, Ronaldo was staying put; Sir Alex had won.

He also came out on top in another confrontation some weeks later, this time with Manchester City. Since the end of the previous season, United had been linked with Tottenham striker Dimitar Berbatov, but the clubs could not reach agreement over his valuation. Suddenly, on transfer deadline day, City made an audacious effort to gazump their neighbours, offering £30 million-plus, and Spurs accepted.

City were the club in the news having been taken over by a company backed by multi-billionaire Sheikh Mansour bin Zayed bin Sultan Al Nahyan. They were being hailed the richest club in the world and wanted to show it by being linked with every big name in the game – including Ronaldo, who they apparently wanted to buy for £135 million! New manager Mark Hughes could hardly believe his luck. When the buy-out happened, he had been at the club for only a few weeks, after replacing Sven-Goran Eriksson; now he had a fortune at his fingertips but little time to spend it.

The transfer deadline was imminent, but City snatched Real Madrid's Robinho from under the noses of Chelsea with a cheque for £34 million, after hours earlier the player had pledged his future to the London club. Then they turned to Berbatov, who was on his way to Manchester, but he was picked up at the airport by Sir Alex and refused to meet up with City. Within minutes of the deadline, with Fraizer Campbell agreeing to join Tottenham on loan as part of the deal, agreement was reached, with United paying a club record £30.75 million.

Berbatov made it clear that he had no intention of signing for anyone but Sir Alex. 'My only goal was to join Manchester United and I am really pleased. My ambitions are big and I want to pursue them with the biggest club in the world. When I heard about the other offer and the money they wanted to spend I was surprised, but it didn't make any difference to me because I always wanted to come to Old Trafford.'

Sir Alex seemed unmoved by events, even the hype surrounding his neighbours. 'What have I made of them? Plenty of talk, but the great thing about my time at this club has been the challenge. There is always a challenge for us. Four years ago when Jose went to Chelsea, it represented a different challenge because up to then it had been Arsenal and Manchester United.

'Chelsea became the new kids on the block and won their first two championships and we had to reassess. We accepted the challenge and got on with our business the best way we could and that is all we can do, to do the best we can. What you see at Manchester United is that it is not an overnight situation. This club has been built up over many years. It's not

Dimitar Berbatov signs for United on transfer deadline day, August 2008, despite a late bid from neighbours City to derail the deal.

December 2008, Ji-sung Park goes past Diego Calderon (l) and Luis Bolanos of Liga de Quito in the final of the Club World Cup. United won 1–0 thanks to a Wayne Rooney goal.

just going to be here for today; it is going to be here for a long time. Four years ago, people were saying United were for the scrap-heap and there was a lot of talk that Chelsea were going to do this and going to do that. We had to accept the challenges, just like today when we accept the challenge from Liverpool, from Arsenal and from Chelsea.

'What we have done is tried to be ourselves. Yes, we have bought big players, but I don't think what you are seeing from Manchester United is a cash cow in the way some clubs are talking. We have seen it before, it'll happen again. It's never changed us. That's the great thing about this club, we've never changed.

'We still play the same way. We still have ambitions. We still have a feet-on-the-ground situation and everybody has a humble approach to their football. We shouldn't concern ourselves about what other people are planning to do, because it doesn't always work. They have spoken about going for Cristiano Ronaldo, which is absolutely absurd.

'It's very difficult to say what is going to happen. When Chelsea were doing the same thing, we worried about it because we saw the quality they were bringing in. At that point, we said to ourselves "they are going to be a handful" and they were. We had to do something about it, and we did.'

The season was already underway when Berbatov arrived, but before it started there had been plenty of activity both on and off the field. Carlos Queiroz, Sir Alex's right-hand man, left the club for a second time to take charge of Portugal's national team. He replaced Luiz Felipe Scolari, who was appointed Chelsea manager when Avram Grant's eight-month tenure was ended. Chief coach Mike Phelan then stepped up to become United's new assistant manager, while on the transfer front Louis Saha was sold to Everton, Mikael Silvestre joined Arsenal and young Chris Eagles moved to Burnley.

The summer tour took the players to South Africa and Nigeria, and once back United retained the Community Shield, beating Portsmouth at Wembley. They failed to win the UEFA Super Cup, though, losing to Zenit St Petersburg in Monaco in a fixture which had a significant effect on the Premier League campaign. It led to the postponement of the home game against Fulham, and for more than half the season United had to play catch-up on their rivals, something that caused early concern for Sir Alex.

'How we manage our programme is going to be a key issue. We'll also have another game to make up when we take part in the Club World Cup in December. That means when we get to the second half of the season if we are involved in everything, it's going to take a great deal of management to make sure we don't get caught in one of those last-gasp, having to play four games in six days, situations like we did back in 1992. That would be unthinkable.'

By mid-September Ronaldo was fit enough to play again and returned for the opening Champions League game against Villarreal, but the transfer talk would not go away. The latest claim was that he had agreed to join Madrid the following summer and in a bid to quash the gossip he appeared on MUTV saying: 'There's always speculation, not just about me, but about the future of players all around the world. People were speaking about me this summer, but that was normal because of what I did during the season.'

He had returned to a side lying 14th in the table, but when he got his first Premier League goal of the season, in a 2–0 win over Bolton, things began to look brighter. Earlier, United had lost 2–1 at Liverpool, but the defeat (during which Nemanja Vidic was sent off) sparked a 12-match unbeaten run which helped Sir Alex celebrate the 22nd anniversary of his appointment in style.

By November, after 10 games, United lay five points behind Chelsea and Liverpool with a game in hand, but a 2–1 defeat at Arsenal halted progress. It also kick-started another unbeaten streak, which began with a 5–0 win against Stoke and included a 1–0 victory away to moneybags Manchester City.

When this run ended, they not only topped the league but were top of the world as well. As winners of the Champions League they were invited to take part in the FIFA Club World Cup, the latest version of a long line of competitions going back to the days when the European Cup holders faced the South American champions in the Inter-Continental Cup. The new format featured champion clubs from each of FIFA's six confederations and was held in Japan. Promoted as the most prestigious club tournament in the world, it struggled to capture the imagination of many in England, but if Sir Alex had any reservations he hid them well.

'We're looking forward to it, but it's a tournament which comes at a very difficult time. We'll be two games behind when we come back, and while that's not the best in terms of us going for the championship, if I was asked if I would like to play in it again next year I would say I would absolutely love to be there, because you only get an invitation if you win the European Cup!

'It's a big challenge to us. When we won the Inter-Continental Cup against Palmeiras back in 1999 we were the first British team to do so and hopefully we can get another success. I hope we can handle it.'

The final game before flying to Japan was a goalless draw at White Hart Lane on 13 December, which left United six points behind Liverpool and five adrift of Chelsea. When last involved in a similar mid-season tournament in 2000, United caused a major controversy because, in agreeing to take part, they had to withdraw from the FA Cup. This time they would be back before the third round, but the manager hoped history might repeat itself.

'We were top of the league when we went to Rio and when we came back we were still there. None of our competitors won while we were away so we had a great break, came back re-charged and went on to win the league. I hope we can do the same this time.'

The European and South American champions were seeded into the semi-finals where United beat Japan's Gamba Osaka 5–3 and Liga de Quito of Ecuador beat Mexico's Pachuca. The final would see the Champions League holders against the winners of the Copa Libertadores – just like it always was.

Sir Alex did not take things lightly. He fielded his big guns, although Berbatov was on the bench after missing the first game because of a virus. Rooney, Ronaldo and Carlos Tevez all started. In defence, young Brazilian Rafael da Silva, one of the season's rising stars who along with his twin Fabio joined United in July, came in at right-back ahead of Gary Neville, with Rio Ferdinand handed the captain's armband. Vidic and Evra completed the back four, with Michael Carrick, Anderson and Ji-sung Park in midfield.

With close to 70,000 filling the Yokohama National Stadium, the final provided plenty of passion, enough to see Vidic sent off in the second half for retaliation, which called for a swift change of plan by the manager. Tevez came off, with promising young centre-back Jonny Evans keeping the defence at full strength.

The move worked. Quito could not crack United, with Edwin van der Sar in fine form, and with a quarter of an hour to go the only goal came. Good work by Carrick set Ronaldo on a swift break down field. His cross-field pass picked out Rooney who scored. Manchester United: world champions!

'It was the collective spirit of the team which won the day,' said an ecstatic Sir Alex. 'With 10 men, we played with great expression and tried to win and that is a measure of the players' ambition. After the sending off, it was important that we didn't lose the ball, to keep passing and hope Ronaldo or Rooney did something special, and Wayne scored a magnificent goal.'

New heights, but just as it was in the 1950s when Matt Busby took those first steps in Europe, the cynics back home cast doubts. Sir Alex claimed attitudes will change. 'In 30 years, you'll look back and see Manchester United's name on the trophy and it will mean something – although I won't be around to enjoy it!'

Rooney was on cloud nine. 'We're the best team in the world. It's a great achievement for the team and something we're all really proud of. It's been a long road, but to score the winning goal in a match like this is a great feeling for me.'

The long road led back to Manchester in time for Christmas, and what had happened while United were away? Liverpool drew at Arsenal, and Chelsea did the same at Everton.

'I reckon those results were predictable,' was the Ferguson view. 'You expected a tight match for Liverpool at Arsenal, but because of Everton's poor record against Chelsea – they haven't beaten them in 20 matches – I was worried. But they played well and might easily have won. So for us it's similar to what happened in 2000, but I have said for a while if we can get within a point or two of the leaders come New Year's Day, we're in with a great chance.'

United had three days to prepare for a trip to Stoke on Boxing Day, an early kick-off game which shortened recovery time after the journey back from Japan, but there were no complaints from the manager.

'The players have actually looked fresh over the last two days. They had the day off after we got back and a good sleep; we never know for certain but if we go back to 1999 when we came back from Japan we beat Everton 5–1, so we'll see what happens. The thing is we're all playing on Boxing Day, so that's the fairness, the only discrepancy is teams are picked for television games and sometimes it can work out unfairly for you. We would probably have preferred it to be a later kick-off, but that's how it is.'

United won 1–0, with Tevez scoring seven minutes from time, while later in the day Liverpool and Chelsea also chalked up victories, leaving Sir Alex to ponder: 'Today could be significant for us. We've now played more away games than home fixtures, which will give us a long programme of home matches during the run-in, very important ones against the top teams.'

Things were going well on all fronts. Through to the knockout phase of the Champions League, in the semi-finals of the Carling Cup, United then had a 3–0 FA Cup third round win at Southampton to set them on their way in that competition. Liverpool were seven points better off, but Chelsea's advantage had slipped to four and United now had two games in hand.

Next up? Chelsea at Old Trafford, but 48 hours before that game came possibly the most bizarre moment of the season. It involved Liverpool manager Rafa Benitez. Earlier, when asked about Liverpool's chances of winning the title, Sir Alex had said: 'I think they'll get nervous in the second half of the season.'

It was a fair comment – the view of a rival manager. No one could have anticipated the reaction it would spark from Anfield. As Benitez faced the media ahead of Liverpool's next game, at Stoke, he produced a sheet of paper, placed it carefully on the desk in front of him then launched into an unprecedented attack on Sir Alex.

'I was surprised by what has been said, but maybe they are nervous because we are at the top of the table. But I want to talk about facts. I want to be clear, I do not want to play mind games too early, although they seem to want to start.'

Benitez then read a long list of claims, alleging Sir Alex escaped punishment for criticising referees, constantly complained about kick-off times for televised games and went as far as suggesting United should not have clinched the title in the final game of the previous season, 'Rio Ferdinand handled the ball, but the referee could not see it.'

He went on. 'Mr Ferguson is complaining about everything, that everybody is against United. We know what happens every time we go to Old Trafford and the United staff. They are always going man to man with the referees, especially at half-time when they walk close to the referees and they are talking and talking. You need to know that I am talking about facts, not my impression.

'There are things that everyone can see every single week. Are they under pressure? Maybe they were not thinking that we would be at the top of the table in January. But we are at the top of the table and they are nervous. I will be watching United's game with Chelsea. The result does not matter to us, if we win at Stoke that result does not matter. I only wanted to explain our position.'

United beat Chelsea 3–0, Liverpool drew. Had what became known as 'Rafa's rant' rebounded? Sir Alex responded reluctantly. Speaking to Sky Sports he said: 'I think you've got to be careful of the venom of it. Hopefully he will reflect and understand what he said was ridiculous. I think he's an angry man. He's disturbed for some reason or another. The things he said are not facts. I'm not going to get into it. At this moment we need to concentrate on catching the leaders.'

Within a week United caught them. Three days after Chelsea came the

Edwin van der Sar saves from John Terry on 11 January 2009. United won 3–0 and the Dutch keeper had added another 90 minutes to his record total of 1311 minutes without conceding in the Premier League.

Teenage debutant Federico Macheda scores in the final moments of United's thrilling comeback against Aston Villa on 5 April 2009.

first of those games in hand, when Wigan were beaten 1–0 at Old Trafford. Victory came at a price. Wayne Rooney scored in the first minute then tore a hamstring and was ruled out for a month. Three days later, another 1–0 win at Bolton saw Berbatov score, this time just before the final whistle, while Liverpool could only draw at home to Everton.

United went top. The pressure was on.

During January's nine games, United reached the Carling Cup final with a 4–3 aggregate win over Derby County and the FA Cup fifth round after beating Tottenham 2–1. In the league they won 5–0 at West Brom (as Liverpool drew at Wigan), then a 1–0 win over Everton at Old Trafford finished things. After trailing by seven points when the month began, they ended it two ahead with still a game in hand.

Unlike their rivals, United were involved on all four fronts. A 4–1 FA Cup win over Derby saw them reach the quarter-finals, while in the Champions League the knockout phase began with a trip to Jose Mourinho's latest club Inter Milan where a goalless draw boosted hopes of retaining that trophy.

By the end of February, the league position also strengthened. Wins at West Ham, then at home to Fulham and Blackburn put them seven points clear of Liverpool and 10 in front of third-placed Chelsea. It was a remarkable transformation. Between the defeat at Arsenal on 8 November and the 2–1 Blackburn win on 21 February, United played 14 Premier League games without conceding a goal, with Edwin van der Sar establishing a new English goalkeeping record for consecutive clean sheets.

As March began, the Carling Cup was won with another final going to penalties, with Tottenham beaten 4–1 thanks to some fine keeping by Ben Foster. A 4–0 win over Fulham in the FA Cup put United in the semi-finals and four days later Inter were beaten 2–0 at Old Trafford and a place in the quarter-finals of the Champions League was secured.

Everything looked fine until, in the space of two games, the picture changed. When Benitez had made his verbal attack, one of his claims was that United players were rarely sent off at Old Trafford. On 14 March he got his wish and much more. Not only did Liverpool end United's run, they destroyed it, winning 4–1 with Vidic again sent off. It was a result that left Sir Alex stunned.

'It's a hard one to take, because I actually thought we were the better team in terms of the football we played and the chances created, but the score doesn't reflect that and quite rightly when you win 4–1 at Old Trafford you deserve all the plaudits and you can't deny them that.'

Despite the defeat United stayed top, but a week later things got worse. Fulham had already been beaten twice in league and cup, but it was third time lucky for the Londoners, who exploited the absence of Vidic at Craven Cottage to crack the best defence in the league and win 2–0. With Chelsea losing at Tottenham, Liverpool roared on with a 5–0 win over Aston Villa, and before United played again took over top spot.

They were at Fulham the night before United's home clash with Aston Villa. They won and the celebrations continued the following afternoon as, with an hour gone, Villa led 2–1 at Old Trafford. With Rooney, Vidic, Ferdinand and Berbatov out through suspension and injury, United eventually fought back to equalise through Ronaldo with nine minutes left. Many would have settled for a draw – not Manchester United.

During the second half Sir Alex had replaced Nani with a 17-year-old debutant Federico Macheda, a tall, powerful Italian striker. With seconds remaining, a Giggs pass found the youngster running in from the left. He controlled the ball, ran inside and bent a perfect shot past the diving Brad Friedel. United won 3–2. If the season had a turning point, surely that was it.

'That's this club. If they're good enough, they'll play,' was how the manager reacted after witnessing an amazing ending. United topped the league by a single point and had eight games to play while Liverpool had seven. Neck and neck.

The grand slam was still on, but a 2–2 home draw against FC Porto jeopardised European progress until a Ronaldo goal in Portugal won a place in the semi-finals. In the FA Cup the luck ran out. The Wembley semi-final against Everton again went to penalties, but this time Foster met his match and Everton won 4–2, but two days later came an uplifting moment in the title race when Liverpool and Arsenal astonishingly drew 4–4 at Anfield.

It was an incredible game watched by Sir Alex, who the next night saw United beat Portsmouth at Old Trafford, only for the scales to tip again three days later as again Liverpool played first, winning their afternoon game at Hull. United faced Tottenham in a late kick-off and, like the Villa game, it looked as though the pressure was getting to them. Spurs led 2–0 at half time – would the title slip through their fingers?

Not so. In a sensational turnaround, they stormed through the second half with two goals each from Ronaldo and Rooney plus a fifth from Berbatov to secure a 5–2 win. United were three points ahead with five games to play.

In a hectic schedule, the spotlight switched to Europe where three of the clubs which reached the semi-finals the previous year got through once again. This time, United were paired with Arsenal while Chelsea faced Barcelona. A repeat of Russia's final in Rome was a possibility. It was not to be.

United went through when a 1–0 win at Old Trafford was followed by a breathtaking 3–1 romp at the Emirates, where Ronaldo stole the show, laying on the first goal for Ji-sung Park after eight minutes, adding a second three minutes later, and a third on the hour.

Sir Alex glowed at the prospect of another European final. 'We got a good start to the game and that made the difference. Two quick goals like that knocked the wind out of their sails. They're a young team and I don't think at whatever level you are playing at teams can recover from two quick goals like that. From the club's point of view, and I have said many times we should have won this cup more than we have, this is another opportunity for us.

'I think we can do it again; I feel we have the quality and we have the energy and ambition to do it. It's a hungry team and when the chips are down they don't let me down.'

United v Chelsea again? No. That opportunity evaporated the following night when, after a 0–0 draw in Spain, Chelsea and Barcelona drew again, this time 1–1 and the Catalans went through thanks to that away goal.

Between the ties the tense league tussle had continued. United won at Middlesbrough, Liverpool at home to Newcastle. Then the Merseysiders threw down the gauntlet with a 3–0 win at West Ham the night before Manchester City were due at Old Trafford. The race for the title was intense, but before Liverpool played again United were champions.

On an afternoon of intense pressure, City were beaten 2–0, with the goals coming in the first half from Ronaldo and Tevez. Few realised this would be their last derby as United players. Ronaldo was still being linked to Real Madrid, while there appeared to be problems surrounding Tevez's contract, whose loan period at United was due to end after the season concluded. United had the option to make the deal a permanent one, but protracted talks with his representatives had left club and player in limbo.

Rather than dwelling on such things, Sir Alex summed up the win over City saying: 'Derby games can either be good games or bad games, and it was a bad game today. I was never comfortable myself, but after getting the second goal on half time we never went for that third to kill it off and that allowed them a lot of possession.

'Liverpool had put us under a bit of pressure. I suppose they have played first on a number of occasions, but what does it matter? If we do our job, that is all we need to worry about. These players have experienced that many times; it isn't as if we're going into the unknown. We find ourselves in a position we are in nearly every season, challenging for the league and whether it's playing before or after another team, it doesn't matter.'

United had 83 points from 35 games, Liverpool trailed by three points with two games left. The time had come to balance the books. Match 36 for United meant a trip to Wigan, where the previous season they had secured the title. A repeat result would not have the same outcome, but would put success within reach, and any claims coming out of Liverpool – from supporters and media rather than football club – that Wigan boss Steve Bruce might make things easy for his former boss were quickly forgotten.

Wigan scored first through Hugo Rodallega and led at half time. Then on the hour a Michael Carrick shot was redirected into goal by Tevez and the equaliser lifted United. They upped the tempo, and with four minutes left John O'Shea laid the ball back and Carrick scored the winner.

'Tonight was a massive three points for us,' said the happy midfielder as around him United fans celebrated. 'I had an up and down game in front of goal, should have scored before I did and mishit a shot which Carlos scored from. After that it was just a case of us getting the winner and happily it was me that got it, but it could have been anyone.'

Carrick and his colleagues were a point away from retaining the title with two games remaining, Arsenal at home and away to Hull City: 'We're not getting carried away. We have to respect Arsenal for how good they are and we've still got a job to do. It looks good at the moment, but we have still got to go and perform again, and hopefully we can do that on Saturday at home.'

Do it they did, in another nerve-filled game played ahead of the weekend's other league fixtures. Arsenal tried their best to spoil the post-match presentation planned by the Premier League and an edgy United also missed several chances, but it finished goalless.

United were champions once again, and Sir Alex had done the virtually unachievable by becoming the first manager to win three successive titles not once but twice, having done so in 1999-2001 as well. No other manager had ever achieved this feat even once.

'It's fantastic. It's that same wonderful feeling when you win a trophy and particularly the Premier League, because it is such a difficult one to win. Credit to the players and the staff, because they have done a fantastic job this year. We've played more games than any other team in the country and

I think it is a great credit to the resilience of the players. When you see the fans celebrating at the end of the game you know that all the hard work and pain was worth it.'

It was United's 18th championship; they had equalled Liverpool's long-standing record of title successes. Neck and neck. If Sir Alex glowed as he looked out on the celebrations, it was with good reason. He had reached yet another milestone as manager of Manchester United.

Like his team-mates, Cristiano Ronaldo also savoured the moment as he pocketed his third Premier League winner's medal. Would it be his last?

'We have to enjoy the moment; we haven't got to care about the other things. It's always good to be at the top and this is a good moment. For the last two years we have played fantastically and we have won a few things and this club needs to carry on. It doesn't matter which players are here, which coach is here, the mentality of this club is always to win and I am very proud to be in the history of Manchester United and I feel very good.'

There were still two games to play, the closing fixture of the season away to Hull City, which saw United go out with a win to end the campaign four points better off than Liverpool, then the Champions League final. Here they fell short of expectations, losing 2–0 to Barcelona in Rome, a result that took some of the gloss off what had been a remarkable season.

World champions, winners of the Premier League, holders of the Carling Cup, but of course Sir Alex Ferguson already had his eyes on the next season.

'Absolutely, you have to here; there's nothing else for it. You just drive on. It's difficult to win a hat-trick of Premier Leagues – we are the only team to have done it and to win it twice is wonderful, but the great challenge is to try and win it next year because that would be something special. It would give us nineteen league titles and without doubt a special place in the club's history,' he said.

As if that place was not already secured!

Sir Alex Ferguson congratulates Ryan Giggs after United's convincing 3–1 victory at the Emirates in the Champions League semi-final on 5 May 2009. Anderson and Gary Neville look on.

Sir Alex leads out his team after United had secured a third successive Premier League title – it was the Reds' 18th title in all.

ROONEY IS TOP MAN

WITH THREE successive Premiership titles under his belt, Sir Alex was the master of English football. But as he approached the start of the 2009-10 season, aiming for a record fourth successive league title, there was some unease in the minds of a section of the demanding supporters, which must have irritated him.

What concerned them was that during the summer United had lost Cristiano Ronaldo to Real Madrid, albeit for an astonishing £80 million fee, along with the energetic and high-scoring Carlos Tevez, but had not replaced them with similar high-profile signings.

Stepping into Ronaldo's shoes was Antonio Valencia, signed for a reported £16 million from Wigan. But the boy from Ecuador, a winger, well built and with a trick or two, didn't yet have the worldwide acclaim of Ronaldo, or so it felt at the time to critical supporters. The new central striker in place of Tevez was Michael Owen, picked up on a free transfer from Newcastle. Given his track record as a prolific goalscorer with Liverpool and England, he was worth a punt, but his catalogue of injury problems was a cause for concern. There was one other signing, as Gabriel Obertan was picked up for £3 million from Bordeaux, courtesy of a former Red, Laurent Blanc, the manager of the French club.

United's decision not to use all of the £80 million Ronaldo fee, which the club insisted was available for Ferguson to spend if he wished, was seized on by fans hostile to the Glazers, the American owners, as somehow being their fault. The Reds had mixed fortunes at the start of their campaign. They won the opening game 1–0 against Birmingham, but lost 1–0 at promoted Burnley, cut loose to win 5–0 at Wigan and then closed the opening month by beating Arsenal 2–1 at Old Trafford.

United were third in the table, but that defeat at Burnley was a shock. Ferguson was having none of the criticisms, though, and hit back to justify his policy. He admitted that he knew some supporters still worried that he had not been out to buy a megastar to replace Cristiano Ronaldo, and that they couldn't quite work out how they were going to compensate for all the goals the Portuguese star used to get. He also conceded that in addition to the challenge of Chelsea and Arsenal, there was another potential rival.

'Competition will be even fiercer this season, with Manchester City's owners raising the bar in the transfer market, and while it is tempting to assume that bringing together a stack of individuals, however talented they may be, doesn't necessarily create a successful team, City do nevertheless pose a new threat,' he explained.

'It would be foolish to ignore developments at Eastlands. We have only to look how well Chelsea did with back-to-back championships after the massive injection of Russian cash to know that money can talk. I think all the leading clubs are looking with interest to see how Mark Hughes handles the situation and whether he can make it work. We are all looking over our shoulders, though as far as Manchester United are concerned at any rate, it is not in fear.

'I am more than happy with our squad, and although we have lost a major, major player, I believe we are on the threshold of a very exciting era for Manchester United. People have focused on the departure of Ronaldo without looking at the bigger picture and appreciating the progress the rest of the squad has made and is still making. We are packed with improving players, youngsters who are showing all the signs of becoming top people, alongside players like Wayne Rooney who are fast approaching real maturity.

'Even over the few months of the close season, there has been remarkable development among some of the young guys. Darron Gibson has been unbelievable in pre-season, and I can't quite believe the way young Federico Macheda has suddenly filled out. He is one very strong boy now. With so many young players developing so quickly, we are going to have a real competitive edge that means I will be selecting teams from a position of absolute strength.

'The media at our last press conference seemed preoccupied with how I was going to keep everyone happy up front, with Michael Owen, Wayne Rooney, Dimitar Berbatov and the youngsters like Macheda and Danny Welbeck all competing for two places. But that really is only half of it, with midfield even more crowded with at least half a dozen major players fighting for two places. I have Ryan Giggs, Michael Carrick, Darren Fletcher, Darron Gibson, Paul Scholes, Anderson and soon Owen Hargreaves on his way back from injury. And that's before we consider the wide players who are also capable of playing midfield, like Ji-sung Park, Nani and Antonio Valencia.

'Now that is what I call a real selection problem! You can perhaps understand why I didn't feel it was necessary to bring in any more big players from a transfer market inflated to the point where true value had gone out of the window. So no eye-catching transfer headlines from Old Trafford, but don't think we have been asleep. A major feature of our transfer policy these days is to go for young players of potential we can develop ourselves,' he added.

Ferguson was disappointed by the one-goal defeat at Burnley, especially when Michael Carrick, the new penalty taker in succession to Ronaldo, had his spot-kick saved by Brian Jensen, but he conceded: 'Burnley have been out of the top division for many years and it was their night, so credit to them.'

He was happy with the five-goal romp at Wigan, especially with Michael Owen scoring, and naturally felt a surge of optimism when his under-fire team beat rivals Arsenal.

'We weren't given the credit we deserved and by the end of the match we were the better side. Arsenal dominated the first half, but I never felt they looked like scoring, apart of course from Andrey Arshavin's brilliant shot that gave them the lead. It was certainly a shock to take in at half time, and we got a break with the penalty, though when you analyse it, in face of a great pass from Ryan Giggs and a brilliant run from Wayne Rooney, their goalkeeper was bound to be in difficulties and the penalty was the outcome.

'There was nothing too wrong with our performance. We have the nucleus of last season's championship-winning team, which I believe can kick on to become better as they mature and as the younger players develop. Nobody should have been surprised that the transfer window shut without any further activity from Manchester United. I said I was satisfied with my squad and the couple of signings I did make, and I saw no reason to change my attitude, even if the vultures had homed in following the blip at Burnley,' he said.

Ferguson's team waved away the vultures in September to go top of the table on goal difference from Chelsea with the help of a particularly dramatic derby that saw the Reds win 4–3 at Old Trafford. Craig Bellamy

Michael Owen celebrates his 96th-minute winner in the 4–3 derby game against City. He may have joined on a free transfer, but to United fans this goal was priceless.

Antonio Valencia, signed from Wigan during the summer of 2009, settled in quickly at United. Here he scores the Reds' second goal against Bolton Wanderers on 17 October.

had put City level in injury time, but Michael Owen capped that late effort with a winner engineered by Giggs. Picking up Owen on a free transfer was looking good.

Winning 2–1 at Stoke while Chelsea crashed at Wigan was the match that pushed the Reds to the top and as Ferguson said: 'Winning at Stoke is never easy. They have a good home record and I always felt that winning there last season was the launch pad for us to go on and win the championship. We showed patience and composure to win the game in the last half hour, with goals from Berbatov and John O'Shea and with Ryan Giggs the inspiration after coming on as a substitute.

'Ryan really does defy time and, like Paul Scholes, has made it clear that he has no intention of giving up on his ambition and determination for more success. I spoke a lot at the start of the season about the development of our younger players, but I meant no disrespect to the older element because I always like my teams to be a balance of youth and experience. I must admit, though, that I didn't really expect the old codgers to be playing such an immense part in what has been a fantastic run of form.

'They have made sure that I won't forget them and I certainly won't. I need them and I'll make sure we do everything possible to get the most out of them for as long as we can. Of course they are fresh at the moment. Injury has stopped Gary Neville from playing a lot and when he does come in he is up and down that wing from full back just as strongly as he did when he first came into the side. Paul Scholes is benefiting from a full pre-season of training and, thanks to staying clear of injuries, his performance levels have been amazingly high.

'Ryan Giggs mystifies me. I just cannot fathom how he keeps going at such a creative level. His enthusiasm is one of the keys plus how he prepares himself. He is helped by his physique and the fact that he is not inclined to put on weight. Age catches us all in the end and it's horrible when you have to give up the game, but there is no sign of a finishing line for the likes of Giggs and Scholes. Naturally I monitor them and, as winter closes in, I shall give them breaks to make sure they stay on top of their game physically so that they can continue to play their part in what we hope will be another great season.'

It was the old guard to the fore again when United turned to the Champions League, with Giggs scoring his 150th United goal on the way to a 2–1 win over Wolfsburg at Old Trafford. After the match the media wanted more words of praise for the man who was playing with all the youthful enthusiasm and enjoyment of someone just starting out on his career and finding everything so exciting, but Ferguson was stumped.

'Honestly I have used them all! The big thing, though, is that however much we laud him, it never goes to his head, and I am sure his after-match thoughts were that Wednesday night saw us take another big step towards going through to the next stage of Europe,' he said.

United had been making good progress in the Champions League towards qualifying from their group for the knockout round, but that did not stop one media man questioning the form of the team. United had just beaten Wolfsburg at Old Trafford and at the press conference afterwards it was put to Sir Alex that United had now won eight successive games but were still not firing on all cylinders. Ferguson was quiet for a moment and then asked him what would make him happy. 'What do you want … blood?' he said.

Later he went on to explain: 'We had been on a terrific run. We had won well at Tottenham when Harry Redknapp said that our football had been unbelievable. Our second half against Manchester City had been tremendous and we could have had six or seven goals. We had been to Stoke and gained a significant win with nearly 70 per cent of play, with Paul Scholes in vintage form. We had navigated a tricky game in Turkey with a win against Besiktas that set us off in fine style in our Champions League group.

'That night at Old Trafford we had just beaten the German champions from Wolfsburg. I do scratch my head at times at people's expectations. Of course there are areas where we can improve, but I feel it is an insult to the rest of football to expect us to run rings round the opposition every time we go out on to the pitch. Our rivals have their own ambitions and nobody in the Premiership is a bad team,' he added.

November brought a significant defeat that was to prove a real setback to their title ambitions. The Reds lost 1–0 at Chelsea and left the manager complaining about the way his men were failing to take their chances. He felt his team should have killed off Chelsea in the first half but didn't, and then lost out through a John Terry goal from a controversial free kick. This was becoming a pattern, and true to his managerial instinct Ferguson moved quickly to improve matters.

He said at the time: 'I am as frustrated as doubtless are our supporters and we are working on the problem. Whether the players feel that they make so many opportunities in the game that they can afford to wait, like missing a bus, but not to worry because there will be another along in a minute, I'm not sure. Patience is a virtue and I have often praised the team, especially in Europe, for their ability to keep plugging away without panicking or losing their quality football. We scored five at Wigan, three at Spurs and four against Manchester City, so it can be done, but that was relatively early in the season and somewhere along the way we have lost the urgency to stamp an early authority on a game in terms of scoring.'

Typically he got the reaction he was looking for, and though at one point United had fallen five points behind Chelsea, and there were defeats against Aston Villa and Fulham, others were faltering, too, and the Reds narrowed the gap to two points to finish 2009 on a challenging note, with Wayne Rooney looking in especially good form, leading the attack.

January was a busy month, with United losing the first leg of their Carling Cup semi-final 2–1 against Manchester City at Eastlands but storming back at Old Trafford a week later with a 3–1 win that took them through to meet Aston Villa in the final, a match they won 2–1 with goals from Rooney and Owen.

Rooney was beginning to score as freely as Ronaldo had and he bagged all four goals in a 4–0 win against Hull City. Rooney was on the scoresheet again at the Emirates against Arsenal, a result that raised hopes that the Reds were title material after all. It was the scoring form of Rooney that was taking the eye, as Ferguson acknowledged when he said: 'Wayne Rooney has been the player capturing the imagination of the headline writers, and rightly so because he has been in devastating form, especially near goal, though I think he would be the first to point out that to a certain extent he is only as good as those around him.

'Take out Rooney and his goals and I find it has been hard to pick out a man of the match, so high has been the level throughout the team, and I think some of the pundits have found it so difficult that they have come up with some crazy marking. I saw that Paul Scholes had been given a six. That really bemused me, because the man who sells dummies to opponents with his eyes has been in compelling mood. He was giving Arsenal the look and sending them all ways to remind me of a game some time ago against Spurs when he looked to head a ball down the line only to let it hit the side of his head and bounce back to Ryan Giggs. All the Tottenham players were heading in the wrong direction and it was so outrageously cheeky that Ryan burst out laughing. Those two continue to confound with the way they defy their ages, so much so that I am no longer thinking that the years are an issue.

'The beauty of the team's recent performances is that it has been a real team effort, with Nani outstanding and the defence finding their feet despite the continued absence of Rio Ferdinand and Nemanja Vidic.

Darren Fletcher battles with Emile Heskey during the 2010 Carling Cup final against Aston Villa.

Dressing-room celebrations as United keep their grip on the Carling Cup for a second year in succession.

Jonny Evans and Wes Brown have come together brilliantly, with Wes particularly deserving full marks for the way he got through at Arsenal despite being ill both before the game and at half time.'

Sir Alex and his players were in good heart and feeling good for Europe when the Champions League reopened for the first knockout round with a tough tie against AC Milan. Their confidence showed when they went to the San Siro and came home with a 3–2 win – including two goals by Rooney – before winning 4–0 at Old Trafford, with Rooney again in sizzling form near goal to score twice.

Sir Alex was purring with satisfaction after the game in Milan and delivered this admiring appraisal of Wayne Rooney: 'I think everyone wondered how quickly we would be able to replace Cristiano Ronaldo following the Portuguese international's move to Real Madrid during the summer. My biggest personal concern was not so much missing the delight of watching him play, but how we were going to maintain the scoring level. Cristiano was not just a specialist with a penchant for scoring from free kicks, but a player with a deadly strike from open play.

'Obviously, I looked at the players available in the transfer market, but I didn't think there was anyone who could help us at anything like a reasonable price and I was certainly not prepared to pay a ridiculous fee because that is not the way to run a football club, or at least it isn't in my eyes. I didn't panic, though, because as I repeatedly stress, I have a great squad giving me several options, plus a number of youngsters on the brink of making that final jump to Premiership level.

'I also had a sneaking suspicion that Wayne Rooney was close to the point of taking a vital step forward in his own career and so it has proved. Ever since we got him, he has performed well, but this season has seen him make dramatic progress to a new level. This was certainly in evidence when we pulled off a remarkable 3–2 win in the San Siro in the first leg of our knockout round against AC Milan. The hallmark of a truly great player is the ability to grab a game by the scruff of the neck when play is deadlocked and it needs something special if there is to be a winner.

'Never was this better underlined when we were 1–1 after coming through a torrid time following the shock of the Italians scoring a deflected goal after only three minutes. Wayne waded into the match to score twice and take his season's total to 25, and leave him perfectly placed the break the 30 mark this season.

'So there you have the answer to the hole left by Cristiano Ronaldo, a player who has not only improved his scoring rate, but who has seemed to

Wayne Rooney scores United's first goal in the second leg of the Champions League tie against AC Milan. Across the two games, he scored four goals to leave the Italian defence in tatters and Sir Alex ecstatic.

have added even more pace to his game, certainly in the way he is running at opponents now. He is terrifying them with the kind of form that is fast putting him up there alongside world greats like Ronaldo, Messi and Kaka.

'Confidence has been the key to his development surge, especially in accepting his tactical role. Rooney in the past has been a bit reluctant to operate in the forward position you now see him in; his youthful enthusiasm to be on the ball all the time took him all over the pitch. You have to admire a top work ethic, but this season has seen him playing with a new maturity in keeping with the growing responsibilities he has taken on in his life away from football. If he continues to improve at his present rate, he will be the complete player ready to join the distinguished band of Manchester United legends,' he said.

So all was going well for the Reds on all fronts, through to the quarter-finals of the Champions League to meet their old rivals Bayern Munich while blasting through March with a string of wins in the league to take 12 points from 12 and sit at the top of the table two points in front of Chelsea and Arsenal.

Then United ran into trouble, and all the wit and wiles of Sir Alex Ferguson couldn't get his team through April without damage. The first hiccup arrived with a 2–1 defeat in Munich, though the manager remained optimistic for the return leg given his club's good form at Old Trafford. Worse was to come, though, because four days later United lost 2–1 to Chelsea at Old Trafford, a defeat that virtually decided the destination of the title.

Later, Ferguson would say that they lost that season's title in the first half against Chelsea because there were too many tired legs from the Bayern game. It confirmed his view that European trips take a lot out of the players involved and that it had become essential to vary his team selections to keep them fresh.

Ferguson has always been one step ahead of the pack in tuning in to the requirements of today's game and it appeared that he finally resolved that he would gamble with his line-ups if necessary in order to achieve his objectives. It's this kind of perception that has helped him achieve so much.

When he first started rotating his squad in the Carling Cup some years ago, he was widely lambasted at times for not picking his strongest possible sides, but Ferguson is not a man to be deflected when he thinks he is right, and the number of trophies he has won tells you he is right more often than he is wrong; indeed, most other managers don't hesitate these days to make full use of their squads in preparation for important fixtures.

Ferguson pioneered the trend; what Ferguson thinks today the rest think tomorrow!

Four days after the Chelsea blow, United went into the second leg against Bayern Munich playing catch-up. They had Rafael sent off for two yellow cards and lost Wayne Rooney after aggravating his damaged ankle, but they still managed a 3–2 win, with two goals from Nani and one from Darron Gibson. It was a brave effort but not quite good enough and they went out on the away-goal rule.

Back in the Premiership, United were running out of games in their efforts to close the gap on Chelsea. They could only draw 0–0 at Blackburn and they went into the final game of the season dependent on Chelsea slipping up. They didn't, and indeed the Londoners slaughtered Wigan 8–0. United beat Stoke 4–0 at Old Trafford, but it still meant that Chelsea had taken United's title by one point in a nail-biting finish to the season. Always graceful in defeat, another Ferguson quality, Sir Alex told the United faithful to banish the doom and gloom.

He said: 'Yes, I know you must have been disappointed as you watched the Premiership title that we have proudly held at Old Trafford for the last three years disappear over the horizon. Yes, I know it would have been a truly great achievement if we had been able to hold off Chelsea for a record fourth successive championship. And I can assure you, our loyal supporters, that on the management and playing side of the club we felt just as devastated as you.

'It's inevitable that we all feel this way, but now as hopefully the wrench of losing our hold on that coveted league trophy fades a little, and the immediate emotional reaction dies down, can I ask you to put on more rational heads and make a realistic assessment of last season.

'As manager, it is my job to cut through the emotion and disappointment to reach honest conclusions on which to base our planning and strategy for the future. I have to analyse what went wrong and what we got right. I must focus on getting everything into perspective so that we can make the right decisions going forward. Naturally I must not fall into the trap of making excuses for any shortcomings, nor must I start to blame bad luck, or even referees. But neither must I panic and rip everything apart, because that would be counter-productive.

'It's all about getting everything into perspective, and now that we have put our regrets behind us I have got to say that I honestly believe we had a pretty decent season last year. We did win one trophy, the Carling Cup, and we did finish second in the league, just one point behind the winners, which isn't really too bad. But there is a lot more to it than that; we have to look below the surface and what I find is encouraging. Overall, there were an awful lot of positives that prompt me to proceed with caution rather than tear everything down.

'I am not being complacent when I say that I am happy with my squad and that spared some of the injury blows we experienced last season that we are more than capable of competing with the best that the Premiership can offer. For instance, we scored more goals this last season than we did the previous year when we won the championship – and this was despite losing Cristiano Ronaldo, the best player in the world.

'I always knew we would miss not only his goals but also the general mayhem he caused in opposing defences, so the fact that Wayne Rooney stepped up to the plate so dramatically was very much a positive. Wayne had a fantastic season to sweep the board with Player of the Year awards from both the PFA and football writers, as well as winning the top-man vote from both the United fans and his team-mates, plus collecting a trophy for United's goal of the season.

'Then there was the achievement of the defence, with the best record in the Premiership, and what's more, achieved despite the loss for lengthy periods of both Rio Ferdinand and Nemanja Vidic. We undoubtedly suffered from a lack of stability that comes from having a settled central defence, and it speaks volumes for the young players who replaced them that we were able to maintain such a mean defensive record. At one point we had Darren Fletcher and Michael Carrick as our centre-backs and they didn't let us down. Jonny Evans, Wes Brown and John O'Shea did well and to come through to finish runners-up in the league was in my book a magnificent effort.

'Our undoing was that black week when we lost at home against Chelsea in the league and then couldn't raise ourselves four days later to go out of the Champions League against Bayern Munich at Old Trafford. We were still under par when we could only draw at Blackburn in the next Premiership match and it proved a costly setback. We lost a few other games that we didn't expect to lose, but I put some of those defeats down to more competitive nature of our league these days. It's a tough competition, quite unforgiving, every team is capable of beating the best.

'We can agonise about things but it doesn't do you any good. At the end of the day we finished a point behind Chelsea and I congratulate them. My message is to stand back, swallow the disappointment and come back next season with high hopes because I am planning to make it a good one!'

25

THE GREATEST
AND CLEARLY SIR ALEX
WAS NOT KIDDING!

THE INDOMITABLE Reds' manager promptly proceeded to steer his team to the Premiership in 2010-11 to give United a record 19th league title, as well as taking them to Wembley for their third Champions League final in four years.

The Premiership success gave Ferguson not only a personal 12th Premiership medal, but the immense satisfaction of finally overhauling Liverpool's title tally and clearly establishing Manchester United as the premier club in the country.

United were decisively beaten by Barcelona in the Champions League showdown, but domestically there is no argument about the way he has taken Manchester United to the top of the tree. Breaking the Liverpool league record was significant, because when he first became United's manager 25 years ago, he knew that his first task, as he graphically put it at the time, was to knock the dominant Liverpool club off their perch.

In fact, he did that some years ago, but here was the clinching argument and though he didn't crow about it, because that is not his style, he couldn't resist saying: 'It was Liverpool's time in the 80s, it's our time now!' There was certainly much rejoicing among the fans.

Europe remains the big challenge, because Ferguson has long felt that United over the years have underperformed in European competition, given the club's domestic achievements, their financial resources and support.

The last few years have seen him devoting much more thought to European tactics and educating his players to the style of play necessary for success on the continent.

Although it would be an exaggeration to say Europe had become an obsession, it's undoubtedly a challenge that plays a part in his refusal to opt for an easier life. In any case, he enjoys his job too much to walk away, and as long as he continues in good health, we can forget about his retirement. He knows that all the big guns will be after him in the league again in 2011-12, with Chelsea, Arsenal, Manchester City and perhaps Liverpool, leading the way with more money than ever before sloshing about in the transfer market.

The big debate for United followers and the critics after the latest Premiership win, once the euphoric cheers had died down, was to examine the merit of his team and assess the worth of niggling criticism that they had played without the flair of some of his previous sides. Some reckoned that United hadn't played 'fantasy football', and that they had fallen short of being a vintage side, a view advanced by Didier Deschamps before United played his Marseilles side in France in the February knockout round.

The United manager was irked by the sniping and vigorously defended the new champions: 'We are an easy target for the media and all I can say is that all teams are different, the game evolves and at the end of the day we proved to be the best team of the season.

'Winning this last championship is special because it means we have won the title more than anyone in the country. It's history and great for the tradition of the club. The players were great and I think they deserved it because there were a lot of outstanding performances. We had the best home record in my time as manager at Old Trafford and we scored more goals. We beat Chelsea four times, our nearest rivals, and we recorded the highest-ever score in the semi-finals of the Champions League. We didn't concede an away goal in Europe until we got to the final, and some of the football we played at Old Trafford during the season was out of this world. We must have been doing something right!'

United certainly finished clear winners in the title race. Arsenal failed to last the pace and while Chelsea revived, after breaking down in mid-season, to come storming up on the last lap, United took the title off them with a 1–1 draw at Blackburn with a game to spare.

The season finished with the Reds on 80 points, nine in front of Chelsea and Manchester City, with Arsenal 12 points behind. The issue wasn't

Wayne Rooney and Sir Alex Ferguson in training in autumn 2010 after the player's surprise transfer request was resolved.

Javier Hernandez heads home an extraordinary goal at Stoke City on 24 October. The Mexican, signed for a bargain £6 million, scored an impressive 20 goals in his first season with United.

always so clear-cut, of course, and there were a number of problems to over-come. Their poor form, relatively speaking, away from home showed up early, with draws at Fulham, Everton, Bolton and Sunderland before winning at Stoke.

The manager warned his players about the need for concentration, but the stutters on their travels were nothing compared to the bombshell dropped by Wayne Rooney in the early weeks of the season when he asked for a transfer. It was the last thing Ferguson expected and the manner of it put manager and player on a collision course, so much so that many critics argued that Rooney would be shipped out before you could say Player of the Year.

But Ferguson hasn't won 12 league titles and made Manchester United the most successful club in the country by acting out of pique. His handling of the situation was a masterclass in brilliant management, because basically he saw Rooney as capable of bringing a lot more outstanding football to the table. So he played it softly-softly, and simply talked the player into withdrawing his transfer request.

Rooney had not been showing the same electric form of the previous season when he collected just about every personal award on offer. Ferguson's reaction was to send him to the Nike Boot camp at the sports company's headquarters in Portland, Oregon, to remove him from the firing line and give him time to think.

The player had upset a lot of fans, especially after press speculation that he might join Manchester City, and some went to his Cheshire home to protest. His time away seemed to bring a new perspective to matters. Later in the season, Rooney would admit his behaviour had been a big mistake, but for the time being, Ferguson slowly but surely concentrated on making sure United got the best out of him. The United manager is brilliant in this kind of situation, handling people in their moments of crisis like a super dad. He had done it with Eric Cantona, after his 'kung-fu' incident, and on many other occasions.

The immediate crisis following Rooney's transfer request was also helped by Dimitar Berbatov, who chose this moment to deliver the kind of football his talents always suggested he was capable of, but who some fans felt hadn't always delivered, because of the Bulgarian's somewhat languid style. Sir Alex had no doubts about his ability, and he had indeed turned down the chance to buy another top player who operated in a similar position, such was his confidence in his striker.

Again it proved to be great man management, because Berbatov simply picked up the Rooney baton and ran with it, to finish the season as the joint highest scorer in the Premiership (with Carlos Tevez) on 20 goals. Crucially, he upped his game when Rooney was injured and before Javier Hernandez had had the chance to get used to life in the Premier League, though the Mexican would go on to strike a tremendously exciting partnership with Rooney that delivered the title in the closing stages of the season.

Ferguson of course was delighted, and after Berbatov had scored five against Blackburn in November to put United on top of the table said: 'It was a timely display that saw us go to the top of the Premier table on the back of the 7–1 win against Blackburn, as our immediate rivals struggled. We have been looking for that kind of rhythm for some weeks, after winning games without turning on the Christmas lights. Dimitar was top of the tree, of course, and I hope he has finally won over the doubters and will find the confidence now to continue to express himself so beautifully.'

Ferguson said United fans should stop worrying about Rooney's failure to capture the previous season's grandiose scoring form and instead revel in the way Berbatov was plundering the goals. A superb hat-trick against Birmingham City and then two against Blackpool in midweek took the Bulgarian's tally to 19 and the manager said: 'Some people are making a meal out of the fact that Wayne Rooney is lagging behind in the goal stakes, and he is, compared with the bucket load he scored last year, but I am not worried.

'It's the scoring partnership that matters and the combination between our two front men has improved beyond all recognition. Last season, Wayne benefited from Dimitar's work, but this year it is Berbatov who is enjoying the last touch. If we finish the season with Berbatov scoring 30 goals and Wayne on say 10 – and those are the targets I have in mind – I will be more than happy. That's what I call a successful strike partnership reminiscent of Andy Cole and Dwight Yorke, and you know what we won when they were hot!

'If I had signed the player we were considering at the start of the season, it would have meant sidelining Berbatov and I wasn't prepared to do that. I determined instead to try to re-energise our man,' he explained. It's testament once again to the manager's judgement and keeping faith in a player.

But even with the Bulgarian international on such good form, the season was far from smooth sailing with what Ferguson described in March as a nightmare spell of two defeats in five days. He said: 'I have no excuses for the poor performance at Liverpool, who were the better team and deserved their win. I was disappointed because we didn't perform to the level I expect

Dimitar Berbatov scores his fifth goal in United's 7–1 mauling of Blackburn Rovers on 27 November 2010 as United continued their unbeaten start to the Premier League campaign.

and which to be fair we generally achieve.

'I certainly reckoned Jamie Carragher deserved to be sent off for his tackle on Nani, and playing against ten men might have helped us. The injury to Nani was a bad one. The gash down his shin was through to the bone and so wide that at first, at any rate, it was impossible to close it with stitches. Nani's absence is a loss, because the boy has had a great season with his crossing, scoring and readiness to open up the opposition.

'The defeat against Chelsea was quite different, and I felt aggrieved, as you might have judged from the comments I made about the refereeing which put me in trouble. I felt sorry for the players because they had taken the game to their opponents and had performed well, only to be undone by the decisions that went against them. And then when I said as much, I faced a charge from the Football Association for what to my mind was simply telling the truth.

'I was disappointed with Graham Taylor, who wrote that I had to take the rough with the smooth, and I think back to when he was England manager and was screaming at a linesman: "You have cost me my job."

'People have short memories. Kenny Dalglish was lecturing me in the papers about the need to respect the referees and that we are all always subject to bad decisions, neatly overlooking the way one of his players had dressed Howard Webb up in a Manchester United shirt not so long ago!'

Sir Alex doesn't win all his battles with the Football Association, who duly fined him and banned him from the touchline for five matches. United were in irrepressible mood though, and one of the reasons was the emergence of Javier Hernandez, or 'Chicharito', which translates as 'Little Pea', the name he wears on the back of his shirt.

Ferguson noted the player's unexpected early impact – he was supposed to be one for development – with the verdict: 'We have always had great players and I am happy to say that it looks as if we have the makings of another fine performer in our midst. I am referring of course to Javier Hernandez, our young Mexican, who has wasted no time showing he knows the way to goal. From his early effort in the Community Shield against Chelsea at Wembley, he has made the most of his time in the team culminating with his two at Stoke that could prove a pivotal moment for us.

'We always knew he had a great scoring instinct, but the way he screwed his body round for his header against Stoke was truly remarkable. Hardly a textbook goal, but exceptionally athletic. People ask me how we came to find the boy hidden away in junior football in Mexico. The answer is that our scout in that part of the world tipped us off, with the result that our

Sir Alex Ferguson bows down to the United faithful after the Reds have seen off Chelsea on 8 May to leave them on the verge of a record 19th title.

chief scout Jim Lawlor spent a month in Mexico at the beginning of the year watching all his games and making the kind of inquiries you need to ask. We did things properly, speaking to the club before the player, with the result that they played it very honourably too and didn't tell anyone of our interest.'

The signing was another masterstroke by the manager and was widely regarded as the bargain signing of the year at £6 million. Hernandez finished the season voted by the fans as their Player of the Year, and there is no doubt that he was a pivotal figure during the closing weeks of the season. It wasn't just his own contribution as a goalscorer – 20 goals in his first season is impressive – but the way Ferguson was able to use him in a tactical switch that was a winner. Chicharito became the front man, with Rooney operating just behind him, rather like an old-fashioned inside forward, and it worked a treat. The Mexican, though not a particularly big man, slipped easily into the role, while Rooney found a new lease of life, and admitted he had never been happier.

Rooney, who won the fans' vote for Goal of the Year with his spectacular overhead kick in the 2–1 win against Manchester City at Old Trafford in February, confessed to what he admitted had been a huge mistake when he was agitating for a move at the start of the season. 'When I look at it now, how wrong was I? It was a long time ago now and hopefully I am now helping the team to be successful,' he admitted.

Ferguson wrote in the match programme at the time: 'The way the whole club has stuck together through the trials and tribulations impressed me. The players tend to be cocooned in their own little football world, and it's only when something like the Wayne Rooney saga explodes that they can judge the enormity of this club. Interest flooded in from all over the world, but they kept their heads down and if anything they were galvanised by events to come up with a good spell.'

Sir Alex confessed to being surprised when he discovered he had overtaken Sir Matt Busby to become the longest-serving manager in the club's history. 'I am particularly blessed to be the manager of this great club. In my mind, Sir Matt was seemingly at Old Trafford for ever. He had brought the club back to life, guided them through the difficult post-war days, launched the Busby Babes and then suffered the tragedy of the Munich air crash. He had to start all over again and remarkably created another super side that went on to win the European Cup. So much drama and success, so many outstanding players, I never thought for a moment that I would be here long enough to match Sir Matt's incredible journey and I am just proud to stand alongside the great man's achievements.'

Maybe Sir Alex felt inspired as his team picked up speed to raise the possibility of capturing another treble of Champions League, FA Cup and Premier League, but a one-goal defeat at Wembley in the semi-final of the FA Cup against Manchester City in April put paid to that dream, and the following month defeat in the Champions League final emphasised just how difficult such an achievement is.

Nevertheless, United pulled off some notable successes in the closing weeks, not least in a league shoot-out against their nearest rivals Chelsea, after being drawn against the Londoners in the quarter-finals of the Champions League. United won all three, decisive results that probably triggered Chelsea into sacking Carlo Ancelotti at the end of the season, as well as delivering a mortal Premiership blow to the Stamford Bridge club.

This is how Sir Alex saw it: 'We have hit top form. It's a really good moment for us and the players are enjoying it. They are relishing the challenges they have got now. You can see the momentum and it's a great thing, with everyone desperate to play.'

The United manager was in good mood as a blitz of injuries cleared and he prepared for the Champions League quarter-finals against Chelsea. United had won the first leg in London 1–0 through a Rooney goal, but a lot of fans feared a backlash at Old Trafford. Their worries proved groundless as the Reds turned in a convincing performance highlighted by two assists from Ryan Giggs that brought goals for Chicharito and Ji-sung Park in a 2–1 win.

United moved further forward on the European trail by beating Schalke in the semi-finals 2–0 away and 4–1 at Old Trafford to go through to the Wembley final.

But the real powerhouse performance on the last lap came when they met Chelsea in the Premier League at Old Trafford for what amounted to a title shoot-out. The Reds played high-octane football that saw Ji-sung Park send Chicharito through to score after only 36 seconds.

Park was inspired, harrying the visitors to give them no rest on the ball and it was not long before Ryan Giggs put in a cross for Nemanja Vidic to head home a second goal.

Chelsea hit back in the second half when Frank Lampard pulled back a goal, but United still created chances and thoroughly deserved their 2–1 win.

As Fergie put it: 'We blitzed Chelsea in that game. I know a lot of people felt that, after beating them twice in the two legs of the Champions League, fate might have evened things up and let Chelsea back into the picture. We were conscious of this factor and we knew we had to go for it, which I think

Rio Ferdinand and Nemanja Vidic leave the pitch at Ewood Park after United had secured the 2010-11 Premier League – the pair had been at the heart of the Reds' defence in winning four titles.

The Old Trafford crowd says it all. When Alex Ferguson arrived in 1986, the total of titles was just seven.

we did, scoring two great goals.'

It was the key moment and left United looking for one point from the final two games to give them their 19th title. It came at Blackburn a week later with a penalty from Rooney and history was made. The last league game of the season, at home to Blackpool, saw team changes but United still managed a crushing 4–2 win that included a goal from Michael Owen, much to the manager's delight, because he had admitted earlier in the season that he had often felt guilty leaving him out of the team.

The season at Old Trafford wound up with a testimonial match for Gary Neville against Juventus in tribute to the player's long and distinguished involvement at the club. Gary left to join Sky as a pundit, but with an invitation from Ferguson to join his coaching staff and act as an ambassador.

Sir Alex enjoyed seeing the return of Neville's old team-mates, including Ryan Giggs, Nicky Butt, David Beckham, Phil Neville and Paul Scholes, to play in the testimonial and reprise their FA Youth Cup success of 1992 that triggered so much for Manchester United. By happy coincidence, United's current youngsters had won the FA Youth Cup by beating Sheffield United the night before to suggest that the club's youth policy is still producing quality goods.

Then, at the end of the week, it was off to Wembley and the disappointment of losing to Barcelona in the final of the Champions League, but as Sir Alex pointed out: 'I had no hesitation seeking out Pep Guardiola at the end to congratulate him and his team on a brilliant performance. Barcelona are a fine team at their peak and any lover of football has got to acknowledge that they are the outstanding team around, certainly the best I have seen in my time as a manager. They are at a tremendous peak in their cycle of development.

'It was a final to grace the game, played in the right spirit and I think we also contributed. I think we can take good memories from the way we faced up to them and our reply to their opening goal with an equaliser so well taken by Wayne Rooney prompted by Ryan Giggs.

'We stuck at it, we didn't give up, we stayed cool in face of some fantastic football and I am proud of our players. They didn't let us down. They did their best; on the night it wasn't quite good enough to win, but that's how it is in football. It was never meant to be easy or predictable, and we have to remember that the Champions League final is the pinnacle of the game.'

So all in all it had been yet another highly successful season, and Sir Alex had indeed delivered on his promise to make it special. He was hard at work during the summer months to strengthen the squad, following the retirements of Gary Neville, Paul Scholes and of course Edwin van der Sar. He signed the Spanish Under-21 international goalkeeper David De Gea, for a reported £17 million from Atletico Madrid, winger and forward Ashley Young for an estimated £15 million from Aston Villa, and Phil Jones, the England Under-21 and Blackburn centre-half for approximately £16.5 million.

There were press reports suggesting United were also interested in one or two other players. As Sir Alex says: 'There's a responsibility as manager of Manchester United that doesn't go away and means that you have to carry on winning. Just because we won a record championship doesn't mean I can now take it easy. We have to carry on, there's nothing else you can do. We have a responsibility and expectation to live up to and that carries on the next season. As I have always said, Manchester United should accept a challenge. We are in fact good at that and next season we'll accept anything that comes our way.'

And of course, it is that readiness for the challenge and the insatiable pursuit of success that on top of all his managerial accomplishments have marked out Sir Alex Ferguson as the greatest manager of all time. We shouldn't be surprised that Graham Stringer, supported by another Mancunian Labour MP, Tony Lloyd, tabled an early-day motion suggesting that the Manchester United manager should be given a peerage… Lord Ferguson!

26

SIR ALEX CELEBRATES
25 YEARS

THE LEAGUE MANAGERS' ASSOCIATION threw a celebratory lunch for Sir Alex Ferguson in February 2011, to mark his long service and achievements in football.

His management colleagues and rivals turned out in force to honour his remarkable career at an elegant meal at the Grosvenor House Hotel in Park Lane, London.

Sir Alex has been in charge of more than 2,000 matches as a football manager, an immense achievement in itself in this day and age of hire and fire, irrespective of the number of trophies he has won along the way. Not that the Manchester United manager has been totting up the games himself – he is far too busy calculating how to win the next one – but it has not escaped the attention of his fellow managers who, despite their constant rivalries, were united in their appreciation of a remarkable career that saw him manage East Stirlingshire for 17 matches, St Mirren 169, Aberdeen 459, Scotland 10 and of course Manchester United, which at the end of the 2010-11 season stood at 1392, and still counting as the 69-year-old long-serving boss continues to defy time.

The LMA had also worked out that he had won 49 European, League and Cup titles, which, as someone pointed out, was probably more than the collective total of the rest of the managers in the room, and there were a lot of them, including England boss Fabio Capello and then-Chelsea chief Carlo Ancelotti.

His old Scottish colleagues, such as Walter Smith, Craig Brown and

Archie Knox, were there, along with former Manchester United striker and then-Fulham boss, Mark Hughes, while his unique treble-winning goalkeeper Peter Schmeichel flew in from Copenhagen to make a personal contribution.

Alex McLeish, once his defensive kingpin at Aberdeen, whose Birmingham City team of mixed fortunes – Carling Cup winners but eventually relegated – had just been beaten 5–0 by United was there and said: 'Sir Alex welcomed me very warmly in his match programme and said nice things about me and my family in his notes and then battered my team.'

McLeish might well have added … but then that's Alex Ferguson, whose competitive qualities were well outlined in the keynote speech and toast proposed by sports writer Hugh McIlvanney, his collaborator in the definitive Ferguson autobiography.

Richard Bevan, chief executive of the LMA, welcomed guests, including Sir Alex's three sons, Mark, Jason and Darren, while chairman Howard Wilkinson outlined the formation of the Association in 1992 and paid tribute to Sir Alex as a staunch supporter of its objectives.

MIKE PHELAN: WORKED FOR FERGIE MAN AND BOY

THE ASSISTANT MANAGER of Manchester United has played for him, he has coached for him and now he serves as his right-hand man. Few in football have been as close to him nor know him better across the 25 years of his time as manager at Old Trafford.

A lot has changed in that quarter century, but he says Sir Alex has kept pace and his principles have stood the test of time.

'Sir Alex signed me from Norwich, along with two or three players from other clubs, because he wanted to change the dynamic of his group of Manchester United players. I had been the captain at Norwich and I think he was on the lookout at that time for straightforward, honest players who were tactically aware and I guess he thought I fitted the bill.

'Looking at him from my position as a player, he immediately struck me as obviously a manager of experience with great knowledge of the game. He was an aggressive coach, but he didn't scare me because you knew the boundaries, which you had the sense not to cross, and he had my respect.

'He taught you discipline and how to conduct yourself, and at the same time he supported you and treated you well, as long as you produced for him with your work. Training was intense, but at the same time relaxing, which you needed because of the big games Manchester United were always involved in.

'I soon felt that this was a place where I could play, which was a remarkable transformation for me, coming from a small club like Norwich to the biggest. The two clubs were polar opposites, one laid back, the other so ambitious, but making you comfortable in new vastly different surroundings, was part of his great man-management skills.

'I enjoyed it as a player at Old Trafford. I liked the manager's honesty, helpful but demanding. He always made it clear what he expected and he helped you grow up. His style was like a blueprint for good management. Eventually my time as a player had run its course and the manager wanted to change the dynamics of the group again, with the introduction of youngsters like Gary Neville, Ryan Giggs, Paul Scholes, David Beckham, Nicky Butt and company, the so-called class of '92 who had won the FA Youth Cup.

'He told me just before the last game of the season on the training ground that he would be letting me go. I was more angry than disappointed, because of course I wanted more of what I had been enjoying so much. You cannot stop a football club evolving, though, and Alex Ferguson was always one step ahead in his thinking, another of his qualities as a manager.

'He made it clear I had played my part and so on I went, playing at West Bromwich and Norwich again before three and a half years in coaching. When I had left Old Trafford, he had given no indication that one day he might bring me back in a coaching capacity. We didn't keep in touch, but looking back, I feel he must have followed my progress, because when I was at Stockport and Gary Megson was sacked as the manager, he invited me to Old Trafford for a chat. Of course I went, and came away with a job as United's reserve team coach.

'I then saw him through the eyes of one of his staff rather than as a player and I have got to say he is just as brilliant managing his staff as he is managing players. I worked for him over a long period in various capacities, alongside people like Steve McClaren, Jimmy Ryan, Brian Kidd and Carlos Queiroz.

'He seemed to have become more relaxed, but perhaps that was because I was a staff man rather than player. His style was still the same, though. He knew what he wanted and just as he insisted that a player had to play, so a coach had to coach. He wanted you to challenge the players. He always used to say bring something to the table that challenges them every day. He would discuss things with you to drive home what he wanted, but once that was out of the way he wouldn't interfere.

'I found it a very refreshing way to work, but he was good at that … managing people. His background before full-time football probably helped there. His experience of handling people with his trade-union work stood him in good stead and instilled things in him. He has high values and is honest with you, while of course expecting honesty in return, but if you

Mike Phelan, Sir Alex and Rene Meulensteen plan their strategy during the summer tour of North America, 2011.

Gary Neville, Gary Pallister, Sir Alex and Mike Phelan share a joke at Carrington, May 2011.

do your work properly he is fine. He will always listen to your views and to your feelings.

'I would say one of his greatest achievements is that he has moved with the times, like bringing in staff of varying ages and embracing developments in football such as the introduction of sports science, nutrition, medical advances and psychology. None of those things existed at a football club when he started out, but he has shown a flexibility that belies his years. He has proved very adept at coordinating all these developments, picking out what is relevant and gathering up all the information. I think I can say he has good staff around him, which helps, but then he chose them.

'I would say he is an even better manager these days, because he has taken on board the fact that we live in changing times. For instance, he doesn't go looking for trouble these days. If it comes to him, he will sort it, but he no longer has to pick a fight to show who is boss because his success commands all the respect a manager needs. He also has a knack for picking out what's relevant.

'He is a better person as well as a manager nowadays, more relaxed, maybe because of the good staff around him. He has a few other interests and knows the place won't collapse if he is not there all the time. This is good because the intensity of the job is relentless.

'His mood swings are not as extreme. He is a lot more mellow, though he does still have his moments. Over the years not many players have answered him back, and of course his "hairdryer" treatment is legendary. Gary Pallister was never afraid to argue, though he didn't win often, because the manager was invariably right. He and Steve Bruce used to catch it at times, probably because they were the two main defenders and English, so he knew they would understand what he was saying.

'I remember him having a real go at Steve because of his habit of chesting the ball down in the penalty area with his arms instinctively closing in on the ball to risk conceding a penalty. He finally warned him that if he saw him do it once more he would bring him off and substitute him!

'We saw him at his hairdryer best one day when we were playing Real Madrid and he was in the middle of his team talk in front of the tactics board in the dressing room. Suddenly the door burst open, nearly knocking Alex off his feet, and in charged Albert, our kit man. He didn't see the manager and he went right across the room to David Beckham, demanding his car keys because Real Madrid couldn't get their bus parked. Now if there is one thing he doesn't like, it's being interrupted in full flow and Albert certainly got the hairdryer that day.

'But though he has become famous for his temper at times, he can be extraordinarily kind and thoughtful. I had played in every round of the League Cup in 1991, but he dropped me for the final against Sheffield Wednesday at Wembley. Neil Webb took my place and naturally I was devastated. Soon after the match, though, he sought me out and even admitted he had made a mistake. He apologised and told me not to worry because I would play in many more cup finals, and I didn't have long to wait, three weeks in fact, when I was in the team that won the European Cup-Winners' Cup against Barcelona in Rotterdam.

'Nevertheless, it was good to have his reassurance after Wembley, because I knew then that my future at United was OK and it was a nice personal touch that was just another aspect of his shrewd man-management technique. He is attentive to everything.

'When will he retire? I don't know because he doesn't give any sign of being tired of Manchester United despite all its ferocious demands and pressures. He is still driven and wants to produce winning teams. Although I said he has mellowed, he will still fight his corner. The focus is still there. There's still the same buzz about him. The intensity of the game has never been fiercer and yet he still relishes it after 25 years.

'Just look at the way the man has driven and led us to success this last season, taking us to the final of the Champions League against Barcelona at Wembley and of course making Manchester United the most successful club in the country with our record 19th League Championship. The fact that he has been the manager behind 12 of those title successes says it all. The man is untouchable!'

SAM ALLARDYCE: YOU WISH HE COULD BE YOUR MENTOR

THE EXPERIENCED Sam Allardyce makes no secret of his admiration for Sir Alex Ferguson, and says when he was manager of Bolton coming up against him was always the greatest challenge of all.

'There was always a welcome for us, and unlike some managers, he could take defeat with a bit of dignity, no doubt helped by the fact that he loses less than anybody else!

'I suppose I have followed his career in England from the start. I first became aware of him during my playing days with Coventry City and Sunderland when he was trying to make an impression at United. Because I have good mates in Bryan Robson and Steve Bruce in particular, I always had an insight into what he was like and how he was progressing the club from the very bottom and how he had got to grips with the job.

'Robbo and Brucie would tell me about what he did and how he drove the team on, the way he was insatiable in terms of his appetite to get the job done. His success was based on what he had done as a manager else-where, but initially that became difficult to put in place at Manchester United, then once he got everybody working his way he really turned it around.

'Then in the 80s I did my full coaching badge with Brian Kidd who was working with United's Centre of Excellence and that gave me an insight into how Fergie was pulling together all the best youngsters, something United had done in the Busby days but hadn't paid as much attention to in the years between. He made life difficult for everybody else when he decided he would

Sam Allardyce, a friendly rival on the touchline with Sir Alex in March 2007.

attract the best crop of young players in the British Isles, and from that we saw that come to fruition with that second batch of what they called "Fergie's Fledglings".

'That group of young players became the core and backbone to the club's success for the next 10 years: the Nevilles, Paul Scholes, Ryan Giggs, Nicky Butt, David Beckham, Keith Gillespie for a while. We had the time when 60 to 70 per cent of his side were the ones he had grown himself. That is why Manchester United became so successful.

'When you become a coach or a manager you look at people who would be your mentors, and when somebody achieves that much you hope you can get the opportunity to meet them and talk to them. I have been fortunate to do that via the League Managers' Association. He is a staunch member and a real driving force behind the rights of managers and how they should and should not be treated. It appears that every area he feels strongly about he is 100 per cent committed to.

'I suppose I haven't really had a lot of dealings with him in terms of the ins and outs of football players, but when I was at Bolton we took Quinton Fortune on board. Before we did, Alex told me how good he was and how if we could keep him fit what a great player he would be and what a super character he is. Stuff like that gives you a true and honest assessment, and I appreciate that.

'Over the years my philosophy has always been to listen and to admire what he has done. I have always said that in modern-day football and for somebody in his time of life, he has managed always to keep up with the changes in the game. He is not old school. He is Alex Ferguson. He always makes sure that he keeps in touch with everything that might be or could be changing in the game, to make sure he stays up there with it or ahead of it, and I think that is the biggest compliment I can pay him.

'Many a manager I have worked under or seen come and go, has been great for a short period of time then has faded away. Instead of keeping up with the times, they have stuck to the way which brought their success and that can very quickly become outdated. Alex moves with the times. He picks up on all the changes and keeps a constant lookout for the different ways people work and have to change, and the game has moved on enormously that way in the last three or four years.

'As for the future, I think it is going to be up to Manchester United to decide when they feel it is time for him to stand down, because I can't see him doing that himself. I am sure he has no desire to pack in and as long as his health is okay who can blame him?'

GARY NEVILLE: YOU NEVER WANT TO LEAVE... EVEN SIR ALEX CHANGED HIS MIND

GARY NEVILLE retired abruptly midway through season 2010-11 after a long and trophy-packed career at Old Trafford, but won't be severing his connections, with coaching, media work and an ambassador role all possibilities for his future.

'Sir Alex has an aura about him and so he should, he is the manager of Manchester United. You listen to him, whether he is telling you something in a nice way or in an aggressive way, because he has been there and done it. Certainly, as a young player you were wary of him. When he walked into the room, everybody went quiet and I am sure it is the same for the kids now, but when you were at United for as long as me, you do recognise the personal side to him.

'I wouldn't say I am close to the Gaffer, but I knew full well I could go into his office and see him whenever I wanted. If someone is in trouble, that is the door you knock on. You might have something in your personal life and he will listen. That's where he wins respect.

'People looking in from the outside might think he has got performances out of his players through fear, but there is more to him than that. He has been a father figure while he has been at Old Trafford and I should imagine it was just the same when he was at Aberdeen. There are past players who are managers at other clubs now who regularly ask him for advice and he is always there to talk to.

Gary Neville celebrates with Sir Alex after United win the 2008 Champions League final.

Sir Alex Ferguson joins the guard of honour for Gary Neville's testimonial in May 2011.

'He is one of those people who will never heap lavish praise on you, but when he comes over and says: "Well done, son," – words which always follow a victory – that is the most important thing. You know you've won and football is about winning.

'He is certainly not one to dwell on sentiment and that is the one thing that has ensured his continued success over the last 25 years, changing the team continually. He almost sees the end for players before they see it themselves and 100 per cent of the time he has been proved correct. Over the years he has let some great players go, sometimes people have agreed with him, sometimes they haven't. There have been players who were considered irreplaceable, but time has proved they were not, because other footballers will always want to come to Manchester United and take on the mantle. When the Gaffer first came here, Norman Whiteside and Paul McGrath were heroes to United fans, but they left. He changed the culture of the club.

'Then he split up the 1994 team to allow untried youngsters to come through, something that was seen as a gamble. It wasn't just Paul Ince, Mark Hughes and Andrei Kanchelskis who went at that time, but other experienced squad players like Mike Phelan, Lee Martin, Clayton Blackmore, yet that side of kids who took over went on to win the "double-double". The manager had great faith in us.

'He had Paul Scholes and Nicky Butt to replace Paul Ince, David Beckham to replace Kanchelskis and me to replace Paul Parker. He showed incredible faith in us, a belief that we didn't even possess ourselves. We had always looked up to those players; we had learnt the ropes off them, we had travelled around Europe with them from about 1992-93, listened to his team talks, watched the players play and eventually they made way.

'He always said they would make way, because he thought we were good enough but at the time it was a huge call for him to make. There are times when you are young that you think you will never leave, but eventually people of my age group left, like Nicky Butt and Becks, and now me! You have to look upon it as a fantastic thing we survived that long.

'The problem is, you never want to leave Manchester United; it is the best club to play for, especially when you have grown up supporting it. Everything about the club is professional and even the Gaffer couldn't leave.

'We thought he was going to retire several years ago, but he surprised everybody by changing his mind. The main reason I was surprised was because he is usually very definite about what he does, but the nearer it got to the time, he was thinking that he couldn't live without this and it would have been the same for anybody in his position. It is a void you cannot fill, whether you leave this club as a player or a manager. It is impossible, losing that excitement, that thrill. Everybody who has ever left Old Trafford will tell you the same.

'This is a great football club full stop. Whether Alex Ferguson is here or not. What the Gaffer has done is take it to a level it should be at, winning championships and FA Cups and being involved in the Champions League, putting the club on to the biggest stage in the world. He will tell you himself that this is the minimum this club should achieve. It's disgraceful to think that this club did not win the league for 26 years, it's an embarrassment considering the resources that were available to the managers over the years.

'So he has now done 25 years in the job, and is still here, but why should he leave? He feels as determined as ever. It is a continual challenge to be at this club. I know that from being a player, I know that from being a fan. That will keep him young. There was a period when people were talking about him retiring but that has gone away. He knows the club, he knows how to make it successful, we have been developing a new side with a lot of young players coming into the squad and hopefully we can continue to bear the fruits of that.

'It would not surprise me if he was to go on for even five more years, but whoever takes over eventually will face a daunting task because there will be so many comparisons, possibly more from outside than from within.'

PAUL SCHOLES:
HE STILL SCARES ME

'IT DOESN'T seem 25 years since Sir Alex took over at Old Trafford and while I've been under him for a large part of that time, it seems to have gone quickly...well, my part has anyway!

'My first memories of him are seeing him around The Cliff when I was a young lad. He would always speak to you, encouraging you, but I remember being very nervous whenever I met him. There he was the manager of Manchester United and I was just one of the school kids, it was great he would take time out to speak to us, but I must confess I was frightened to death of him – and I still am!

'I suppose he has mellowed slightly, with age everyone does, but with him the players definitely come first. He would never slag anyone off in public. If he has got something to say, he will say it to you and it stays in the dressing room and that is how it should be. These days a lot of managers seem to have a go at their players publicly, but he has never done that and I am sure he never will. He knows how important players are and gives them his full support. He sticks up for us to the hilt, and is always behind you. He makes players feel wanted and I think that is important.

He does not bear grudges. If someone does something wrong and he is not happy about it, if you go to him and apologise there is always room to forgive. He protects you, but if something is not right and he is not happy with it, he will let you know about it, then once it is dealt with he forgets about it. That's a good thing because it keeps you on your toes. You know you have to perform or you will know about it.

Paul Scholes and Sir Alex in training ahead of the 2011 Champions League semi-final against Schalke.

'He looks forward rather than back and is also someone who will not rest on his laurels. He is always looking to improve and that is something which has never changed after all this time. Even when we won the treble, that quickly became something which had happened in the past. By the start of the next season, it had gone. You had won a European Cup but it didn't make any difference, he still wanted to win the next year. That is still the same today. What comes next is important, what has been done before doesn't really matter.

'People talk about the future and how long he will go on, but who knows? I don't think he is looking any older and I am sure he enjoys coming out on the training ground every day, even when it is freezing cold. He still loves it and it's going to be a while yet before he calls it a day.

'I have often been asked if I have any special memories about the Gaffer, anything which stands out during the 17 years I have been with the first team, but to be honest there isn't one in particular; just being involved with such a person and the things he has achieved and to have been a part of that has been fantastic.

'I can't imagine what this club will be like without him. Obviously one day that is going to happen, but I don't think it is going to be too soon. He has been fantastic for Manchester United and has made the club what it is today and when somebody else takes over they will have a big gap to fill.

'When my grandchildren ask me what Sir Alex was like, I will tell them he was a great man, someone who gave young lads a chance and made me what I am today, as well as doing the same for a lot of other younger players.'

David Gill, Eric Cantona, Paul Scholes, Sir Alex and Pelé line up ahead of the United No 18's testimonial on 5 August 2011.

STEVE MCCLAREN: I WILL ALWAYS BE IN HIS DEBT

STEVE MCCLAREN was United's coach when they won the treble in 1999 before leaving to manage Middlesbrough and subsequently England. He has not lost his admiration for his old boss and looks back fondly on his time at Old Trafford:

'I found my time as assistant manager at Manchester United both challenging and rewarding. It was a big jump moving from Derby County to Old Trafford, but one I had to take. I never really knew Alex before I went there and he didn't know me, but we had a two-hour meeting somewhere outside Sheffield, got on like a house on fire and we went from there.

'I agreed there and then to take the job, joined the team at the hotel and went the next day to Nottingham Forest, sat on the bench and watched them win 8–1. I was left wondering: "How can you improve on that?"

'Manchester United is a fantastic club and he is such a great person to work for, but he was always the boss, the man in charge, the one who made the decisions and the one who picked the team. That was always so, but I remember on my first day, going up to his office and asking him what kind of work he wanted during the training session, and he just said: "You're the coach, go out there and coach."

'That was the beauty of it. He very much left me to my own devices. That was him. The big word he used all the way through the time I worked with him was "trust". He trusted his players when they crossed the white line, he trusted me to coach and when you are given that trust and responsibility you appreciate it and it seems to get the best out of you.

Former England coach Steve McClaren and United manager Sir Alex discuss matters with two of their key players, Wayne Rooney and Rio Ferdinand.

That first season I was at United could not have been better. To finish with the treble was incredible. They were in a great situation when I went and obviously there was a lot of pressure on me to sustain that and not be the one who messed things up, but it was a wonderful period and there was such a great spirit in the club and a feeling of invincibility as momentum gathered.

'He led that very well and I saw first hand how he did it. To go on three fronts and rotate the squad, pick different players and leave players out, then pick different teams and change games in such a heavy schedule was a fantastic education. I learned a lot from him but as I have often said, you couldn't really write the lessons down.

'What happens is you come across things in your role as a manager and it suddenly clicks that you have had a particular situation before and had seen Alex deal with it. You ask yourself, "What would he do?" and you have the answer. That impression has stayed with me.

'I had also worked with Jim Smith and found he and Alex to be similar people. They are the old-fashioned type of managers who have both adapted to the modern game. Very passionate. Driven. Ambitious. Winners. Alex has managed to sustain that for 25 years at the biggest club in Europe and that is an incredible achievement. You can build a team, but to build three or four teams and make them as successful as they have been…there is no one better in the world.

'I had three great years at United, but decided to move after Alex had announced he was going to retire. Once again, he really looked after me in that period. He knew I had ambitions, but it was a very uncertain time at Man United and when an opportunity arose for me, he allowed me to take it. I will always be in his debt for that.

'As things worked out, he carried on and I could understand that because he is such a footballing man who has Manchester United at heart. It must be very difficult to leave that job.

'I went to Middlesbrough and enjoyed my time there and once or twice finished up on the winning side when we faced United. It was then I saw another side of Sir Alex Ferguson. We are all bad losers, but he has great humility and that is what makes him a great manager. He understands football and he knows things like that happen and just moves on and gets on with it.

'As for Alex Ferguson the person, there is a lot of misconception about him in the media and from the public, and it is not until you know the man properly that you appreciate what he is really like. He is a great man to work for. He is generous, loyal to his staff and trusting, and I think that is the key to his success.

'He treats everyone of his staff the same, from the tea ladies through the full spectrum all the way up to the top. That is what has made him sustainable in all his years at that big club.'

PICTURE CREDITS

The publishers would like to thank the following for their kind permission to reproduce the photographs in this book:

Manchester United Football Club Limited
2–3, 7, 11, 15, 21, 33 (bottom), 43 (bottom), 92 (bottom), 98 (top), 104, 113 (top), 122, 124 (bottom), 127, 129, 145, 149, 152, 161, 168, 172, 177, 178, 181, 185, 187, 189, 191, 192, 195, 201, 205, 209, 215, 221, 225, 229, 231, 237, 240, 244, 251, 255, 258, 262, 264, 268-9

Empics
17, 24, 26 (top), 29 (bottom), 33 (top), 39, 43 (top), 47, 51, 57, 59, 65, 68, 73, 80 (top), 82, 84, 88, 91, 98 (bottom), 101 (bottom), 113 (bottom), 116, 120, 131, 134, 159

Getty Images
26 (bottom), 29 (top), 75, 80 (bottom), 92 (top), 101 (top), 106, 124 (top), 141, 157